Dysfunctional Organizations

Dysfunctional Organizations

How to Remove Obstacles to Psychological Safety

David D. Van Fleet

BEP

BUSINESS EXPERT PRESS

Leader in applied, concise business books

Dysfunctional Organizations: How to Remove Obstacles to Psychological Safety

Copyright © Business Expert Press, LLC, 2024

Cover design by Charlene Kronstedt

Interior design by Exeter Premedia Services Private Ltd., Chennai, India

First published in 2024 by
Business Expert Press, LLC
222 East 46th Street, New York, NY 10017
www.businessexpertpress.com

ISBN-13: 978-1-63742-602-9 (paperback)
ISBN-13: 978-1-63742-603-6 (e-book)

Business Expert Press Human Resource Management and Organizational Behavior Collection

First edition: 2024

10 9 8 7 6 5 4 3 2 1

Description

Dysfunctional organizations result from the behavior of individuals and the culture they develop. Many American workers have directly experienced some form of dysfunctional behavior while at work, including trauma from nonfatal workplace violence. Bullying and harassment, violence, unsafe work practices, and other unacceptable workplace behaviors pose significant problems and result in dysfunctional organizations.

To deal with these unacceptable behaviors and to prevent organizations from becoming dysfunctional, psychological safety is recommended. Psychological safety is not the only way to prevent dysfunctional organizations, but it is a critical way. This book outlines in simple and direct words the major forms of behavior that act as obstacles to developing psychological safety in organizations as well as how safety efforts also impact psychological safety. Then it provides practical guidance for what can and should be done to remove those obstacles.

To assist in that guidance, a unique framework (V-REEL) is outlined to enable you to better understand how and why certain behaviors are associated with dysfunctional organizations. Originally developed as a practical guide for entrepreneurs to think through what they know (and need to know) in order to assess their potential for creating value in their respective environments, the framework is used here to indicate the value of having a psychologically, psychosocially, and physically safe workplace. The use of the framework helps the reader to carefully identify factors that erode or chip away psychologically, psychosocially, and physically safe workplaces as well as those factors that serve to enable or help to create those workplaces.

Keywords

abusive management; bullying; costs; dark side behaviors; dysfunctional; enabling factors; eroding factors; harassment; offender; perpetrator; sex related complaints; terrorism; violent behavior

Contents

Testimonials

"Dysfunctional Organizations is a book that is both necessary and likely to remain necessary as long as people form organizations. The presence of dysfunction within organizations is a fact of organizational life that comes with multiple facets. David Van Fleet examines those facets with clarity and precision while offering methods to address and mitigate the dysfunction. His use of the V-REEL framework to provide an overarching model to address dysfunction in organizations is a creative and useful application of the framework that pulls together the factors to both diagnose and treat the dysfunction. This will become another book that I keep as a point of reference for insights when working with managers and executives who want to raise the performance bar in their organizations."—**David Flint, Educator, Serial Entrepreneur, Author of Think Beyond Value—Building Strategy to Win (2018, NY: NY, Morgan James Publishing)**

"In this book, Dr. Van Fleet brings together his extensive scholarly knowledge and his critical insights to address a challenge of increasing importance facing both business and nonprofit organizations across Western democracies."
—**Ernie Stark, Former Editor, Journal of Behavioral and Applied Management**

"Understanding the causes and consequences of dysfunctional behavior in organizations has continued to grow in importance. Since the COVID-19 pandemic, there has also been increased awareness of the significance of psychological well-being. Dr. Van Fleet has developed an important perspective on these two constructs, and his book promises to be invaluable to managers everywhere. Indeed, his approach to these issues, combined with his strong expertise, promises a breakthrough book."—**Ricky W. Griffin, Distinguished Professor of Management and Blocker Chair in Business, Mays Business School, Texas A&M University**

"*David Van Fleet has penned an intriguing analysis of dysfunctional organizations, replete with insights and guidance for today's corporate world. As with his previous work, this is a valuable addition to our understanding of modern organizations and their successful management.*"—**Arthur G. Bedeian, Boyd Professor Emeritus at Louisiana State University and A&M College**

"*Frequently, delving into the dynamics of less successful and poor-functioning organizations can be just as enlightening, if not more so, than studying thriving ones. In this regard, David Van Fleet embarks on a comprehensive exploration of dysfunctional organizations. I wholeheartedly recommend reading his book, as the invaluable insights he imparts will equip you with the wisdom to navigate the challenges of dysfunctional work environments and, most importantly, steer clear of them altogether.*"—**Christopher P. Neck, W. P. Carey School of Business, Arizona State University**

"*My career has been more as a trench guy working in sales and paid largely on commission. Too many owners and managers have their fiefdoms. For me, it was easier to stay below the fray and focus on earning a living. How I wish managers and owners understood the concepts in this book. This subject or book should be a required class for managers and owners.*"—**Steve Nemeth, Realtor—Broker RE/MAXOne**

Preface

Dysfunctional organizations exist as a result of the behavior of individuals in those organizations as well as the culture permeated by that behavior (Lagios, Nguyen, Stinglhamber, and Caesens 2022; Alemu 2016; Griffin, O'Leary-Kelly, and Collins 1998). The behavior leading to the dysfunction generally results from forms that violate accepted norms in the workplace and comes in several forms and goes by many names—bullying, harassment (verbal, racial, sexual, sexual orientation, gender, religious, physical, ability-based, age-based), abuse, blaming, criticism, gaslighting, judging, name-calling, threatening, lying, retaliation, mobbing, intimidation, and more. Almost a third of adult Americans (30%) indicate that they have directly experienced some form of such behavior while at work (Namie 2021b).

Among the most common forms of such behavior are bullying and harassment, particularly sexual harassment, workplace violence, and unsafe practices. Bullying is experienced by about 10 to 20 percent of workers (Einarsen et al., 2011; Rayner 2002) and is recognized as an adult workplace problem (Gurchiek 2005). Namie (2021b, 5) reports that "two-thirds of adult Americans are familiar with workplace bullying—ranging from a painfully intimate immersion to a superficial recognition of the term without knowing many details." It is not just individuals who are impacted; in extreme cases, the whole organization can be threatened (Goldman 2009, 2010). These behaviors' impacts are felt both emotionally and physically (see, e.g., Dombeck 2020; Tracy, Lutgen-Sandvik, and Alberts 2006; Lewis 2004; McCarthy and Mayhew 2004; Vaez, Ekberg, and LaFlamme 2004; Rayner, Hoel, and Cooper 2002; Vartia 2001).

"According to the Bureau of Labor Statistics, 20,050 workers in the private industry experienced trauma from nonfatal workplace violence in 2020" (https://tinyurl.com/ycy2955s). The National Safety Council reports that "there were 1,176,340 nonfatal injuries and illnesses that caused a private industry worker to miss at least one day of work in

2020" (https://tinyurl.com/y3k6tbye). Wiefling (2019) refers to this as a global epidemic. Clearly, bullying and harassment, violence, unsafe work practices, and other unacceptable workplace behaviors pose significant problems and are what result in dysfunctional organizations. Numerous books and articles have been written about bullying, harassment, workplace violence, safety, and the many other forms of abusive unacceptable behavior in the workplace (see the Reference section of this book). The plethora of labels and, in many cases, having different labels for the same sort of behavior makes it difficult for organizations to address the problems resulting from those behaviors. "As a result, writing distinct policy statements is almost certain to cause confusion when policymakers and legislators need to reach a consensus" (Van Fleet and Van Fleet 2022, *xi*).

Despite the prevalence and impact of these behaviors on organizations, they are seldom reported to management. Identifying and reporting these behaviors does not seem to be influenced by age, gender, experience, language at home, or having been bullied (Van Fleet and Van Fleet 2012). Failing to report may be because individuals feel threatened by the perpetrator if they do so. They may simply not know how or to whom they should report such behaviors. Finally, they keep silent because of "a small set of common, largely taken-for-granted beliefs about speaking up at work" (Edmonson 2019, 32). As Edmonson (2019, 34) notes, "no one was ever fired for silence." So, not reporting any incidents seems to be a safe option, especially for those who were only observers.

To deal with these unacceptable behaviors and to prevent organizations from becoming dysfunctional, scholars and consultants increasingly recommend that organizations create psychological safety. Psychological safety is not the only way to prevent organizations from being dysfunctional organizations, but it is a critical way (Helbig and Norman 2023; Manning 2021; Clark 2020; Edmondson 2019; Radecki, Hull, McCusker, and Ancona 2018). In this book, I indicate what is involved in psychological safety, then drawing on nearly 30 years of my research with my wife (Ella 9/22/1941-8/7/2022) and others, I outline the major forms of behavior that act as obstacles to developing psychological safety in organizations, how safety efforts also impact psychological safety, and what can be done to remove those obstacles.

The Journey

This book is the result of a long scholarly journey. My first work concerned the economic conditions of governmental organizations. But I became curious as to how those organizations were structured, so I turned my attention to organizational arrangements, particularly the span of management or control. But structures are developed by individuals and groups so that, in turn, quickly led me to study organizational behavior. One of the predominant forms of behavior in developing structures would be that of the organization's leader or leaders. So, I next turned my efforts to studying organizational leaders and leadership in general. Those leadership studies focused on good and or effective and ineffective leadership behaviors with particular emphases on mismanagement and workplace safety. At this point, the linkage between an organization's leader and the safety of those in the organization became my concern.

As I learned more and more about ineffective leadership and mismanagement, terrorism in the workplace came into focus as an extreme consequence. Then the combination of mismanagement and its negative results led me to refocus my efforts on workplace violence in general. In collaboration with a management consultant who specializes in workplace violence, we developed a book (Nater 2023) focused on reducing or eliminating workplace violence. My late wife and I also collaborated on a book focused on bullying and harassment (Van Fleet and Van Fleet 2022). That effort captured much of our work on those forms of abusive behavior but did not specifically consider psychological safety as a potential part of the solution to reducing those behaviors in the workplace. This book closes that gap and brings it all together and so the journey continues.

Pedagogy

This book can be valuable to a single reader but even more valuable if used in a group or classroom setting where concepts and reactions can be discussed and debated. Each chapter begins by asking you, the reader, to make some notes or form a definition regarding the contents of the chapter based on the chapter's title. You will be asked to look back on those to compare your thinking after having read the chapter. Each chapter also has a short case designed to highlight and make more relevant the chapter's contents. Then at the end of each chapter, there is a set of key points or key takeaways designed to both highlight the important points made in the chapter and suggest their use to you as well as your organization. There is also an extensive glossary as well as a bibliography and reading list to assist in your further exploration of dysfunctional organizations.

Acknowledgments

This book is based on the research and opinions of the author and is meant as a source of valuable information for the reader; however, it is not meant as a substitute for direct legal assistance. If such assistance is required, the services of a competent professional should be sought.

The anecdotes and cases, unless otherwise noted, are based on surveys and correspondence by the author and earlier work, Van Fleet and Van Fleet (2022), *Bullying and Harassment at Work: An Innovative Approach to Understanding and Prevention* (Northampton, MA: Edward Elgar Publishing) and Van Fleet and Van Fleet (2014), *Violence at Work: What Everyone Should Know* (Charlotte, NC: Information Age Publishing).

CHAPTER 1

Introduction

Make some notes of what you expect in this chapter. Write down what you feel is a definition of a dysfunctional organization. Keep that definition in mind as you read this chapter.

Definition

What is a dysfunctional organization? One definition is that it is an organization that "works in a way that is not consistent with the goal it's supposed to pursue" (Montgomery 2016). Yet, many others would argue that, in the case of a business firm, for example, the organization could be accomplishing its goal of making a profit but still be dysfunctional, in that it is a horrible place to work. Another definition focuses on too much communication and lack of trust (Thomas 2018). While another indicates that a dysfunctional organization is "the product of structural, cultural, or leadership patterns that undermine the purpose, health, wholeness, safety, solidarity, and worth of an organization or its stakeholders" (Carroll 2016), others also focus on leadership (Cano 2019; Dandira 2012; Alemu 2016; Paul, Strbiak, and Landrum 2002). A dysfunctional organization brings harm or intends to bring harm to its employees or stakeholders (Giacalone and Greenberg 1997, vii). These latter concepts would seem more in line with common usage.

Characteristics

Various authors provide lists that indicate characteristics of dysfunctional organizations. So, as a starting point, consider the diverse characteristics noted in many of these lists. Here are some lists that seem particularly insightful.

Yones at the Institute of International Management (Yones n.d.) provides three extensive lists that would indicate a dysfunctional organization. First, there are dysfunctional leadership symptoms and warning signs:

- Dictatorial Leadership: Management that does not allow disagreements out of insecurity or arrogance.
- No 360-Degree Feedback: There is limited or no leadership performance feedback.
- Personal Agendas: Recruitments, selections, and promotions are based on internal political agendas, for example, hiring friends to guarantee personal loyalty at the expense of other highly performing and more qualified employees.
- Political Compensation: Stock options, bonuses, and perks are not fairly linked to performance.
- Inefficient Use of Resources: Budgets are allocated between business units or departments based on favoritism and power centers rather than actual business needs.
- Empire-Building Practices: Managers believe that the more people they manage and the bigger the budget, the higher the chance that they will be promoted. This results in raging battles around budgets, strategies, and operations.
- Unequal Workload Distribution: You'll find some departments are underutilized, while other departments are overloaded.
- Too Much Management: There are many management layers in the organization, thus hindering communication and resulting in slower execution.
- Fragmented Organization Efforts: Interdepartmental competition and turf wars between rival managers lead to the emergence of silos, which results in communication gaps. Management silos almost always result in fragmented and duplicated budgets and projects, thus wasting valuable company investments.
- Too Much Talk: Plans are heavy on talk but light on action. In a political corporate culture, image management becomes far more important than actions.

- Ineffective Meetings: Argumentative and heated cross-divisional meetings with discussion and language focusing on point scoring and buck-passing rather than sharing responsibility and collaborating to solve the problem.
- Lack of Collaboration: Every person for himself/herself. A low sense of unity or camaraderie on the team. The key criterion for decision making is "What is in it for me?"
- Low Productivity: Management wastes more time and energy on internal attack and defense strategies instead of executing the work, innovating, and overcoming challenges. Critical projects fall behind on deadlines, budgets, and performance targets (e.g., sales, market share, quality, and other operational targets).
- Constant Crisis Mode: The management team spends most of its time on firefighting instead of proactive planning for next-generation products and services.
- Morale Deterioration: Muted level of commitment and enthusiasm by other teams. Even successful results cannot be shared and celebrated due to animosity and internal negative competition.
- Backstabbing: Backbiting among executives and managers becomes common and public.
- Highly Stressful Workplace: There is a high rate of absenteeism and a high employee turnover rate.

Then there are bad politics and performance risks:

- When employees feel discriminated against, abused, or unappreciated, they may resort to one or more of the following harmful options:
  o Defecting to competition
  o Resort to sabotaging the company, for example, by sharing confidential information with competitors or the media
  o Employees may become emotionally distant and have no interest in the success of the company
  o They will display passive–aggressive behaviors, become uncooperative, work less, or produce substandard results

- Key talent will leave the company. Good honest workers generally don't have the skills or disposition for functioning in a highly political environment.
- The company develops a reputation for being political and an unpleasant place to work, making it more difficult to recruit good talent to compete effectively.
- Employees will lose faith and motivation. When the leadership comes up with good initiatives, they are met with skepticism and resistance. The bottom line: Business performance will suffer. The worst thing that could happen to a company is when the staff loses confidence in the leadership team. The two critical questions every leader must ask:
  - How many of the previously-listed symptoms are present in our organization, department, or teams?
  - How best to manage workplace politics and improve team performance?

Something to Think About

A public service agency employs 250 members of whom around 100 have direct face-to-face contact with the public on a daily basis. While the agency provides a number of different services, its primary service is providing information, coordinating research requests of clients, and operating as a clearing house for sizeable research requests and needs of those clients. The day-to-day working environment at the agency was rather turbulent. Some members of the agency strove to be innovative and forecast the needs of clients, but others were content to hold on to the past and responded to things only when requested. These opposing *past* and *future* orientations stirred up emotions and caused fear among some. Over time, an atmosphere of hostility and suspicion began to emerge, particularly at the lower levels of the organization. Is this a dysfunctional organization? (Adapted from McConkie 1980).

Finally, it is difficult to treat dysfunctional organizations.

- Many times, the leadership team is part of the political game.
- There is a lack of consensus on the correct strategy: strong conflicting views or conflict of interests.
- New leaders cannot assess who is right or wrong because of a lack of information or misinformation.
- Changing the culture requires performance–rewards system reengineering, which may be faced with serious resistance.
- It takes substantial time and effort to heal the wounds, reestablish broken communications, and rebuild trust and collaboration.

Roumeliotis (2022) also has an extensive list focused on poor leadership. His list is:

- Poor customer service.
- No unique selling/value proposition.
- Operational deficiencies—various ailments and no structure.
- Absence of or very little communication between staff and management.
- Divisions aren't well coordinated and do not function as a team.
- No transparency—There is hardly any openness from management.
- Unethical practices—short-term selfish objectives in search of market share.
- Lack of proper execution of decisions and new products/ services.
- Lack of productivity incentives to boost results and employee morale.
- Creativity is practically nonexistent.
- No clear vision/strategy.
- A weak sales force along with an unattractive compensation plan.
- Favoring nepotism and bias.

- Poor hiring practices.
- Slow/delayed decision making process—too many layers—overwhelming bureaucratic structure.
- High turnover.
- Management is in a state of denial about their organization's shortcomings—remaining with the dysfunctional status quo.
- No specific and/or stable channel strategy.
- The hidden game—corporate politics—is power played by a handful of individuals for their own benefit to the detriment of their colleagues and the company.
- Misrepresentation of the brand(s)—too much hype—empty promises—not delivering on expectations.
- Weak financial controls—cash flow dilemmas—overleveraged/undercapitalized (high debt-to-capital ratio)—not reinvesting a certain percentage of profits for future growth.
- Absence of sound marketing program(s) and/or brand strategy.
- Growing too fast and not staying on course as the company grows.
- Lack or very little employee training and development.
- Deficient control systems—reactive rather than proactive.
- Lack of continuous improvements or complacency.

Daskal (2016) presents a list of 50 characteristics. Her list consists of the following:

1. Personal problems overwhelm effectiveness
2. Withdrawing support
3. Hiding resources or withholding information
4. Ongoing turf wars
5. Pouting and yelling
6. Taking undue credit
7. Misrepresented roles
8. Frequent and senseless reorganizations
9. High turnover
10. Undeserved promotions
11. Being careless about quality
12. Backbiting and backstabbing
13. Gossiping and rumors
14. Favoritism and preferential treatment
15. Bigotry and prejudice
16. Hiring quotas
17. Refusing to establish procedures
18. Inflexibility in procedures

19. Failing to take initiative

21. Breaking confidentiality

23. Low productivity

25. Confusion about goals

27. Squandering time

29. Focusing on self instead of the greater good

31. Not confronting

33. Perfectionism

35. Hubris and arrogance

37. Excessive delegation

39. Lack of diversity

41. Overpromising and underperforming

43. Paralysis by analysis

45. Reinventing the wheel

47. Inaccessibility and unavailability

49. Isolation

20. Hearing what is said, not what is meant

22. Bullying and tyrannical behavior

24. Disloyalty and undependability

26. Filtering bad news

28. Mistaking abusive behavior for toughness

30. Constant alibis

32. Excessive fear of change

34. Smugness and conceit

36. Shooting the messenger

38. Undue emphasis on speed

40. Emphasizing equal results instead of equal opportunity

42. Mismanaging the dysfunction

44. Unfriendliness and hostility

46. Undue emphasis on results

48. Ascribing bad motives

50. Paranoia and suspicion

Wolf (2016), on the other hand, lists only nine signs of a dysfunctional organization:

1. There are secrets in the organization or work unit, and it is not OK to talk about these issues openly.
2. Feelings are not discussed in the workplace.
3. Never say exactly what you mean to a person who needs to hear it. In other words, speak in code and doublespeak.
4. Make one mistake and you are gone.
5. Leadership will take credit for your good ideas and punish you for failures.
6. Everything you are belongs to the organization.
7. Do as we say and not as we do.
8. You're not here to enjoy yourself; you're here to work.

9. Don't rock the boat.

Newman (2012) identifies eight signs of dysfunctional management as:

1. Because I Said So—assigned a task with no explanation.
2. Passive–Aggressive—showing up late to meetings, forgetting to share important details, or consistent excuses for not getting things done all indicate that the person doesn't care about or for what the meeting is about.
3. Narcissistic—management only cares about its success.
4. Noncommittal—rather than committing to a strategy or plan, it is changed constantly.
5. Turnover—high turnover suggests problems.
6. Division—pitting one unit or group against another also suggests problems.
7. Politics—when members of the organization use office politics for personal gain.
8. (Mis)Communication or Lack Thereof—sending the wrong message or no message at all.

Rozell (2015) lists six signs of dysfunction:

1. Unwritten and unspoken rules   2. Narcissism
3. Passive–aggressive behavior   4. Communication issues
5. Turnover   6. Lack of delegation

Finkle (2018) also identifies six but they are quite different from those of Rozell (2015). She notes these characteristics:

1. Strategy or idea of the day (or week or month....)—always scrambling for change and looking for the new greatest hit.
2. Putting lipstick on the pig—making superficial, cosmetic changes to a product or plan to disguise its fundamental problems.
3. Favorite children mentality—certain individuals are treated differently than others and can do no wrong.
4. No accountability, except when you want it—no one is accountable until disaster strikes, at which point everyone is accountable until things get back to normal and again, no one is accountable.

5. Analysis paralysis—overanalyzing or overthinking a problem or situation so no solution or course of action is decided upon.
6. Fiefdom mentality—everyone concentrates on only their work or group with no communication as to what's best for the whole organization.

Stanislaw (2022) and Banks (n.d.) have the same list consisting of only five characteristics: (1) absence of trust, (2) fear of conflict, (3) lack of commitment, (4) inability to hold each other accountable, and (5) inattention to results. However, Banks (n.d.) adds three more: (1) silos where individuals make decisions without informing affected groups, (2) top-down decision making or the highest paid person in the office (HIPPO) principle stifles communication, and (3) artificial harmony where everyone is just *doing great*. Kolko (2015) suggests that dysfunctional organizations have layers of bureaucracy and management, siloed functions, and a culture of friction and defensiveness. Van Fleet and Griffin (2006) suggest that in a dysfunctional organization, one may find inappropriate attire, alcohol use, smoking, inappropriate behaviors, loud talking or loud radio playing, tardiness, sabotage, or "violent behavior directed toward one or more individuals or the organization as a whole" (p. 699).

All of these lists are a bit mind-boggling, but the *top 10* would seem to be the following:

1. High levels of turnover—particularly when good individuals are leaving the organization.
2. Communication issues—too little, too much, or miscommunication.
3. Dictatorial management—do as I say or top-down decision making; abuse of power (Burton 2002).
4. Politics—using influence for personal gain.
5. Isolation—silos where the group concentrated only on their work, ignoring what was needed by the whole organization.
6. Not confronting issues, including poor performance or fear of conflict (Harvey, Martinko, and Douglas 2006).
7. Favoritism—individuals or groups are treated differently (Proyer, Oyler, and Odom 2013).
8. Too many layers in the organization—bureaucracy.

9. Lack of commitment—failure to stick with a strategy, plan, or decision.
10. Narcissism—selfishness, involving a sense of entitlement, or a need for admiration (Ouimet 2010).

Something to Think About

Justin was the newly hired chief executive officer (CEO) for a group of 25 nonprofit schools. He was anxious but eager to get started as he took over the reins of Leg Up Learning Centers. He had researched the organization and done Google searches during the recruiting process, and as a result, he felt that he understood the organization and its strengths as well as the challenges it faced in the future. As a result of his research, he knew that there were four major challenges to be dealt with—(1) some people issues, (2) financial uncertainty, (3) family and employee concerns, and (4) inadequate rigor around accountability. He thought he was prepared, but within six weeks, the staff, the executive team, and the board all shared grievances. Longstanding and unaddressed problems were found, and everyone hoped that Justin would somehow fix everything all at once. He found himself confronted with awful behavior, safety violations, and uneven financial performance. What would you do if you were Justin? (Adapted from Yazbak 2017).

Consequences

Dysfunctional organizations lead to a good many unwanted results. Some of the more obvious consequences of a dysfunctional organization are:

- Scandals (Elliott 2002)
- Adverse working conditions in terms of health and job satisfaction (Larsson, Berglund, and Ohlsson 2016; Alpass et al. 1997)
- Individual stress, long working hours, and constant availability (Fors Brandebo and Alvinius 2019; Burke and McAteer 2007)
- Tyrants and workplace bullying (Langan-Fox and Sankey 2007)

- Unauthorized taking or using the organization's property for personal use, for example, employee theft (Tomlinson and Greenberg 2007)
- Toxic behavior (Goldman 2008)
- Unethical behavior (Jurkiewicz and Giacalone 2016)
- Immediate, deferred, and intangible costs (Van Fleet and Griffin 2006)

Consider each of them in a bit of detail.

Scandals

Scandals almost always involve the leader or leaders of the organization and money although sometimes, as with the case of Father Ritter, money was not involved. One of the most notorious scandals associated with a dysfunctional organization was the U.S.$2.8 billion accounting scandal at HealthSouth that went on for six years (McCann 2017). L. Dennis Kozlowski, the CEO of Tyco, helped build Tyco into an international conglomerate, and then, he and his financial advisor Mark H. Swartz falsified company records to conceal U.S.$14 million in improper payment to himself (Sorkin 2002). John Rigas formed Adelphia Communications Corporation, which became one of the largest cable television providers in the United States. He then speculated with its stock, and in 2002, it was disclosed that Adelphia was liable for U.S. $2.3 billion in debts and that the Rigas family embezzled at least U.S.$1 billion from Adelphia (Partridge 2019). Scandals do not happen just to business firms.

After the 2010 earthquake in Haiti, the Red Cross raised U.S.$488 million for relief efforts, but it was shown that it broke promises, squandered donations, and made dubious claims of success (DiGangi 2016). Father Bruce Ritter founded *Covenant House* (CH) in 1972 to create a safe shelter for homeless teenagers, but between 1989 and 1990, he was accused of having sexual relationships with individuals while they were under his care (Couzzo 2018). In 1992, William Aramony resigned amidst allegations that he siphoned money from United Way of America through spinoff companies he helped to create (Meleen 2020).

Unfortunately, the list goes on and on including business organizations such as Enron (Elliott 2002), Volkswagen, Lehman Brothers, British Petroleum, Uber, Apple, Facebook, Valeant Pharmaceuticals, Kobe Steel, and Equifax (https://tinyurl.com/4wyc4pjs), plus nonprofit organizations like Planned Parenthood, the Sierra Club, and the Boy Scouts of America (DiGangi 2016).

Adverse Working Conditions

Adverse working conditions involve "unreasonable, oppressive, hostile, or punitive working conditions, including inadequate or unsafe physical facilities, unsafe working environment, and harassment" (www .lawinsider.com/dictionary/adverse-working-condition). These would include cuts in financial resources, layoffs, yelling, excessive criticism, mobbing, physical and mental abuse, threats, and fear of losing one's job (Psychogios et al. 2019). Long hours and low pay could also contribute to adverse working conditions.

Adverse conditions impact both the physical health and mental health of members of an organization. Adverse conditions such as no written contract of employment, lower wages, and experiencing insults or threats can lead to worsened physical health and increased levels of depression (Drydakis 2022). Adverse job conditions were related to workers' mental health (ten Have, van Dorsselaer, and de Graaf 2015). Daily hassles add up to severe problems (Larson, Berglund, and Ohlsson 2016). An adverse working environment was shown to be related to poor mental health, particularly when organizational support was lacking (Blanchard et al. 2022). Adverse psychosocial and physical working conditions were associated with higher long-term sickness absence due to mental disorders (Heinonen et al. 2022).

Poor working conditions may result in dangerous health effects, lead to absenteeism, early retirement, increased pension costs, and decreased worker productivity. Those working conditions can also cause occupational accidents, sickness, and absenteeism (Nappo 2019). Those who are low paid, in poor-quality jobs, and have a lack of control over their work are disproportionately employed in physically demanding or hazardous jobs (Fasanya 2020). Job satisfaction is impacted (Alpass et al. 1997).

Organizational environments with risks and hazards, physical demands, and complexity are related to burnout, engagement, and safety issues (Nahrgang, Morgeson, and Hofmann 2011). A negative workplace with adverse working conditions could also contribute to suicide (Baumert et al. 2014).

Individual Stress

The National Institute for Occupational Health and Safety (NIOSH) defines job stress "as the harmful physical and emotional responses that occur when the requirements of the job do not match the capabilities, resources, or needs of the worker. Job stress can lead to poor health and even injury" (https://tinyurl.com/25wnnp9r). The World Health Organization (WHO) defines work-related stress as "the response people may have when presented with work demands and pressures that are not matched to their knowledge and abilities and which challenge their ability to cope" (https://tinyurl.com/2z7f7xee).

Workplace stress is a pervasive problem (Tams et al. 2015). Uncongenial workplaces contribute to stress (Kendrick et al. 2020). Stress can lead to soft tissue injuries. More soft-tissue injuries are filed on Mondays than on other days of the week where *soft tissue* refers to issues such as *bruises/contusions, headaches, nausea, sprains/strains, unspecified illness, carpal tunnel disease*, and *emotional/stress/mental disorders* (Butler, Kleinman, and Gardner 2014). The expression "The harder I work, the behinder I get" unfortunately conveys the feelings of too many workers who feel overwhelmed by the demands of their jobs (quote source—https://quoteinvestigator.com/2021/04/04/behinder/). Long hours can also lead to individual stress (Burke and McAteer 2007).

Organizational dysfunction is the result of dysfunctional individual behavior (Fors Brandebo and Alvinius 2019). Stress can have a detrimental impact on workplace safety (Ventiv Technology 2023). Work-related problems such as procrastination and perfectionism are associated with severe distress and high psychosocial costs (Steinert, Heim, and Leichsenring 2021). The proliferation of information and communication technologies such as instant messaging, e-mail, calendar task reminders, Internet telephony, and smartphones is all constantly calling for peoples' attention increasing their stress in terms of actually doing their jobs (Tams et al. 2015). Certain kinds of workplace stress have been shown to be associated with a higher frequency of depressive symptoms in employees (Bilkser 2006).

Tyrants and Workplace Bullying

Workplace bullying is generally defined as repeated, health-harming mistreatment by one or more individuals in an organization, specifically abusive conduct that takes the form of verbal abuse; or behaviors perceived as threatening, intimidating, humiliating; sabotaging one's work; or in some combination of the above (https://workplacebullying.org/). Bullies are a type of tyrant (Langan-Fox and Sankey 2007). Workplace bullying is a concern for many employees in their everyday working lives. Research shows that it is a widespread phenomenon, with rates of 5 to 28 percent across Western countries (Lutgen-Sandvik, Tracy, and Alberts 2007). Workplace bullying results in anxiety, depression, absenteeism, and turnover (Hogh, Mikkelsen, and Hansen 2003).

Closely related with similar negative impacts are abusive supervision (Tepper 2000 and 2007), incivility (Cortina et al. 2001), bullying/ mobbing (Einarsen et al. 2011), harassment (Nielsen, Glasø, and Einarsen 2017), emotional abuse (Keashly 1998), ostracism (Williams 2007), and social undermining (Duffy, Ganster, and Pagon 2002). Workplace bullying can lead to stress, depression, and employee turnover (Akella 2016). It can cost an organization up to U.S.$300 billion in medical claims, lost productivity, employee turnover, absenteeism, and legal costs (King 2019). It has been shown to be "A severe and pervasive problem with devastating effects, both personally and professionally" (Carbo and Hughes 2010, 387).

Workplace bullies assert their power and influence through targeted aggression and personal attacks that are uninvited, undeserved, and unwarranted (Foote and Barash 2021). In total, 79 percent of working professionals reported that they had experienced workplace bullying (Woolf 2021). It is happening not just in organizations in the United States but in countries throughout the world—European employees

(Einarsen 2005), India (Kompella 2022), China (Sims and Sun 2012), Sweden, Norway, Finland, UK, Australia Denmark, South Africa, New Zealand, and Asia (Ciby and Raya 2015).

Employee Theft

The term employee theft refers to the unauthorized taking, transfer, or use of property of an organization by a member of the organization. "The five most common ways employee theft occurs are petty theft, data theft, cash larceny, skimming fraud, and fraudulent disbursements" (Picincu 2020). A recent report notes that 75 percent of employees have stolen from their employer at least one time (Counterpart 2022). Employee theft may result from an individual's effort to restore justice (i.e., perceptions of fairness) following a provocation by an organization and/or its managers (Tomlinson and Greenberg 2007). Wilkie (2019) notes that many excuses are in line with this explanation—"Corporations don't have feelings"; "No one got hurt"; and "If my company's going to cut my benefits, it owes me." Thus, a common explanation for employee theft is being treated unfairly (Langner 2010).

Many dishonest employees are younger, part-time, untenured, and dissatisfied (Hollinger 2017). While individuals appear unlikely to steal from other individual members of an organization, they are likely to steal from the organization itself (Greenberg 2002). It is not just the organization that bears the costs of employee theft, but society also has costs associated with increased business failures, the resulting losses in jobs and tax revenues, and higher prices passed on to consumers (Lipman and McGraw 1988).

Retail organizations typically have slim profit margins, so theft occurring there is particularly impactful (Bailey 2006). Despite the prevalence of employee theft, employers may prefer not to admit or address the problem because it may damage the organization's reputation, cause trouble with unions, and suggest their own incompetence as managers (Sparks 1982). Managers may also feel it is the duty of auditors or the organization's board to guard against fraud, misappropriation, and embezzlement perpetrated by the employees (Hemraj 2001).

Something to Think About

The store manager of a shoe store pleaded guilty to stealing nearly U.S.$80,000 from her employer by creating almost 800 fraudulent receipts over a period of more than three years. Frustrated by what she perceived as unnecessary rules, regulations, and policies that caused her to waste her time, she decided to *get even* by taking what initially was small amounts of cash. When she initially was not caught, she began to do it regularly. In a court proceeding, she disclosed that she had processed false refunds for shoes and other merchandise using the names of friends or names she got from other receipts. She would then take the cash out of the store's register and use it to buy things for herself, mostly clothes. How could this behavior have been stopped? How could it have been prevented?

Toxic Behavior

When an organization becomes dysfunctional, it is often due to an outgrowth of toxicity in the workplace (Goldman 2008, 2009, 2010).

> A toxic work environment is one where negative behaviors—such as manipulation, bullying, yelling, and so on—are so intrinsic to the culture of the organization that a lack of productivity, a lack of trust, high stress levels, infighting, and discrimination become the norm (Sandhu 2023).

"Toxic work environments breed unrest, competition, low morale, constant stressors, negativity, sickness, high turnover, and even bullying" (Career Contessa n.d.). So, many of the behaviors already noted would also fit in this category.

Toxic corporate cultures have been shown to be better predictors of an organization's attrition rate than compensation (Sull, Sull, and Zweig 2022). A survey of 800 managers and workers in 17 industries indicated that when subjected to incivility, 66 percent said that their performance declined, 48 percent intentionally decreased their work effort, 38 percent intentionally decreased the quality of their work, and 12 percent resigned (Porath and Pearson 2013).

Individuals in toxic environments will spread negative feelings among others, leading to harassment, bullying, and ostracism, which in turn result in unnecessary stress, burnout, depression, and anxiety among the workers (Rasool et al. 2021). Toxic organizations have increased costs resulting from the loss of a positive company image, low self-esteem, low morale, high turnover, high absenteeism, poor employee health, and lowered productivity (Anjum et al. 2018). While under federal law, an employer can be sued for creating or hosting a toxic work environment that must have impacted a particular protected group (Nakase 2019).

Unethical Behavior

Unethicality is systemic, so dealing with it requires an in-depth analysis of the organization (Jurkiewicz and Giacalone 2016). Unethical behavior in organizations violates generally accepted social and ethical standards. Examples would include data falsification (McCrum 2019), false advertising (Zaleski 2017), and falsified performance (Hakim and Ewing 2015). Common unethical behaviors are rule violations (29%), lying (27%), unhealthy work environments (also 27%), sacrificing safety (9%), discrimination (3%), stealing (3%), and bullying (2%) (Ivcevic, Menger, and Miller 2020).

Women are less tolerant of unethical behavior than men (Klein and Shtudiner 2021). Job instability may motivate employees to engage in unethical actions if they believe doing so may protect them from losing their jobs (Elshaer, Ghanem, and Azazz 2022). Nonprofit organizations can be more susceptible to fraud due to having fewer resources available to help prevent and recover from a fraud loss as well as less oversight and usually a lack of internal controls (Association of Certified Fraud Examiners 2020).

Relative to lower-class individuals, individuals from upper-class backgrounds behaved more unethically (Piff et al. 2012). A high identification with the organization has been shown to create unethical work behaviors by instigating feelings of psychological entitlement (Naseer et al. 2020).

Unethical behavior can be costly. Ethical failures (bribery) resulted in the German company Siemens agreeing to a U.S.$1.6 billion settlement and Royal Dutch Shell (misrepresenting information) paying U.S. $150 million (De Cremer 2014).

Costs

Should any of these behaviors become extreme, they could result in legal actions, worker's compensation claims, or even civil liability for negligent hiring. If violence occurs, the organization will incur immediate and direct costs—injury or death; cleanup, repair, and replacement; hiring and training of new personnel; increased insurance premiums; lost wages; and the like. "But there also would be less immediate and more difficult to measure costs, including decreased efficiency, productivity, and quality; interruption of business operations; and possibility of a decreased reputation and credibility for the organization" (Van Fleet and Griffin 2006, 699).

Mental health issues can result in lost workdays, lower employee productivity, and high job turnover rates that increase the costs of organizational staffing and health benefits (Maki et al. 2005). These are known as hidden costs. "On average, there are $20,000 of annual per-person hidden costs in organizations. In technology companies, this can easily exceed $80,000 per person annually" (Irwin 2020). If the dysfunctions lead to conflict, costs go even higher. "U.S. employees spend 2.8 hours per week dealing with conflict, equating to approximately $359 billion in paid hours in 2008" (Hayes 2008).

The costs associated with employee turnover alone can be considerable when you consider that they include advertising fees, recruiter fees, management's time for decision making, human resource's recruiting time, selection, training, overtime expenses from other employees needed to pick up the slack, lost productivity and sales, decreased employee morale, and disgruntled customers (Wallace and Gaylor 2012). In a dysfunctional organization:

> Projects will be routinely delayed, costs will routinely be revised
> upward, quality will be at risk of being forgotten in the quest for
> profitability and timeliness, products will be at risk of many and/

or severe defects, and customer satisfaction will lag behind more capable and less dysfunctional competitors (Prosser 2008).

Framework

The organization's culture has been mentioned as important in determining whether it is dysfunctional as is the behavior of people in the organization. Culture and people interact in such a way that determining which is the factor that initially moved the organization toward becoming dysfunctional cannot be determined. As shown in Figure 1.1, as they interact, there are clear indicators of dysfunction, including unsafe workplaces, bullying and harassment, workplace violence, and even internal terrorism. This book will focus on the issues in Quadrant 2 and how to prevent or correct them using psychological safety.

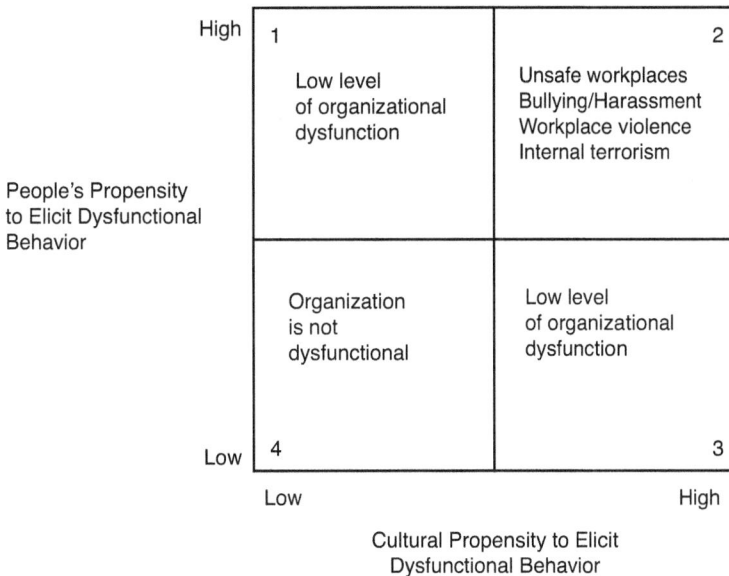

Figure 1.1 *Organizational dysfunction framework*

Rethinking This Chapter

Look at the notes and definition of a dysfunctional organization you wrote down at the beginning of this chapter. How might you change that definition now? With any changes in mind, respond to the

following questions and actions. Managers, human resource professionals, and students should do this carefully in order to be prepared to
deal with violent incidents. Even if you are not currently employed,
your responses should be made as if you are working in an organization.
In a classroom setting, your responses should be shared and compared
through discussion with others.

Chapter Questions

1. Have you ever experienced the sort of behavior that might lead to a
   dysfunctional organization?
2. Have you ever witnessed the sort of behavior in your organization
   that might lead to a dysfunctional organization?
3. What specific actions could, or should, you or your organization
   take to prevent it from becoming dysfunctional?

Introductory Actions

1. Draft a policy statement for your organization that could defray its
   becoming dysfunctional.
2. What specific information should be collected by your organization
   to support your policy?
3. Who in the organization should keep records regarding dysfunctional behavior, for how long, and for what purpose(s)?

Case to Consider

Charity Organization

A charity organization had been quite successful under the leadership of
Mary Kosmalski who encouraged and facilitated suggestions from members of the organization regarding tactics and strategy. However, when
Sam Smith took over, that changed. Sam focused on fear and intimidation to get things done and paid scant attention to what others in the
organization thought. If someone questioned a decision made by Sam, he
not only tended to ignore it but rebuked the person for daring to question

him. Meetings of the board for the organization became simply approving of Sam's suggestions provided to them ahead of time.

At one point, Sam seemed to sense that the organization's strategy needed to be reexamined; however, instead of convening a group of senior staff to consider it, he brought very junior members who would simply agree with whatever he suggested. He also moved his office to the middle of the workspace where he could easily keep an eye on what was going on and who was talking to whom. However, this also meant that some of his conversations that should have been private were overheard by others. One female director tried to question one of his decisions, but he simply interrupted her and talked over her. She was so frustrated that she resigned from the organization.

He lost the respect of the staff, and the organization's reputation suffered. While it previously was known for its innovativeness and leadership, it now became a weak follower of what other charities were doing.

(Adapted from Boddy 2017)

Case Questions for Discussion

1. Is this organization dysfunctional? Why or why not?
2. If you were a member of this organization, how would you react to Sam's style of leadership?
3. Do you think that this organization will continue under Sam's leadership? If not, when and how might it change?

Chapter 1 Takeaways

- A dysfunctional organization brings harm or intends to bring harm to its employees or stakeholders and generally it is an unpleasant place to work. Is your organization an unpleasant place to work?
- Dysfunctional organizations have high levels of turnover, communication issues, and dictatorial management, where some people feel isolated, while others play favorites, and leaders are bureaucratic and narcissistic. Are there elements in your organization that are dysfunctional?

- When the propensity to elicit dysfunctional behavior is high for both people and culture, results may include unsafe workplaces, bullying/harassment, workplace violence, or even terrorism. Are there unsafe conditions in your workplace?

Recommended Reading

In addition to the many sources used in this chapter, the following case and article could expand your understanding of the chapter's material:

Case: Edmondson, A.C. and M.A. Roberta. 2022 "Executive Decision Making at Zola." https://hbsp.harvard.edu/product/622074-PDF-ENG.

Article: Kolko, J. 2015. "Dysfunctional Products Come From Dysfunctional Organizations." *Harvard Business Review Digital Article.* https://hbr.org/2015/01/dysfunctional-products-come-from-dysfunctional-organizations?autocomplete=true.

CHAPTER 2

Culture

Make some notes of what you expect in this chapter. Write down what you feel is a definition of culture. Keep that definition in mind as you read this chapter.

Concept

An organization's culture refers to the shared beliefs and values that enable its members to understand what the organization stands for, how it does things, and what it considers important (Deal and Kennedy 2000). While culture cannot be objectively measured or directly observed, it can be inferred from the organization's documents and the behavior of those in the organization. The organization's culture both shapes the way people in the organization behave and is, in turn, shaped by their behavior. Organizational culture is about the relationships that exist among organizational members and how people in the organization connect and interact with one another as they perform their organizational activities. However, there can be both an intended culture and an actual culture, which in many cases can be vastly different.

Importance

The leaders of an organization felt that it had outgrown its old building. Everyone liked the casual and relaxed atmosphere, but it was getting crowded. So, it moved into a nice, new, modern office building with operations spread over three floors. Soon, members of the organization noticed that the culture was beginning to change and that they did not like it. The leaders were isolated, and everyone missed the informal chance meetings in the halls. As soon as it could make the arrangements, the organization moved out of that building and into one that would again foster informality. There also is a park adjacent to the building where employees converge for lunchtime conversations. With this move, the old culture returned.

An organization's culture defines the *feel* of the organization. It is a powerful force in organizations that can shape the firm's overall effectiveness and long-term success. IBM executives are thought of as wearing a white shirt and dark suit. Texas Instruments, on the other hand, talks about its *shirt-sleeve* culture, where ties are rare and few managers even wear jackets. Further, large organizations can have different cultures for different units. Sales and marketing are quite likely to have a different culture from operations and manufacturing. Nevertheless, organizations that develop and maintain strong cultures, such as those at Hewlett-Packard and Procter and Gamble, tend to be more effective than those that have trouble developing and maintaining a strong culture.

Determinants

Long lists of determinants of culture can be readily found (Anonymous 2023), including artifacts, attitudes toward foreign goods and services, behavior, beliefs and attitudes, customer preferences, customs and taboos, economic philosophy, education, ethical norms and systems, etiquette, geography, history, language, norms, organizational structure, political philosophy, religion, social structure, symbols, technology, and values. Gordon (1991) notes that environments affect an organization's culture, and the important aspects of the environment are the assumptions about customers, competitors, and society. So, changes in the environment may change those assumptions and lead to confusion and resistance by those in the organization until the culture changes as well. Such change can be for the good, though. Dey (n.d.) suggests that:

- Culture includes acquired qualities. This refers to the qualities, habits, ideas, and so on that are acquired through socialization.
- Culture is found only in human societies. While animals have social groupings, they do not appear to have cultures.

- Culture is communicable. Because aspects of a culture are communicated, a new generation can benefit from the experiences of an older one, which enables the culture to become stable over time.
- Culture is not individualistic but social. Culture is a social or group phenomenon and not a characteristic of individuals.
- Culture is idealistic. This suggests that culture includes ideal behavior patterns or rules that the members of the organization try to follow.
- Culture satisfies certain needs. Culture satisfies the moral and social needs of those in the organization.
- Culture is capable of adjustment. Cultures change as environments change.
- Quality of integration in culture. Cultures bring about order and unity, so any new element tends to be subsumed within it.

Something to Think About

Our organization created teams called Happiness Teams, which meet once a month to develop programs and events and to re-evaluate the organization's culture as the organization grows. Teams from different parts of the organization also come together as needed to arrange organizationwide volunteer events for local charities. In addition, the organization encourages members to occasionally bring a family member with them so that they can get to know the member's coworkers as real people rather than just names they here. Would this culture be functional in your organization?

For the purposes of this book, three basic factors are indicated as determining the culture of an organization. The first and perhaps the most important refers to the values held by leaders of the organization. If the leaders are antagonistic toward the regulations and the government, if they want to eliminate any competing organizations, or if they just want to succeed at any and all costs, they set a certain tone for the organization that is likely to be dysfunctional (Van Fleet and Griffin 2006). On the other hand, if they want to cooperate with regulators, if they want to coexist peacefully with similar organizations, or if they want to treat users of the organization's products or services honestly and fairly, a very different culture will prevail.

A second factor in determining the organization's culture is its history. "Culture and its evolution can be shaped by history" (Nunn 2012, 11). An organization founded by a strong personality tends to develop a history following the example of the founder (Eddleston 2008; Morley and Shockley-Zalabak 1991). Someone like that will leave a mark on the organization that will continue even in their absence. For example, Steve Jobs left an indelible imprint on Apple Computer, Sam Walton at Wal-Mart, and Ross Perot at Electronic Data Systems. Even older companies such as Ford still carry the traces of their founders.

The third factor is the vision of the organization's leaders. "What the leader can do is to build, to steer the management culture, to provide a coherent and credible organizational environment and what performances are requested from its members" (Chirimbu 2014, 44). If the leaders decide that the organization needs to undertake significant new approaches, their vision will permeate the entire organization. Likewise, if the leaders are content to maintain the status quo, that, too, will shape the culture.

Origins

How does a culture come about? Where does it come from? Typically, it evolves over a long period of time. Its starting point is often the organization's founder. Founders typically have a considerable impact on the development of an organization's culture. Behavioral norms gradually emerge when they are consistent with the organization's values as established by the founder. In some organizations, conflicts occur openly and are resolved so that everyone can learn from them; on the other hand, some organizations settle conflicts quietly behind closed doors.

The culture of the ice cream company Ben and Jerry's is usually traced to that of its founders, Ben Cohen and Jerry Greenfield. Microsoft was noted for its aggressive nature, which was usually traced back to Bill Gates. Still, under Satya Nadella, "In 2021, Microsoft was awarded as the Best Places to Work in Seattle, Best Global Culture, and Best Company Outlook" (Le n.d.). James Cash Penney believed in treating employees and customers with respect and dignity while employees are still called associates rather than employees, and customer satisfaction is important. However, as an organization grows, its culture will evolve and be shaped by new members and the environment (Brahm and Poblete 2022).

The success of any organization and the experiences shared by its members contribute to the organization's culture. The culture of Hallmark Cards was shaped by its success in the greeting card industry. The company talks about personal contact and inspiring people to express their emotions (https://werkenbijhallmark.nl/en/about-us/culture/). As Zappos grew from a small online shoe company to one selling shoes, clothing, handbags, accessories, and more, it developed such a strong culture that before anyone is hired, they must go through a cultural fit interview (https://tinyurl.com/mrjddr5x).

New members of an organization learn the culture implicitly through interaction with others in the organization. They unconsciously imitate others to fit into the social environment. Communication and interaction with others lead to the new member learning the norms, values, symbols, and ways of doing things in the organization. Of course, conditioning and reinforcement also come into play. Behaviors that lead to positive outcomes tend to be adopted, while those that lead to negative outcomes disappear over time.

Components

How are these differences translated into a culture? In general, they shape some basic components that can be used to characterize an organization's culture. First are shared experiences. These are the common events that people participate in that become a part of their thinking while part of the organization. For instance, a group working closely together for an extended period, putting in 12-hour days and seven-day weeks to develop an event, creates part of the culture. Even after the group breaks up, its members will remember the experience and talk about it with others. So, the experience becomes part of the culture. This and other shared stories also become a part of the culture. "Do you remember...," "That was the time...," and "This company has always..." are common beginnings to stories that have become part of the organization's tradition.

Along with shared experiences and stories, shared beliefs are part of the culture as well. These are beliefs that those in the organization accept as actual truths about or characteristics of the organization. "We can do anything we put our minds to," "We are too big to fail," and "More is always better" are examples of such beliefs (https://tinyurl.com/yey8c97t). Similarly, shared norms are generally accepted ways of doing business. The Washington State Bar Association has a set of 14 communication norms, including "Assume the best of others," "Aim for clarity; be complete, yet concise," and "Focus on reaching understanding and finding solutions to problems" (Nussbaum 2019). Finally, shared actions are day-to-day behaviors that most people perform. Other common actions involve work hours, social interactions, and so forth.

Types

Boogaard (2022) identifies four distinct types of cultures along with good aspects and bad aspects of each with examples. They are as follows (adapted from Boogaard 2022).

Type 1: Clan Culture

Clan cultures (also called *collaborate cultures*) result in friendly working environments where teamwork, togetherness, relationships, morale, participation, and consensus are the focus. Those in positions of leadership are regarded as mentors, and everyone in the organization thinks of the organization as a *family*. The advantages of clan cultures are high morale and good communication. The disadvantages are that a great deal of interaction can lessen productivity and that difficult decisions are not made because members' feelings might get hurt. An example of a clan culture is the online shoe and clothing retailer Zappos (Hsieh 2010).

Type 2: Adhocracy Culture

Ad-hoc cultures (also called *create cultures*) are common among start-up organizations in which things move fast, and procedures are frequently broken and replaced with newer versions that also could soon be broken. They are entrepreneurial work environments where members take risks. The advantages of ad hoc cultures are innovation growth and psychological safety. The disadvantages are a lack of stability and a sense of intimidation for new members who haven't experienced this sort of culture. Examples of ad-hoc cultures are Google and Facebook.

Type 3: Market Culture

Market cultures (also called *compete cultures*) emphasize results. Members of the organizations are highly goal-focused, and those in charge typically are tough and demanding. The advantages of market cultures are that members are highly motivated, and the performance of the organization is high. The disadvantages are that intense competition can create a toxic work environment, and members of the organization can burn out due to the high stress. Amazon might be an example as it is known for its harsh work culture (www.entrepreneur.com/business-news/amazons-allegedly-harsh-work-culture-has-made-headlines/312942).

Type 4: Hierarchy Culture

Hierarchy cultures (also known as *control cultures*) are very structured and process-oriented. There is an emphasis on roles, rules, and procedures. Those in charge emphasize stable results and reliable delivery. The advantages of hierarchical cultures are clear communication and members having a good sense of security with paths to advancement clearly outlined. Disadvantages are inflexibility and little innovation. Examples are government organizations.

Characteristics

The Workhuman Editorial Team (2022) has identified what they feel are the seven elements of a great organizational culture (adapted from Workhuman Editorial Team 2022). They are:

1. Core Values. First and foremost, core values suggest to members of the organization how they should behave and perform. Usually included as part of the organization's mission statement, they should also be in a handbook for new members. They also recommend that these core values be included in meetings or team-building exercises to ensure that they are readily observable.

2. Leadership. Not just any leadership but good, effective leadership that is supportive, motivates those in the organization, and embodies the core values. A good leader sets an example and acts ethically.

3. Unified Sense of Purpose. A unified sense of purpose is necessary for a productive work environment. It provides focus and motivates those in the organization. Purpose lets everyone know why they are in the organization and how their efforts matter.

4. Accountability and Autonomy. To avoid alienated and dehumanized members, the organization should provide them with a sense of independence and ways to communicate with those in charge of the organization. The Workhuman Editorial Team suggests using a software tool like Moodtracker to get insights into members' thoughts regarding the organization.

5. Recognition and Appreciation. Use positive reinforcement to recognize members' performance. Recognition could be a simple thank you, a complimentary post on the organization's web page promotions, or pay increases. Workhuman provides tools like Social Recognition or Service Milestones that can assist in providing positive reinforcement in the organization.

6. Communication. Communication is necessary—up, down, and laterally—all are vital to keeping an organization from becoming dysfunctional. This is increasingly important as organizations become more diverse with very different communication styles. 360 degree feedback has been shown to improve communication and assure justice in the organization (Karkoulian Assaker and Hallak 2016).

7. Environment. A healthy environment consists of both physical and psychosocial aspects of work and the workplace. Developing a sense of belonging will prevent the organization from having an oppressive or dull environment. Keeping healthy is necessary, and so many organizations are providing reimbursements for home gym equipment (Goth 2021).

Core Values

Forsey (2022) identifies 18 core values that would inspire members of the organization and prevent it from becoming dysfunctional. They are integrity, boldness, honesty, trust, accountability, commitment to customers, passion, fun, humility, continuous learning, ownership, constant improvement, leadership, diversity, innovation, quality, teamwork, and simplicity.

Something to Think About

The Predictive Index, PI, has a set of cultural values known as THREADS: teamwork, honesty, reliability, energy, action, drive, and scope (adapted from https://tinyurl.com/4ky5ek6n). These values embody everything that makes a perfect member of the PI organization. These values are mission-critical to the organization. To encourage the adoption of THREADS, PI actively rewards behaviors associated with these values. The culture is even a part of the hiring process as a dedicated THREADS interviewer asks questions specific to this set of values. If a candidate satisfies all of the job requirements but isn't a culture fit, they likely won't thrive at PI. Would this culture be functional in your organization?

Drivers of Culture

Expanding on the work of the Gallup organization (Gallup 2018), Corey (2021) identifies nine drivers or *seeds* of culture. They are:

1. Values. Values help those in the organization understand what it stands for and what is expected of them. They act to guide everyone in their daily behavior in the organization. Values may include creativity, innovation, transparency, collaboration, and diversity.
2. Rituals. Rituals are not just special events but also parties and informal get-togethers. Rituals may be more formal as reward ceremonies or ringing a bell when something significant is accomplished, but they may be simple, like a morning coffee run or celebrating birthdays or anniversaries. They serve to help people to feel more deeply involved in the organization.
3. Communication. This refers to not only the methods by which individuals in the organization communicate but also to how and how often they do so. Communications should be transparent. And, of course, there should be two-way communication; feedback should be provided.

4. Management practices. These are not just the behaviors of those in authority but also refer to all of the policies and practices of the organization. They include things like offer letters, organization handbooks, sickness and absenteeism policies, and similar documents that indicate the practice of management in the organization.

5. Job and structure design. The way assignments are handled and the degree of *layers* in the organization impact the culture. They indicate how much trust the organization has in its members and how much autonomy and responsibility those in the organization have. Do decisions tend to be made by those in authority or by anyone in the organization with the knowledge necessary? Is everything in written documents or is most everything done more informally? Answers to these types of questions have a sizable impact on the type of culture in an organization.

6. Reward and recognition. What are the consequences of actions in the organization? What gets rewarded or punished is another important driver of an organization's culture. Examples include a bonus (financial incentive in addition to their compensation), profit-sharing, stock options, merit pay, fringe benefits such as parental leave or member discounts, public recognition, paid leaves, or leaves (perhaps with pay) for professional development training.

7. Workspace. How are workspaces arranged and/or decorated if at all? Is personalization normal and permitted or frowned upon and prohibited? Thoring(n.d.) provides an example of a global software organization that spent millions of dollars redesigning its headquarters only to discover that the members hated it. The new open design did not match the existing culture nor the work requirements of its members who needed privacy for client conversations.

8. Informal *collisions*. "Do you pull together and support one another, or do you point fingers, do you sort it out at the leadership level, or bring in a group of people from across the organization?" (Corey 2021, 17). Clearly related to communication, as mentioned earlier, examples include casual catchups, coffee chats, water cooler conversations, brainstorming sessions, and other unplanned contacts among members of the organization.

9. Leadership. The leaders in the organization must act to support the culture or it will never become functional. They must understand their roles and their impact and commit to the culture, "Effective leadership results in individuals being willing to set aside, to an extent, their personal agendas in order to tackle tasks that move the group's agenda forward" (Kwantes and Boglarsky 2007). Leaders can maintain the organization's culture or move to innovate and change it (Trice 1991). By reinforcing the organization's values while simultaneously holding people accountable, leaders maintain the culture. Changing the organization's culture is more difficult. Memon (2022) suggests that it involves six parts: (1) invite the whole organization to be part of the cultural change process, (2) create a safe and trusting environment for people to share their thoughts and opinions, (3) ensure everyone feels heard, (4) help people find their own *whys* for the change, (5) visualize your common dream about the future together, and (6) make it clear how people can be involved throughout the change journey.

Consolidation

It should be apparent that culture is a complex concept. When trying to itemize some aspect of culture, the same aspect is labeled differently by different writers. The keywords used are:

- Accountability
- Beliefs
- Environment
- Habits
- Leadership
- Patterns
- Rules
- Stories

- Actions
- Change
- Experience(s)
- Ideas
- Norms
- Purpose
- Shared
- Unified/unity

- Autonomy
- Communicate/communication
- Group(s)/groupings
- Integration
- Order
- Recognition/appreciation
- Social
- Values

However, even without a quantifiable way of measuring culture or a precise of it, one can still understand its importance and consequences.

Consequences

So, just, what are the consequences of culture? Although relevant research is mixed, it seems clear that to avoid a dysfunctional organization, there should be a strong organizational culture. The first and perhaps the most significant consequence is that the organization's culture impacts the organization's effectiveness. The culture transmits a clear, strong message to those in the organization. There is probably not a single best culture, but it is important that everyone in the organization understands what the culture is. The success of firms such as IBM, Digital Equipment, Disney, and Delta is frequently attributed to the organization's culture.

It is important that the culture is shaped by the organization's leaders to fit the strategy of the organization. The organization's effectiveness will be enhanced if the corporate culture is consistent with the organization's strategy. When they are not in sync, the organization becomes dysfunctional, and its effectiveness suffers (Van Fleet and Griffin 2006). "Almost all the companies which have failed seem to possess an organisational culture, which is 'by default' and not consciously, professionally well designed" (Rao 2022). Further, the organization's leaders must keep the culture flexible so as to respond to changes in the organization's environment.

Another consequence of a culture that is an extension of the first is that it provides a guide to actions for new members of the organization. A new employee at Texas Instruments can look around the office and know immediately how he or she should dress the next day. The actual dress code at TI is "Clothing should be both practical for the work situation and suitable to a business environment. Employees should dress for safety and comfort, and ensure they are dressed appropriately for customers and visitors" (https://tinyurl.com/uv7cjxu3).

Something to Think About

As I was finishing my master's degree, I began interviewing a variety of organizations. One that I especially liked went well, and the recruitment company extended me an offer. Even though I had never been to the organization's location, I immediately accepted the offer as the organization had a great reputation, and the situation seemed to fit me perfectly. For my first day, I had my best suit cleaned and pressed so that I would look exceptionally sharp and ready to go. When I arrived at the office, however, I quickly noticed that no one was dressed as I was; indeed, few of the males even had no ties, let alone suits! During lunch, one of them asked me if I was attending a funeral after work. Will this person fit this culture?

The shared values and beliefs of the culture influence employees' motivation, satisfaction, and commitment to the organization's goals (Tsai 2011). A positive organizational culture will help an organization survive in even extremely difficult environments. Nguyen and his colleagues (Nguyen et al. 2019) also found that an organization's culture was positively related to innovation by members of the organization.

The social theory (Salin 2003) indicates that the relative powerlessness between members of an organization influences who becomes a victim and why they become one. Individuals from a variety of cultures with different beliefs, values, and attitudes must work together in stressful situations. Frequently, in situations such as these, those in charge of the organization may feel that they should be able to resort to any method to get results. In addition, organizational cultures with an intense focus on results may unintentionally trigger higher levels of anxiety that undermine the organization's purpose (Yip et al. 2021). In those cases, the organization may well become dysfunctional.

Managing Culture

Given the importance and consequences of an organization's culture, it must be managed in some way. The organization's leaders must understand the current culture, and then, with communication with everyone in the organization, decide if it should be maintained or changed. Only by understanding the organization's current culture and everyone's reaction to it can leaders take appropriate actions. At Hewlett-Packard, the values represented by *the HP way* still exist (Packard 1995). They not only still exist, but they also guide and direct significant activities undertaken by the organization. The principal tools organizational leaders have to manage culture are by rewarding and promoting people whose behaviors are consistent with the existing culture and by articulating the culture through slogans, ceremonies and so forth.

On the other hand, if the leaders of the organization feel a change in the culture is necessary, they must first have a clear idea of what it is they want the changed culture to be. Over the years, many organizations have attempted to create a culture like that espoused by Ouchi in his Theory Z (Ouchi 1981), Peters and Waterman in their excellence framework (Peters and Waterman 1982), or Kanter's Change Masters (Kanter 1983). While each of those approaches represents a form of organizational culture, it may or may not be appropriate for the particular organization. Involving everyone in the organization to get ideas should be considered. Yet, another way to shape culture is to bring outsiders into important positions in the organization. Bringing in new leadership is a clear signal that things will be changing. Consultants may also be useful in easing an organization from one culture to another. Of course, adopting new slogans, telling new stories, staging new ceremonies, and breaking with tradition will also lead to a changed culture.

As noted earlier, managing an organization's culture involves reinforcing desired behaviors or characteristics and punishing or providing negative outcomes for those not desired. Care must be taken in the latter circumstances. Discipline is often the trigger that precedes violence. But discipline is a necessary part of work life in order to avoid chaos. Some companies maintain a discipline-based culture where even minor indiscretions are penalized; others have a laissez-faire attitude giving the employees enough rope to hang themselves. The ideal is probably a balance between too lax and too heavy-handed (Mantell and Albrecht 1994). Even minor emotional pain suffered from public embarrassment, face threats, and reprimands by superiors may turn increasingly toxic as the contagiousness of negative emotions rubs off on coworkers and colleagues escalates and permeates organizational culture (e.g., see Goleman 2000).

Additional problems with employee relationships have resulted from the diversification and stratification of the workforce. Our shrinking world is leading to a growing "collision of cultures, political ideologies, religious doctrines, economic struggles, and national-security measures" that increases the likelihood of organizations becoming dysfunctional and individuals resorting to terrorism (Bowman 1994, xvii). Trying to understand the latter is extremely difficult because there are so many different types in so many different cultures across so many different time periods (Post 1990).

One clearly noticeable form of diversification is more women entering the workforce. Men may have less *support* at home, which may make them inclined toward disruptive or even violent behavior—and women are frequently the objects of that violence. Historically, women identified with relationships—home, husband, and children, while men identified with their chosen job or profession. Both are changing in today's society. As the number of women in organizations increased particularly in positions of leadership, they have become targets for men. In most cases, these sorts of feelings are kept in check, but when the situation changes such that a man feels helpless, he may totally lose control.

But men are not the only ones who have developed bias and resentment as women have increased in numbers at work. Women, too, feel harassed; they frequently feel they are not being treated fairly in terms of opportunities and compensation. They frequently end up in lower-wage, higher-risk jobs in the service industry, which, because of its openness to customers, is more vulnerable than factory work to violent perpetrators from the outside. Men (particularly white males) who have outdated attitudes toward females and males of other colors/races may feel threatened by the increased diversity in organizations. If they mistakenly perceive that these groups are promoted or rewarded at their expense, frustration and anger increase.

Of course, diversity includes more than just sex or race. Employing individuals with sexual preferences different from the majority, especially if one or more have acquired immune deficiency syndrome (AIDS), can elicit fear and dissension among uninformed workers and unprepared managers. Other forms of diversity include age, disability, religion, and even culture from foreign members of organizations. Each of these can lead to problems if groups are highly heterogeneous and not properly educated.

Clearly, people are important. Which ones—the leaders or managers of the organization who can help to assure psychological safety, other members of the organization, customers or clients of the organization, or suppliers to the organization? Actually, all can be involved in determining whether or not an organization is dysfunctional, as will be seen in the next chapter.

Rethinking This Chapter

Look at the notes and definition you wrote down at the beginning of this chapter. How might you change those now? As you rethink the material, focus on the culture of your organization or on that of an organization with which you are familiar. With those changes in mind, respond to the following questions and actions. Managers, human resource professionals, and students should do this carefully in order to be prepared to address issues that arise when individuals' actions aren't aligned with the organization's culture. Even if you are not currently employed, your responses should be made as if you are working in an organization. In a classroom setting, your responses should be shared and compared through discussion with others.

Chapter Questions

1. How would you describe the culture of an organization that you would like to be a member of?
2. When interviewing for a position with an organization, what questions might you ask to determine if you would fit in with the organization's culture?
3. What happens in your organization when someone makes an error or does something wrong?

Introductory Actions

1. Draft a set of cultural values for your organization.
2. What *signs* would you look for to determine the culture of an organization?
3. Who in the organization should monitor the fit of the culture with the performance of members in the organization, and how should they do that?

Case to Consider

Asia Pacific International Limited (APIL)

Asia Pacific International Limited (APIL) is headquartered in Shanghai, China, but has offices in Asia, Europe, and South America. It is a global leader in trade regarding agricultural and food products. APIL trades a wide variety of products internationally through an extensive network of suppliers and distribution chains. As of 2013, it had an integrated supply chain for 15 products and a direct presence in 58 countries. The company has a shared vision embedded in a common culture. Its mission is to deliver exceptional, personalized, first-class service to its clients by always ensuring excellent product quality, reliability, consistency, trust, traceability, and other value-added services. This has allowed APIL to grow and become the supplier to many of the world's most prominent brands. The reward system adopted by the organization is focused on value generation (short-term profit) rather than a long-term strategy for the company. This emphasis on value orientation has led, at times, to the organization neglecting its customers when it chooses the cheapest shipping line rather than one that would better serve its customers. Thus, there is a clash between value orientation and customer orientation in the company impacting the mission of high service to customers.

(*Source*: http://api-globaltrade.com/ and Naikal and Chandra (2013). Organisational Culture: A Case Study. *International Journal of Knowledge Management and Practices*. 1. Available at: https://tinyurl.com/58w5vrw7.)

Case Questions for Discussion

1. Is this culture sustainable? Why or why not?
2. If you worked for APIL, how would you reconcile the value of profit with that of customer service?
3. Consultants recommended decentralizing the organization and developing new pay systems. Do you feel that those will help?

Chapter 2 Takeaways

- Organizational culture is about the relationships that exist among organizational members and how people in the organization connect and interact with one another as they perform their organizational activities. Describe the culture in your organization.
- Organizations that develop and maintain strong cultures tend to be more effective than others. Is your organization's culture strong?
- Three basic factors are indicated as determining the culture of an organization—values held by leaders, its history, and the vision of the leaders. What are the values of leaders in your organization?
- Organizational culture evolves over a long period of time, starting with the organization's founder. Who founded your organization, and what was his or her vision for the organization?
- Cultures involve shared experiences, stories, and shared beliefs. Describe some of the shared stories for your organization.
- There are four types of culture—clan, ad hoc, market, and hierarchical. Which type of culture exists in your organization?
- The principal tools for managing culture are by rewarding and promoting those whose behaviors are consistent with the desired culture and by articulating the culture through slogans and ceremonies. How does your organization reward behavior consistent with the culture?

Recommended Reading

In addition to the many sources used in this chapter, the following case and article could expand your understanding of the chapter's material:

Case: Konrad, A. n.d. "Organizational Culture, Values and Fit in the Workplace: Making the Right Job Choices." https://hbsp.harvard.edu/product/W11240-PDF-ENG.

Article: McKee, A. 2019. "Keeping your Company's Toxic Culture from Infecting your Team." *Harvard Business Review Digital Article.* https://hbsp.harvard.edu/product/W11240-PDF-ENG.

CHAPTER 3

People in Organizations

As with previous chapters, make some notes of what you expect in this chapter. Identify the different groups of people that could contribute to an organization becoming dysfunctional. Keep those notes in mind as you read this chapter.

Introduction

Culture and safety both involve people. It is the behavior of those in the organization that largely determines whether the culture will be functional or dysfunctional. Likewise, the behavior of members of the organization will be associated with a safe place or an unsafe place. So, a closer examination of those people is necessary. However, there are several types of individuals in or associated with organizations that need to be considered—the leaders or managers of the organization, the members or employees, customers or clients, and even suppliers. Each of these has a unique impact on whether or not the organization is dysfunctional.

Leaders/Managers

Those who are in charge of the organization, and perhaps were even the founders, have tremendous and long-lasting impacts on every aspect of the organization—the purpose of the organization, the people in the organization, how it is structured or arranged, and how it functions on a day-to-day basis. It is these leaders or managers who have the most profound impact in determining whether or not the organization is dysfunctional. There are costs associated with dysfunctional leaders, including (1) a failure to develop employees, (2) increased stress and decreased productivity, (3) demotivation and low morale, and (4) a lack of team cohesion (Dranitsaris 2021).

Dysfunctional leaders set bad examples for others in the organization. They may be "abusive or bullying leaders; those who quickly assign blame and don't set priorities; those who make the same errors over and over; those who claim that they 'don't know' or have bad information; leaders who worry about 'my watch' rather than long-term organizational effectiveness; those who think that apologizing is all that is necessary to 'make things right'; and those who cook the books, pad their expense accounts, and behave unethically if not illegally" (Van Fleet and Griffin 2006, 705). Dysfunctional leaders rely on coercive power and ego, are unpredictable, and frequently are not even aware of their dysfunctional nature (Shuck, Rose, and Bergman 2015). Long-term consequences of dysfunctional leaders include high turnover, low morale, decreased performance, and a decreased reputation for the organization (Holland 2020).

Dysfunctional leaders may be classified by one or more of the following—authoritarianism, narcissism, abusive supervision, unpredictability, or Machiavellianism (Savas 2019). Another somewhat overlapping classification is narcissistic, bipolar, psychopathic, and obsessive-compulsive (Kets de Vries and Rook 2018). Using two case studies, Goldman (2008, 2006) describes how a narcissistic personality disorder or an antisocial personality disorder can cause a dysfunctional organization. Narcissism may well be the driving force of leaders, but high levels lead to dysfunctionality. A leader with an antisocial personality disorder can set a pattern in the organization such that personal aggression, verbal abuse, loud altercations, and physical confrontations become commonplace. While it may take an expert to document these disorders, anyone can witness their effects. Dysfunctional leaders created environments in which organization members feel discouraged, unenthusiastic, unappreciated, and undervalued with feelings of injustice, negative emotions, stress, little trust, low levels of commitment or collaboration, and a decline of creativity and innovation within the organization (Mehraein, Visintin, and Pittion 2023).

One aspect of narcissism is that individuals think more about themselves and their own discomforts, needs, and ambitions and so neglect the perspectives of others (Gunderman and Sechrist 2018). This toxic behavior degrades performance, undermines teamwork, reduces satisfaction, and drives people away, resulting in higher turnover rates. Narcissistic leaders tend to be grandiose, entitled, self-confident, risk-seeking, manipulative, and hostile (O'Reilly and Chatman 2020). "Organizations can be required to devote considerable resources to support the vainglorious vagaries of senior managers who are too involved with themselves to make good staff and organizational decisions" (Furnham 2007, 33). Autocratic leaders and petty tyrants who rely on fear as a way to motivate those in the organization are likely to cause the organization to become dysfunctional (Langan-Fox and Sankey 2007).

Something to Think About

Charlie loved working at his charity organization, but when a new director arrived, he began to wonder if it was such a great place to work. The new director tended to work alone in his office and if anyone intruded, he wasn't particularly pleasant in his responses. He did come up with a few new ideas, but if anyone raised a question or concern about them, he would storm off in a huff. It wasn't long until several of Charlie's coworkers left. Noting that questions seemed to go unanswered or led to loud rebukes, Charlie decided to try a different approach. He would agree with the boss and say nice things about him in his presence. The result didn't seem to improve his situation and indeed made it worse because increasingly, his coworkers were no longer chatting with him or inviting him to lunch. Now Charlie was in a bind. He could try to keep on good terms with the director or try to restore relations with his coworkers, but he couldn't do both. He decided that his relations with coworkers were more important and began to join them in criticizing the director. Nevertheless, work was no longer fun. He began to be depressed and the quality of his work suffered, so eventually, he exercised what he thought was his best option—he quit. Would you have handled this differently?

As indicated in Chapter 1, there are numerous warning signs and symptoms of dysfunctional leaders (Yones n.d.). Stroup (n.d.) suggests that there are five important warning signs: (1) a lack of transparency in decision making, (2) an overemphasis on the leader's personal success,

(3) inconsistent messaging where the leader says one thing but does another, (4) a lack of accountability where the leader refuses to take responsibility for errors, and (5) a toxic culture. If one or more of those signs or symptoms are present, something will need to be done to prevent organizational dysfunction. In addition to those, other intrapersonal and interpersonal symptoms (e.g., perfectionism, difficulties working in a team, or delegating responsibility) can also be indicators of problems in the workplace (Kyrios et al. 2007). However, it may be difficult to see the signs through layers of employees upon whom blame can lie and miscommunications (Shapiro and Von Glinow 2007).

To differentiate effective leaders from dysfunctional ones, Gottfredson (2018) argues that four mindsets serve. Those mindsets are:

- Fixed Mindset: These dysfunctional leaders do not believe that they are able or even need to change or improve their talents, abilities, or skills.
- Closed Mindset: These leaders do not listen to the ideas and suggestions of others presuming that they are right while stubbornly and illogically holding on to their own points of view.
- Prevention Mindset: They seek to avoid problems, avoid risks, and maintain the status quo.
- Inward Mindset: They are more important than others and take rather than share credit.

However, Alemu (2016) indicates that four variables will serve that same purpose. "Namely, decision making, organizational goal achievement, modeling, and meeting ethical expectations were found to be critical leadership characteristics that distinguish leaders of functional organizations from those leading dysfunctional organizations" (p. 7). Or one could look for the habits of dysfunctional leaders as warning signs. Proce (n.d.) identifies those habits as:

- Habit #1: Refusing to Make Decisions—analysis paralysis.
- Habit #2: Not Doing What You Say You Will Do—being two-faced.

- Habit #3: Not Doing What You Know You Should Be Doing—not actually taking the lead.
- Habit #4: Avoiding Responsibility—ignoring problems.
- Habit #5: Passive Aggressive Behavior—talking behind someone's back.
- Habit #6: Playing the Victim—passing the buck.
- Habit #7: Resume Building—making their C.V. look good.

Bird (2020) suggests seven ways of dealing with or surviving dysfunctional leaders. They are:

- Make the decision to stay or go—if you stay, be prepared.
- Do the work; don't be a target—perform well so the boss has no reason to pick on you.
- Don't get drawn in—be polite and honest but keep your distance from those who complain.
- Don't gossip—as stated earlier, do not get involved.
- Keep detailed records—if you become a victim, keep honest and accurate records of all that transpires.
- Don't derail your career—bite your tongue and do your best to follow the boss's orders.
- Remember, it's not forever—dysfunctional leaders are always trying to move up the organization's structure so you may not have to endure him or her for long.

Even with functional leaders, the organization could become dysfunctional because of others in or associated with it—members, customers, and/or suppliers. Probably the most important of those are the members or employees of the organization.

Members/Employees

Technically, dysfunctional employees are those who have a diagnosable personality disorder, but more commonly they are disengaged, say one thing and do another, create problems that they will then solve, or refuse to identify obvious problems (Bauer 2023). Over the years, different labels have been used to describe the behavior of dysfunctional workers: counterproductive work behavior (Raver 2013), workplace deviance (Bennett and Robinson 2000, 2003; Robinson and Bennett 1995), organizationally directed aggression (O'Leary-Kelly et al. 1996; Vardi and Weiner 1996).

According to Alemu (2016), dysfunctional organizations are the result of the behavior of their employees. Dysfunctional members of an organization can direct their behavior toward the leaders of the organization, others in the organization, or against the organization itself (de Bruijn 2021). The behavior of those individuals is likely to be toxic as "94 percent of individuals have experienced a toxic person in the workplace" (Sutton 2010, 8). "Globally, nearly 90 percent of workers are either NOT engaged or are actively disengaged—actually working against their own organizations! In the United States, where engagement is highest, it still averages a pathetic, approximately 30 percent" (Wiefling 2019). Unfortunately, even Christian-led organizations can have dysfunctional workers (White 2017).

The costs of dysfunctional behavior include increased insurance premiums, capital replacement costs, injury payouts, lawsuits, lost productivity, costs associated with stress, and a tarnished reputation for the organization (Dunlop and Lee 2004). Turnover alone has cost U.S. businesses more than U.S.$223 billion over five years (Sanchez 2020).

What exactly is a dysfunctional member of an organization? How would you identify them? Emmerich (2004) suggests that there are 10 indicators:

- No. 1: People being at odds with each other with no desire to fix it
- No. 2: Saying one thing and meaning another
- No. 3: Giving lip service to new ideas, then undercutting them in private
- No. 4: Defensiveness at reasonable suggestions
- No. 5: Attraction to Chaos
- No. 6: Not following through on commitments
- No. 7: Deflecting blame

- No. 8: People pretending like they *never got the memo*
- No. 9: Refusing to deal with conflict directly
- No. 10. Gossiping and backstabbing

Writers have different ways of classifying dysfunctional employees. Miller (2008) discusses five categories of dysfunctional employees:

- Shrinkers and clingers—overly dependent and constantly use the time of leaders
- Emoters and reactors—overreact and cause chaos in the organization
- Preeners and predators—narcissistic individuals who try to make themselves look good
- Oddballs and spoilers—passive–aggressive individuals who cause problems
- Detailers and vigilantes—obsessive–compulsive or paranoid individuals who nit-pick so much that they do not accomplish much

Reed (2015) also identifies five types:

- The office whiner—constantly finding something that needs to be changed in his or her favor
- The know it all—you can't tell them anything because they already know it all
- The one who wants your job—smiles to your face but stabs you behind your back to make themselves look better
- The behind the *scener*—these individuals spread negative gossip to make you look bad
- The yes man—the boss pleaser

Farmer (2014), on the other hand, names only four types: (1) the self-promoter who is always noting how good they are, (2) the lazy lug who does as little as possible, (3) the saboteur who likes to see others fail, and (4) the drama master for whom everything is earth-shattering.

Something to Think About

George had a problem. He doesn't seem to get along with his coworkers. He loves the company and, for the most part, enjoys his work, but increasingly, he is having difficulties with his fellow workers. The salary is good, and the field is a bit crowded, so another job might be difficult to find, so he is biding his time and hoping that somehow relations will improve. He doesn't hate his coworkers; he just doesn't feel connected to them. He tells them no thanks when he is genuinely too busy to engage in conversation or join in betting pools for local sports events. One of them just seems to not have anything to do as he always seems to be around gossiping and complaining. Another has bad breath and insists on getting close and speaking quietly. George is thinking that if he will occasionally go for a beer with some of them after work, they will accept his reluctance to interact much on a day-to-day basis.

Needless to say, nonprofit and volunteer organizations also may have dysfunctional members. Robotham, Plaza, and Windon. (2021) suggest such individuals become problematic for their organizations for four reasons:

1. A lack of or poor communication and feedback from the leaders of the organization
2. Leaders who have negative attitudes or approaches to their roles
3. The individual(s) simply are not engaged with their assignment of the goals of the organization
4. The individual(s) have certain personality traits (e.g., negativity, egotism, petulance) that make them difficult to work with

Jones (2019) suggests that dysfunctions occur in four stages: Stage 1: Ambiguities are not questioned; Stage 2: Inconsistencies are ignored; Stage 3: Ambiguities and inconsistencies are undiscussable; and Stage 4: Undiscussability is undiscussable. He then provides a checklist that can be used to assess the extent of dysfunction that might exist in your organization. That checklist is:

- Communication is indirect.
- Conflicts are not stated openly.
- Secrets are used to build alliances.
- Gossip is used to excite and titillate.
- Corporate memory is lost or forgotten.
- Requests for policy clarification are ignored.
- The open expression of true feelings is absent.
- People look for direction on how to act and react.
- The search for the cause of a problem is personalized.
- Friendship between professional colleagues is lacking.
- Meetings have long agendas and end up going in circles.
- Inconsistent application of procedures is not challenged.
- Complex procedures are initiated by electronic messaging.
- Mundane announcements are given more time at meetings.
- Promises of better times ahead seduce people into a status quo.
- Dualistic (us versus them) thinking creates conflict and sets up sides.
- Perfectionism creates an atmosphere of intolerance for mistakes.
- Judgments are made about people and things being *good* or *bad*.
- Isolation by management keeps them from seeing what is happening.
- Management isolation is used as the basis for decision making by cliques.

One form of dysfunctional behavior that seems to get less attention is ostracism. "Workplace ostracism presents an act of omission—the actor withdraws or omits their social interactions with the victim" (Liu 2020). There are three different types of ostracism: social exclusion, social rejection, and psychological exclusion, but all have negative effects on the organization. Workplace ostracism has been found to bring negative consequences on employees' attitudes toward work, particularly lower job satisfaction and a higher intention to leave the organization (e.g., Liu and Xia 2016; Ferris et al. 2015).

Emmerich (2004) suggests that to cure dysfunctional behavior, you need to follow the three Cs—clarity, consistency, and consequences. Be clear about what individuals are expected to do, have a zero-tolerance policy for dysfunctional behaviors, and have firm and systematic penalties. On the other hand, if you are a functional person but find yourself in a dysfunctional organization, there are certain steps you should take (Battaglia 2015). The four steps are:

- **Seek realignment and clarity in job processes**—Be sure to have a clear goal and then work diligently toward that goal.
- **Get creative**—Develop new routines and work habits to overcome the monotony of your work.
- **Control what you can; don't worry about what you can't**— Get involved and focus on issues rather than individuals.
- **Commit (in or out)**—If you believe in your organization's goals, work to help accomplish them; if you don't, it is time to move on.

As mentioned earlier, there are still other groups of individuals that can contribute to an organization becoming dysfunctional. One such group consists of the clients or customers of the organization.

Customers/Clients

In dealing with customers, the Iron Triangle rule is frequently mentioned. The Iron Triangle essentially says: "We can do it fast. We can do it cheap. We can do it well. But we can't do all three. So, choose any two" (https://tinyurl.com/nxtxtd4y). If the organization strives to do all three, it may create such conflict among units (the budget, sales, and production/operations) that it becomes dysfunctional.

Likewise, organizations that blindly follow the saying "The customer is always right" may become dysfunctional. A customer coming into a print shop may say "I want you to do this" without realizing that there may be better and possibly less expensive ways of providing them with what they want.* Further, customers can be dishonest or have unrealistic expectations. Hueffner (2022) suggests five particular reasons why the saying should not be blindly followed. They are:

- It can be demoralizing to team culture. The leaders may advocate it but those who have to actually work with the clients may find it impossible to adhere to.
- It can lead to poor customer experiences. Trying hard to satisfy one customer may result in others getting less attention.
- It was never meant to be taken literally. It was meant to mean that customers should be listened to, not that they were always right.
- Customers are sometimes just wrong. They may lack the information to truly understand the product or service and so need explanations rather than blindly following their requests.
- It can lead to unrealistic expectations and set your team up for failure. Customers can be simply wrong or as noted above, dishonest so blindly following the saying could be harmful to the organization.

Czerwonka (2022) echoes these in arguing that the saying is wrong for several reasons. His reasons are:

- It puts undue stress on employees.
- It strains the management–employee relationship.
- Some customers will hurt your business.
- It results in poorer customer service.
- Some customers are wrong.

---

* In the 1890s, the hotelier César Ritz maxim was "Le client n'a jamais tort" or the customer is never wrong. The more recent saying was popularized by retailers Harry Gordon Selfridge (London-based department store, Selfridges), John Wanamaker (Philadelphia department store, Wanamaker's) and Marshall Field (Chicago-based department store, Marshall Field's) in the early 1900s (https://en.wikipedia.org/wiki/The_customer_is_always_right).

On the other hand, Dalpes (2023) suggests why the saying should be followed. Her suggestions are:

- Meeting customers' standards gives you an edge over the competition. Sixty percent of customers indicate that they would switch after a bad experience.
- Happy customers lead to better retention metrics. Seventy-seven percent of business owners say that satisfying customers is vital to maintaining them as customers.
- Satisfying your existing customer base can help you attract new customers. Eighty percent of surveyed businesses plan to increase their customer service budgets to attract new business.
- There is a direct link between happy customers and business performance. Sixty percent of customers purchased a particular brand because they expect that it will be better.
- Loyal customers are less likely to churn. Sixty percent of customers who interact with customer support indicate that if they have a bad experience, they may turn to a different source in the future.

Something to Think About

Sarah had to take a trip for her company. The travel department made all of the arrangements for her, including transportation to and from the airports on both ends of her journey and, of course, her hotel reservation. When she checked in to her hotel, she noticed a sign indicating that they had a 100 percent satisfaction or a money-back guarantee. That started her thinking. She mulled over the guarantee each day of her three-day stay and decided that she could save the company some money by taking advantage of the guarantee. So, as she was checking out, she told the clerk that she wanted a refund as the noise from the bar had been too disconcerting for her to get to sleep easily; indeed, she told them that at least one night it had kept her awake for almost all of the nights. The hotel refunded her visit with no questions asked. When she returned to work, she relayed the episode to her boss and noted how she had saved the company the money for the hotel. What can or should be hotel do about this sort of customer behavior?

However, a large proportion of customers in the hospitality and service industries are dysfunctional (Hwang, Yoo, and Kim 2021). These customers adversely affect employees, generating psychological stress, damaging their self-esteem, and making the service employees engage in counterproductive behaviors (Van Jaarsveld, Walker, and Skarlicki 2010; Harris and Reynolds 2003). If they are deliberately engaging in disruptive behavior, they are termed jaycustomers (Harris and Daunt 2004; Lovelock 1994), and they cause problems for the organization, its members, and other customers. Those effects while generally short lasting can lead to long-term problems (Xiao et al. 2022). Consumer misbehavior is not limited to the service industry nor to only face-to-face interactions but exists online as well (Wu, Zheng, and Zhao 2021).

Consumers at times can simply act unfairly. Shoplifting is a clear example (Krasnovsky and Lane 1998). Berry and Seiders (2008, 30) identify consumer unfairness as "when a customer behaves in a manner that is devoid of common decency, reasonableness, and respect for the rights of others, creating inequity and causing harm for a company and, in some cases, its employees and other customers." They suggest that unfair behavior can be differentiated from bad manners or bad judgment by three factors—the severity of harm, the frequency of the behavior, and intentionality (p. 30). Overreacting to such unfair behavior could cause the organization to become dysfunctional.

In addition to customers, suppliers can also be a contributing factor to an organization's becoming dysfunctional.

Suppliers

In a supply chain setting, relationships develop through partnerships or buyer–seller relationships. A supplier partnership in the supply chain implies an agreement between a manufacturing firm and its suppliers or subcontractors. However, due to the extensive interactions required for the supplier to adapt to the buyer's specific requirements, conflicts occur (Gulati, Lawrence, and Puranam 2005). Those conflicts can result in one or both of the organizations becoming dysfunctional.

There seems to be inherent buyer–supplier distrust that predisposes antagonism and dysfunctional conflict (Prince et al. 2016). The dysfunction occurs when buyers are reluctant to implement suppliers' ideas that reduce costs. The buyer may like a supplier's idea but won't agree to it because they feel that it won't translate to price increases for the consumer. Dysfunction may also result from pressure to come up with new ideas for customers (Moore 2015).

Close buyer–supplier relationships are a double-edged sword because mutual benefits are bought with a greater dependency (Aßländer 2010). That dependency can easily result in negative relationships. Negative buyer–supplier partnerships can occur especially if the two organizations have value structures that don't match (Davis-Sramek, Fugate, and Omar 2007). Close buyer–seller relationships tend to have relatively high instability rates and generally fail (Das and Tang 2000). Dissatisfied managers report that unfulfilled promises, deceitful behavior, unreasonable demands, and difficulties in changing the terms of the collaboration spoil the relationship (Piercy and Lane 2006).

Villena and her colleagues (Villena, Choi, and Revilla 2016) identify the sources of risk in buyer–supplier relationships that could lead to conflict and, hence, dysfunctional organizations. Those risks are:

1. Loss of objectivity—This happens when the buyer organization places too much trust in their supplier organizations and thus becomes less objective.
2. Partner opportunism—On the other hand, buyers who trust their suppliers too much are prone to reduce their monitoring efforts, and suppliers may take advantage of it.
3. Knowledge redundancy—In every situation, when information becomes repetitive or redundant, the value of that information will decrease.

They also suggest that those risks could be reduced if the organizations adopt three mechanisms. Those mechanisms are:

1. Set challenging goals—Setting challenging goals tends to reduce overconfidence and promote new ways of thinking.
2. Implement a rotational policy—Changing or rotating purchasing managers by the buyer organization avoids excessive camaraderie between the organization's employees and their counterparts in the

supplying organizations, and it also tends to ensure more accurate supplier performance data.

3. Use contracts as a coordination and control tool—having clearly defined contractual terms benefits both organizations by promoting objectivity, reducing incentives to misbehave, and avoiding dysfunctional relationships.

Buyer organizations that deal with suppliers from other countries should comply with the Foreign Corrupt Practices Act (*FCPA*). FCPA prohibits companies from bribing foreign officials in an effort to obtain or retain business, and it requires that companies maintain adequate books, records, and internal controls to prevent unlawful payments (www.sec. gov/securities-topic/foreign-corrupt-practices-act). But dysfunctional organizations may fail to comply with FCPA. Chen (n.d.) identifies signs of ineffective compliance programs. They are:

- *Lack of Financial and Organizational Discipline.* Dysfunctional organizations lack enterprise resource planning (ERP) tools, have no centralized visibility into financial transactions, have out-of-date databases, have inadequate controls of payment methods, and have ledgers that are both duplicative and incomplete.
- *Legal Dominated Compliance.* These organizations are less interested in whether their programs actually work than how it looks as a legal defense.
- *Citing Sentencing Guidelines as the Standard.* These organizations are trying to be just good enough so that if caught, no one goes to jail.
- *Counting Training Completion Rate (and other invalid or incomplete metrics).* Rather than measure actual compliance, these organizations count training instead.
- *Focus on Due Diligence Rather Than Management.* Organizations focusing on initial due diligence instead of ongoing management of their programs fail to recognize that due diligence is the beginning rather than the end of a continuing process.

- *Single-Statute Compliance.* Focusing only on one agency's regulations does not prevent unethical behavior.
- *Disproportionate Focus on Gifts–Meals–Travel–Entertainment.* Just because gifts, meals, travel, or entertainment are not accepted, again, does not prevent some other form of unethical behavior.

People in organizations can contribute to the organization becoming functional or dysfunctional. The next several chapters examine in more detail how those individuals influence their organizations in ways that cause them to become dysfunctional. How people can contribute to improved psychosocial conditions and psychological safety are covered in the final chapter.

Rethinking This Chapter

Look at the notes you made at the beginning of this chapter. How might you change those now? As you rethink the material, focus on the various people in your organization or on that of another organization with which you are familiar. With those people in mind, respond to the following questions and actions. Managers, human resource professionals, and students should do this carefully in order to be prepared to deal with the different groups of individuals discussed in the chapter. Even if you are not currently employed, your responses should be made as if you are working in an organization. In a classroom setting, your responses should be shared and compared through discussion with others.

Chapter Questions

1. Have you ever experienced or witnessed a situation where the leaders of the organization were dysfunctional? What about others in the organization, customers, or suppliers?
2. What specific actions could, or should, you or your organization take to reduce the negative effects of those individuals?

3. What costs or impacts to you or your organization concern you the most? Why those particular costs?

Introductory Actions

1. Draft a set of behavioral *rules* for your organization.
2. What information should be collected by your organization to monitor or possibly predict the types of behaviors described in this chapter?
3. Who in the organization should keep those records for how long, for what purpose(s), and to whom should those records be made available?

Case to Consider

Keeping the Hotel Clean

Working as a maid in a hotel isn't glamorous, but it pays for medications, rent, and other bills. Recently, the new manager has been making it more difficult. She expects us to clean rooms faster than we ever had in the past. Other cleaning workers have quit, so we are understaffed. When several of us complained about the increase in work, especially with no increase in pay, he said it was "orders from the top" and there was nothing he could do about it.

In the hotel business, there are two types of customers—stayovers and checkouts. A stayover refers to someone who has booked for several days. For them, my job is relatively easy. I remake the bed, touch up the bathroom, and take out the garbage, and can be done in about 15 minutes without any back-breaking work. I'm essentially just doing some minor touchups so that the customers will feel good when they come back at night. A checkout, on the other hand, requires more.

When someone checks out, it can be more of a chore unless it was a business traveler. They are usually there for only a day, so their rooms are not very dirty. But for others, it can be a lot of work. You have to change the sheets on both of the beds and also change the towels and washcloths. You have to see that there is a new box of tissues and a new roll of toilet paper folded in a little point. While all of that isn't horrible, if the room has been occupied by a family with kids, the garbage alone can be bad. Every trashcan will be full, and there will be stuff all over the floors. The bathroom will be disgusting, requiring chemicals that burn our noses and hands while we scrub down every surface to ensure it will be clean and sanitary for the next guests.

When we were fully staffed, the work was split among us so that each of us had some stayovers and some checkouts. We each did about 15 rooms each day. Now I have to clean 17 rooms a day, and the pressure is almost overwhelming. I am so tired all the time now that when I'm home, I just want to lay in bed or sit on the couch and do nothing. My kids want me to spend time with them, but I'm just too worn out to do anything. I'm so tired that I don't even cook anymore; we just do takeout from local fast-food places, which is not healthy but all I can do. I don't like it but can't quit without something else already lined up.

(Adapted from www.motherjones.com/politics/2021/09/our-hotel-ceo-made-tens-of-millions-of-dollars-and-furloughed-us/)

Case Questions for Discussion

1. Is the manager a dysfunctional leader? Why or why not?
2. If you were the person in this case, what might you have done differently? Why?
3. If you were advising the manager, what advice would you provide? Be specific.

Chapter 3 Takeaways

- Costs associated with dysfunctional leaders include a failure to develop employees, increased stress, decreased productivity, demotivation, low morale, and lack of team cohesion. What costs associated with leaders can you identify?
- Dysfunctional leaders set bad examples for others in the organization. What bad examples can you identify?
- Dysfunctional leaders are authoritarian, narcissistic, abusive, and unpredictable. Have you encountered any dysfunctional leaders?

- Dysfunctional workers may engage in counterproductive work behavior, workplace deviance, or organizationally directed aggression. Have you encountered any dysfunctional workers?
- The costs of dysfunctional member behavior include increased insurance premiums, capital replacement costs, turnover, injury payouts, lawsuits, lost productivity, costs associated with stress, and a tarnished organizational reputation. What costs associated with members can you identify?
- Dysfunctional customers adversely affect employees, generate stress, and make service employees also engage in counterproductive behaviors. What costs associated with customers can you identify?
- The risks in buyer–supplier relationships that lead to conflict are loss of objectivity, opportunism, and redundant information. What risks in buyer–supplier relationships can you identify?

Recommended Reading

In addition to the many sources used in this chapter, the following case and article could expand your understanding of the chapter's material.

Case: Manzoni, J.-F. and Barsoux. n.d. *Strike at British Airways: Unavoidable or Set-Up-To-Fail.* https://store.hbr.org/product/strike-at-british-airways-unavoidable-or-set-up-to-fail/IMD451.

Article: Gallo, A. 2013. "How to Manage Someone You Don't Like." *Harvard Business Review Digital Article.* https://hbr.org/2013/08/how-to-manage-someone-you-dont.

CHAPTER 4

The Role of Safety

As with previous chapters, make some notes of what you expect in this chapter. Write down what you feel is meant by safety. Keep that in mind as you read this chapter.

Introduction

Dysfunctional organizations are inherently unsafe. They are psychologically unsafe as well as physically unsafe. It should be apparent that any of the topics previously addressed—poor or harsh cultures, dysfunctional people—would lead to dysfunctional organizations and unsafe working conditions. The organization needs a culture based on safety, a safe working environment, and prevention programs. A safety culture would minimize the impact of dysfunctional people in the organization.

To create such a culture, there are specific guidelines that should be followed. The first is to recognize and follow the guidance of the Occupational Safety and Health Administration (OSHA). The Occupational Safety and Health Act of 1970 (OSH Act) requires that "[e]ach employer shall furnish to each of his employees employment and a place of employment which are free from recognized hazards that are causing or are likely to cause death or serious physical harm to his employees" (Section 5, Duties). This is known as the *General Duty Clause*. Relying on the General Duty Clause, OSHA cites employers who fail to address issues of workplace violence (https://tinyurl.com/37y3xeh9). To follow its guidance and prevent being cited, OSHA suggests adopting five *building blocks* for an effective violence prevention program. The five are (1) management commitment and employee involvement, (2) worksite analysis, (3) hazard prevention and control, (4) safety and health training, and (5) recordkeeping and program evaluation (OSHA: 3148-06R 2016, 2016). To achieve a safety culture where people do the right things for the right reasons, the organization must involve everyone in the process of learning from events, both good and bad.

Why Safety

Following inspections of worksites, OSHA publishes a list of the top 10 most frequently cited standards (/www.osha.gov/top10citedstandards). The only industry that stands out is the construction industry. Correcting these would go a long way to prevent injuries, illnesses, and deaths at work, so organizations should pay particular attention to these causes of accidents. While these data generally do not include volunteers, no organization should neglect them as they are just as likely to suffer from accidents as paid members of an organization.

1. Failure to have proper fall protection, particularly in the construction industry.
2. Failure to have proper respiratory protection in general rather than associated with a particular industry.
3. Having unsafe ladders and their use, particularly in the construction industry.
4. Failure to have proper hazard communication in general rather than associated with a particular industry.
5. Having unsafe scaffolding, particularly in the construction industry.
6. Failure to have proper fall protection training in the construction industry.
7. Failure to have proper control of hazardous energy (lockout/tagout) in general rather than associated with a particular industry.
8. Failure to have proper eye and face protection, particularly in the construction industry.
9. Having unsafe powered industrial trucks in general rather than associated with a particular industry.
10. Failure to have proper machinery and machine guards in general rather than associated with a particular industry.

Morrison (2016) has identified seven workplace hazards that are seen again and again by members of the National Safety Council. They are:

1. Working at height—this doesn't simply refer to scaffolding and ladders but includes working on roofs or high equipment without proper railings or other safeguards.
2. Poor housekeeping—clutter, leaks, or standing water contribute to slips, trips, and falls, as can improperly storing items.
3. Electrical extension cords—*Daisy-chaining* extension cords and using them more or less permanently can lead to fires and trips.
4. Forklifts—too large a load, being in a hurry, or simply being distracted can lead to accidents.
5. Lockout/tagout—this refers to practices and procedures that are necessary to disable machinery or equipment to prevent hazardous energy release and, if not properly implemented can cause serious injury.
6. Chemicals—not just the chemicals but also improperly storing them or having chemicals that are not really necessary.
7. Confined spaces—the major issue is the atmosphere, which could be deadly if not properly ventilated.

Something to Think About

Harry, a student at a nearby college, worked as a carpenter in the summers to pay his tuition and fees. Recently, he was working for a real estate development company building new houses. While he was working on the second floor, trying to set up rafters for the roof, he slipped. Unfortunately, he was also near a stairway opening, so when he fell, it was all the way to the first floor. Unfortunately, the first floor was still just the concrete foundation. As a result of his fall, he suffered a skull fracture with serious brain injuries. To add insult to injury, neither he nor his employer had accident insurance so instead of earning money for tuition, he had to pay a great deal of money for medical bills. How might Harry's fall have been prevented?

The conditions identified by OHSA and Morrison would clearly render an organization dysfunctional. Yet, those conditions exist and even persist in far too many organizations. If more organizations worked to improve psychosocial conditions and develop psychological safety for their members, there would be fewer and fewer dysfunctional ones. Hopefully, a fuller understanding of health and safety will encourage organizations to strive for psychologically safe cultures.

The National Safety Council reports the following data for work injuries and deaths in the United States (Table 4.1). Once again, the construction industry is notable for having the highest number of deaths, although transportation and warehousing are close to it. Utilities and information industries have the lowest—only about 4 percent of that in construction.

Table 4.1 Preventable injuries at work by industry, United States, 2021

| Industry division | Hours worked[a] (millions) | Deaths[a] | | Deaths per 100,000 full-time equivalent workers [a] | | Medically consulted injuries |
		2021	Change from 2020	2021	Change from 2020	
All industries	284,100	4,472	9%	3.1	3%	4,260,000
Agriculture[b]	4,600	435	-10%	18.9	-8%	110,000
Mining[b]	1,300	94	22%	14.5	41%	10,000
Construction	21,000	946	-1%	9.0	-8%	260,000
Manufacturing	29,600	347	16%	2.3	10%	490,000
Wholesale trade	6,900	150	6%	4.3	2%	90,000
Retail trade	28,200	164	18%	1.2	20%	510,000
Transportation and warehousing	13,500	900	20%	13.3	6%	310,000
Utilities	2,100	32	88%	3.0	100%	20,000
Information	4,900	35	30%	1.4	17%	20,000
Financial activities	20,600	72	11%	0.7	17%	80,000
Professional and business services	35,700[c]	188[c]	NA[c]	1.1[c]	NA[c]	200,000
Educational and health services	44,600	132	19%	0.6	20%	890,000

Industry division	Hours worked[a] (millions)	Deaths[a]		Deaths per 100,000 full-time equivalent workers[a]		Medically consulted injuries
		2021	Change from 2020	2021	Change from 2020	
Leisure and hospitality	19,800	150	-2%	1.5	-17%	290,000
Other services[b]	12,400	183	31%	3.0	20%	100,000
Government	38,900	311[c]	-2%	1.9[c]	-6%	880,000
Industry not reported by BLS		333				

[a] Deaths include persons of all ages. Workers and death rates include persons 16 years and older. The rate is calculated as: (number of fatal work injuries × 200,000,000/total hours worked). The base for 100,000 full-time equivalent workers is 200,000,000 hours. Prior to 2008, rates were based on estimated employment—not hours worked.
[b] Agriculture includes forestry, fishing, and hunting. Mining includes oil and gas extraction. *Other services* excludes public administration.
[c] BLS did not report the total number of deaths for several industry sectors. The NSC estimate is based on the partial data reported for this industry by injury event.
Source: NSC analysis of data from the BLS CFOI surveillance program.
Source of table: https://tinyurl.com/23rpykcc.

More recently, Georgiev (2023) presents health and safety information in a more detailed way that draws more attention to the problem than the data shown in the table. He notes that:

- Each year there are 3.5 fatalities per 100,000 full-time workers.
- Every second in the United States, 14 workers are injured.
- Private sector workers experience nonfatal job-related injuries and illnesses at a rate of 2.7 per 100 full-time employees.
- In 2019, accidental death grew by 2 percent.
- In 2019, exposure to harmful substances or environments accounted for almost 37,000 injuries at work.
- In 2019, 70 million workdays were lost due to injuries and deaths at work.
- In 2019, the cost of work-related injuries was U.S.$171 billion.
- In 2020, 2.8 out of every 100 full-time workers suffered injuries at work.

- In 2020, there were 266,530 sprains, strains, and tears.
- In 2020, there were 4,764 fatal deaths at work, but it rose to 5,190 in 2021.
- In 2020, about every 111 minutes, a worker in the United States died.
- In 2020, deaths associated with transportation were the leading cause of death at work.
- Only 3 percent of workplace injuries are the result of fires or explosions.
- Slips, trips, and falls account for 26 percent of all nonfatal injuries at work.
- Each year, over 2.4 million workers require a trip to an emergency room after an injury at work.
- Those 55 years of age or older account for 35.5 percent of fatal workplace injuries.
- In the United States, an average of 14 workers die on the job each day.
- Workplace incidents resulting in death have dropped 66 percent with the passage of the OSH Act of 1970.
- Each worker must produce U.S.$1,100 of goods to offset the costs associated with accidents.

What To Do

The organization should conduct annual inspections of its physical facility(ies) as part of a worksite analysis to evaluate and determine any vulnerability to workplace violence or hazards. Such an analysis will determine corrective actions that should be taken to reduce any and all risks. As part of a prevention system, critical security factors such as closed circuit televisions (CCTVs), access controls, doors, and locks must be properly functioning. The organization should routinely check these and other components such as emergency phones, emergency lighting, security escorts, panic buttons or switches, video monitoring, and metal detectors. Organizations that invest in these safety and security devices are likely to avoid being dysfunctional and have safe and violent-free workplaces.

To deal specifically with accidents, both potential and actual, organizations should develop safety management practices (Fugas et al. 2012). However, there are different approaches to safety. It may be seen as a job-specific phenomenon. In that context, it involves the design of equipment (safe design or safety in design), the design of jobs, attitudes, awareness, and the like (Howard 2008; Peterson 1980). This approach to safety involves the improvement and reduction of ergonomic factors that contribute to an employee's psychological and physical stress (Fargnoli 2021; De la Garza and Fadier 2005; Rosen 1985). It reduces the need for other safety procedures or administrative controls. Even with proper equipment, some organizational members may not use it. For example, personal protective eyewear use seems to be a function of personal risk perception (Lombardi et al. 2009).

Nevertheless, it is possible to reduce workplace incidents through systems reengineering. Applying process reengineering principles to safety looks like this (Joly 2020):

1. Identify a process, product, or experience your company is engaged in.
2. Consider the constraints that safety concerns are imposing on the process, product, or experience.
3. Keeping your company's purpose front and center, imagine ways to overcome or work around these constraints, typically with the help of digital technology.
4. Reassemble your process and test it in the real world to verify its effectiveness and economics.
5. Using safety to reengineer a company's processes or products can drive innovation on multiple dimensions.

Regardless of what the organization may do, individuals may engage in job crafting. Job crafting is when individual members of the organization take action themselves to achieve a better match between their own circumstances and their jobs (Wrzesniewski and Dutton 2001). Job crafting may be done by task crafting (shaping the number of tasks), relational crafting (modifying who the individual interacts with on the job), and cognitive crafting (changing the way the individual feels or thinks about the job). While finding some differences between permanent and temporary members of organizations, psychological safety was important to both (Plomp et al. 2019). Job crafting has been shown to improve both psychological and physical safety (Nascimento et al. 2022; Lee 2022; Kim and Kim 2022; Renkema et al. 2022; Demerouti et al. 2020; Jiang, Zhang, and Feng 2019).

Something to Think About

A 14-hour shift proved fatal for Robert Dietz. Dietz worked for the Lower Bucks County Joint Municipal Authority in Pennsylvania. He had worked for over 20 years as a maintenance worker, but seniority didn't prevent him from regularly working long hours doing manual labor, including jackhammering, repairing water main breaks, and cutting tree roots. Nearing the end of an especially grueling day, Dietz collapsed. First responders could not resuscitate him. Shortly after, he was pronounced dead. Some doctors explained that Dietz's preexisting conditions put him at high risk for a heart attack, while others stated his conditions, paired with extraneous physical labor, caused his death (adapted from Trimedia Environmental and Engineering at https://tinyurl.com/kc5yucdv). What could have been done to prevent this sort of occurrence?

At other times, safety is dealt with at an organizational level involving the presence or absence of unions, type of industry, and so on (Misch 2015; Conchie, Moon, and Duncan 2013). Yet another viewpoint is to deal with safety at the supervisor's level. The importance of the relationship between supervision and work injuries has been noted (Haas 2020; Prest 2020). Additional numbers of supervisors were found to be associated with lower work injuries in most cases, and the cost of such additional supervision was found to be partially justified in terms of the reduced costs of work injuries, although there was considerable variation across industries (Rinefort, Van Fleet, and Van Fleet 1998; Rinefort and Van Fleet 1993). Indeed, when an organization reduces the number of supervisors by downsizing to the extent that an organization's safety record is a measure of its health, downsizing may be hazardous to an organization's health (Rinefort, Van Fleet, and Van Fleet 1998).

Sustaining a culture that is strong on safety is never-ending, but supervisors play key roles in maintaining the organization's safety plan. Supervisors help to ensure that workplaces are free from unnecessary hazards and conditions. The province of Ontario, Canada, has developed a training program for supervisors dealing with health and safety (https://tinyurl.com/bdems8ft). The program involves the following five steps.

1. Make a difference—describe the health and safety roles and responsibilities of the employer, supervisor, and worker.
2. Lead the way—show that they are required to support the rights of workers.
3. Know the supervisor's toolkit—incorporate the recognition, assessment, control, and evaluation of hazards when planning and organizing; communicate about potential or actual hazards and how to work safely; look for hazards and listen to and respond to members' concerns; make sure everyone follows the rules and wears protective equipment; what they should do if something goes wrong; and know the legal consequences if they don't fulfill their legal obligations.
4. Know you are not alone—identify sources of information, such as policies, the safety committee, government regulations and associations, and other associations.
5. Be a role model—set a good example to influence others in the organization.

Supervisors should also be aware of domestic violence spilling over into the workplace. Its impact on the workplace may include lost productivity, health care costs, absenteeism, and employee turnover.

Planning

An emergency action plan (EAP, also known as an emergency preparedness plan) is required by particular OSHA standards (https://tinyurl.com/yc2e2u7a). Many companies already have EAPs to deal with substance abuse, rising health and safety costs, and increased stress in the workplace, but EAPs should also cover fires, hazardous materials spills, tornadoes, floods, and the like. The purpose of an EAP is to facilitate and organize the actions of members of an organization during emergencies. Generally, an EAP will have assessed risks members of the organization may face and how to respond to them. Of course, it will specify policies and procedures, how the plan will be communicated to those in the organization, and what sort of training and testing will be required to ensure that the plan will work. An EAP should specify evacuation procedures, escape routes, and floor plans as well as how and to whom emergencies should be reported, including visitors.

OSHA suggests that an EAP should be comprised of the following components (https://tinyurl.com/bdevzb92):

- It must be in writing and available to all members of the organization although those with fewer than ten members may communicate the EAP orally.
- It should have procedures for reporting a fire or other emergencies.
- It should specify procedures for emergency evacuation, including the type of evacuation and exit route assignments.
- There should be floor plans or maps clearly showing emergency escape routes.
- There should be color coding to aid individuals in determining the particular route they should follow.
- It should have procedures to be followed by members of the organization who must remain in order to carry out critical operations before they evacuate, that is, power and water supplies or other essential services that cannot be shut down or have to be shut down in stages.
- It should have procedures to account for all members of the organization after evacuation to be certain that no one is left behind.
- There should be procedures for performing rescues or medical tasks.

- It should identify the name or job title of everyone who may be contacted by those needing more information about the plan or an explanation of responsibilities under the plan.
- There must be a working alarm system that is regularly kept functional.
- The alarm system must have distinctive signals for each purpose and comply with the requirements in Section 1910.165 of OSHA regulations (https://tinyurl. com/2sms8vkk).
- Some members of the organization must be trained to assist others in a safe and orderly evacuation.
- There must be an adequate number of employees available at all times to act as evacuation *wardens* in times of emergencies. One *warden* for every 20 employees should be available.
- These *wardens* must be thoroughly aware of the organization's layout, places of refuge (interior and exterior), and any and all handicapped or disabled members who may need extra assistance.
- Leaders in the organization must review the EAP with each member of the organization who is covered by the plan when the plan is developed, when the member's responsibilities under the plan change, and when the plan is changed in any way.

Having a safety plan is of little value if those in the organization are not familiar with it. In 2020, 30 percent of respondents indicated that they were not even aware of their organization's safety plans (Dobrilova 2021). Even in health care where you might think that everyone would be concerned about safety, 58 percent of employees fear speaking up about safety problems (Murphy 2012). Women are less likely to speak up than men, and virtual environments seem to make matters worse (Tulshyan 2021). Suggesting a solution to a safety issue may not be conducive to maintaining good relations with others in the organization. This sort of failure to speak up is an important contributing factor in communication errors and adverse events (Sutcliffe, Lewton, and Rosenthal 2004). Young workers explain their reluctance to an underlying fear of being fired, their inexperience and newcomer status, and relatedly, a belief that they were powerless to bring about improvements in safety (Tucker and Turner 2013). One study (Hurt and Dye n.d.) suggested that members of organizations are reluctant to speak up because (1) people don't think leadership wants their ideas, (2) no one asks, (3) they lack the confidence to share, (4) they lack the skills to share, and (5) people think nothing will happen. In any event, if you want to move toward a safety culture where people do the right things for the right reasons, they must feel involved in the process of learning from events, both good and bad.

Not only do individuals not report problems that could lead to accidents, but some even fail to report injuries when an accident has occurred. In one study (Moore et al. 2015), 27 percent indicated that they had failed to report a work-related injury in construction work. The five most commonly endorsed reasons for not reporting were (a) "My injury was small, so I don't need to report it"; (b) "I accept that pain is a natural part of my job"; (c) "Home treatment, anti-inflammatories, pain medication, heat, and so on are sufficient to deal with my problems"; (d) "I am not sure if my pain or symptoms are the result of work activities"; and (e) "I am afraid I won't be hired again by the same or another contractor if I file a claim."

To overcome this reluctance to speak up organizations could set rules that people don't interrupt one another in meetings (Tulshyan 2021). Those meetings should encourage member participation, but there should also be ways to report any near-miss situations. Chew (2019) suggests that for members to speak up, two conditions must exist and the responsibility for creating these conditions rests with the leaders of the organization. The conditions are (1) meetings with employee participation and (2) the presence of psychological safety. Another suggestion (Baker 2020) is to be SMART in making suggestions—specific, meaningful, action (ask for something to be done), realistic (don't expect the impossible), and time (provide a deadline if possible).

Safety Systems

Health and safety systems should consist of the following (Maine Department of Labor 2013):

- Leaders who are committed to making the system work
- Involved members of the organization
- Ways in which to identify and control hazards and potential hazards
- A system that is in accordance with OSHA regulations and suggestions
- Training for everyone in the organization on safe work practices
- A strong safety culture with mutual respect, caring, and open communication
- Continuous improvement

The U.S. Department of Labor identifies 10 steps to get your safety system started (https://tinyurl.com/5ew28txd):

1. Establish safety and health as core values in your organization—clearly explain why a safety and health system is important.
2. Lead by example—also make clear the roles and responsibilities of those in the system.
3. Establish a reporting system—be sure to include procedures to encourage members to report any concerns.
4. Provide training—for everyone in the organization.
5. Conduct inspections—the system should call for periodic inspections.
6. Involve everyone—getting suggestions and information from everyone, but especially those who are not leaders, is important to a successful system.
7. Establish controls—the system should include procedures to control potential hazards.
8. Address emergencies—the system should identify potential emergencies (e.g., fires, floods, chemical spills, angry outsiders) and how to respond to them.
9. Actively ask for suggestions about workplace changes—once again, the system should involve everyone in obtaining about how to improve conditions.
10. Make improvements—ask questions to make sure everyone understands the system and periodically take steps to make it better.

Something to Think About

Farming isn't easy, particularly if it involves working with large animals. On a pig farm, a sow can weigh from 300 to 500 pounds. Sows can also be unpredictable and even aggressive at times. They have been known to injure people by running into them, trampling them, and even biting them. Joe thought he knew enough to be safe but when one unexpectedly charged him, he ended up fearing for his life. He was lucky though; his back and knees were severely damaged, and he almost lost a leg. Thankfully, his leg only required surgery and not amputation. *Could this sort of accident have been prevented?*

As a vital part of your health and safety system, a safety team should be established. It may be called a committee, but the label *team* carries more of what is desired from such a group. When establishing your team, be sure to provide it with a statement of what is expected from the team, its purpose, what decision making authority, if any, it may have, and be sure that it has access necessary to deal with problems or issues that may occur. In establishing your safety team, be sure that each member understands the responsibilities of the team. Kleinpeter (2019) identifies seven common responsibilities of the safety team. Those responsibilities are that the team:

1. Has a focus on learning—learning and improving conditions in the organization in four distinct areas: failure, learning from mistakes or errors; near misses, no one is injured, and no property is damaged, but something still needs to be corrected; positive experiences, suggest what should be repeated; and observations, paying attention and asking questions to learn what might be done to improve conditions.
2. Be committed—everyone on the team should be setting a good example and have a positive attitude about the safety system and health and safety practices.
3. Communicates—both oral and written media should be employed to ensure that everyone understands the importance of health and

safety but also how to act safely. Communication should also be two-way to ensure that everyone is heard.

4. Embrace consistency—team members should be consistent in carrying out their responsibilities.

5. Be understanding and tolerant—errors, mistakes, and even accidents should be seen as opportunities for learning and tolerated to some extent unless, of course, the individual who made the error ignored safety procedures or equipment.

6. Have patience—learning and change take time, and team members need to recognize that and not react too quickly when individuals seem to be slow in learning.

7. Follow through—the team should always be sure that suggestions or procedures are put into practice.

Strikwerda (2022) provides a long list of what a safety team could accomplish, although some of the items could also be accomplished by other organizational units. Her list is:

- Establish best practices for safe operations
- Develop health and safety orientation and training programs
- Conduct safety training
- Develop programs to increase everyone's safety awareness
- Encourage individuals to voice their concerns about safety issues
- Conduct investigations of safety incidents (e.g., injuries, accidents, and close calls)
- Prepare safety manuals and other documents related to the health and safety system
- Perform inspections of workplaces
- Take action to alleviate problems that could cause accidents
- Review claims regarding incidents that have occurred
- Develop policies and procedures for resolving disputes that may occur
- Develop safety checklists
- Actively support health and safety
- Obtain feedback from those in the organization

- Assist collaboration between leaders and others in the organization
- Conduct evacuation, shelter-in-place, active shooter, and other drills
- Make certain that the organization is in compliance with all health and safety-related legislation

Global Issues

The United States is not the only country where organizations face challenges in dealing with health and safety (Schulte 2020; Meswani 2008). The challenge of developing safe workplaces in numerous countries has been addressed, including Greece (Rinefort et al. 2014), China (Petrick and Rinefort 2004; Petrick, Rinefort and Yen 2008), Croatia (Wollan, Rinefort and Petrick 2013), India (Rinefort and Petrick 2015), Mexico (Petrick and Rinefort 2006), Russia (Rinefort, Petrick and Schukin 2001), the UK, France, Germany, the European Community (Rinefort and Petrick 2004), and other Asian countries (Rinefort and Petrick 2006).

The International Labor Organization has identified specific challenges faced by seven key occupational groups (International Labor Organization 2023b). Those groups and their challenges are:

- Food system workers—these workers endure risks, generally are in poverty, and are poorly covered by any sort of social protection.
- Health workers—they are exposed to psychosocial, physical, and psychological risks with low remuneration and pay gaps.
- Retail workers—most of these are self-employed, without social protection coverage, have irregular work schedules, and work long hours.
- Security workers—these workers face risks of violence and harassment, work excessive hours, and frequently develop physical and psychological illnesses as a result of their work.
- Warehouse workers—they generally have low pay, work on temporary assignments, and have high turnover with little chance for advancement.

- Cleaning and sanitation workers—these, too, frequently are temporary and low-paid, as well as facing contamination.
- Transportation workers—their long hours at work contribute to significant safety and health risks.

Unsafe working conditions, regardless of where they occur, lead to dysfunctional organizations. Psychological safety and psychosocial safety are necessary to reduce and prevent conditions that lead to unsafe conditions in organizations.

Rethinking This Chapter

Look at the notes and what you wrote down at the beginning of this chapter. How might you change those now? Has your conception of safety broadened to include people, practices, and things? With those changes in mind, respond to the following questions and actions. Managers, human resource professionals, and students should do this carefully in order to be prepared to deal with health and safety issues. Even if you are not currently employed, your responses should be made as if you are working in an organization. In a classroom setting, your responses should be shared and compared through discussion with others.

Chapter Questions

1. Have you ever experienced or witnessed an unsafe situation in your organization?
2. What specific actions could, or should, you or your organization take to improve the health and safety of those in your organization?
3. What safety issue impacts you or your organization the most? Identify your *top five*.

Introductory Actions

1. Outline a safety plan for your organization.
2. What information should be collected by your organization for each safety violation?

3. Who in the organization should keep safety records, for how long, and for what purpose(s)?

Case to Consider

Shocking Development

Harry, a 30-year-old male, was an electrical technician. He was helping a company service representative, George, a 50-year-old male, in a test of the voltage-regulating unit on a new piece of equipment. They needed the service manual for the equipment, so Harry left the area to get it. While he was gone, George opened the cover of the voltage regulator control cabinet to prepare to trace the wiring in question. The wiring was not color-coded, and he didn't see the need for using personal protective equipment.

George then climbed on a nearby cabinet over the voltage regulator control cabinet so that he could better see the wires. When Harry returned, he began tugging on wires so that George could attempt to identify them from his higher vantage point. Harry was reading inside the control cabinet near exposed and energized electrical conductors at this point.

Soon, George heard Harry making gurgling sounds. He looked down to see what Harry was doing and saw that he was shaking as though he were being shocked. As George climbed down to check on Harry, Harry fell to the floor. George noticed that Harry was unconscious and having difficulty breathing. When George checked his pulse, it seemed very weak. So, he sounded an alarm and then began cardiopulmonary resuscitation (CPR) on Harry. Harry was pronounced dead almost two hours later in the emergency room. Apparently, he had accidentally made contact with an energized electrical conductor (*Source*: adapted from Miller, 2019).

Case Questions for Discussion

1. What do you think of the actions of Harry and George?
2. If you had been George, what might you have done differently? Why?
3. If you had been Harry, what might you have done differently? Why?

Chapter 4 Takeaways

- Dysfunctional organizations are psychologically unsafe and physically unsafe. Is your organization safe?
- Common workplace hazards are working at height, poor housekeeping, *daisy chaining* extension cords, forklifts, lockout/tagout, chemicals, and confined spaces. Are any of these possible hazards in your workplace?
- Organizations should conduct annual inspections of physical facility(ies) to evaluate and determine any vulnerability to workplace violence or hazards. Does your organization conduct annual inspections?
- An EAP is required by OSHA. Does your organization have an EAP?
- A safety team or committee should be established. Does your organization have a safety committee?
- Training should be conducted. Does your organization do safety training?
- Countries other than the United States face challenges in dealing with health and safety. How familiar are you with issues overseas?

Recommended Reading

In addition to the many sources used in this chapter, the following case and article could expand your understanding of the chapter's material:

Case: Lee, S.H., M. Mol, and K. Mellahi. n.d. *Apple and Its Suppliers; Corporate Social Responsibility.* https://hbsp.harvard.edu/product/W16147-PDF-ENG.

Article: Michaels, D. 2023. "Worker Safety Needs to Be Central to Your Company's Operations." *Harvard Business Review Digital Article.* https://hbr.org/2023/09/worker-safety-needs-to-be-central-to-your-companys-operations.

CHAPTER 5

Bullying and Harassment[*]

As with previous chapters, make some notes of what you expect in this chapter. Write down what you feel are definitions of both bullying and harassment. Keep those definitions in mind as you read this chapter.

Introduction

Bullying and harassment unfortunately have become increasingly significant problems in our workplaces (McGill 2016; Vardi and Weitz 2016; Carbo and Hughes 2010; Crouthers and Lipinski 2014; Einarsen et al. 2011; Parzefall and Salin 2010; Rayner and Cooper 2006; Rayner and Keashley 2005). They impact not only individuals but also organizations, lowering morale and productivity while increasing dissatisfaction, stress (c.f., Cortina and Magley 2009; Lutgen-Sandvik *et al.* 2007; Tepper 2000), turnover, and even fatigue (Hogh *et al.* 2003). Bullying has been identified as an all-too-common problem in organizations (Einarsen *et al.* 2011; Rayner *et al.* 2002; Schat *et al.* 2006) that can threaten an entire organization (Goldman 2009, 2010). It can lead to post-traumatic and other forms of stress (Hansen *et al.* 2006; Hogh *et al.* 2003; Mikkelsen and Einarsen 2002a and 2002b), and its impact can last for years (see, for example, Vartia 2001; Lewis 2004; McCarthy and Mayhew 2004; Vaez *et al.* 2004).

The frequency and associated costs of bullying and harassment make it imperative to educate ourselves and others about these behaviors. Once we understand them, we can learn to avoid them. We can also ensure that others avoid them. And, of course, we can be change agents (Specht et al. 2018; Gerwing 2016) in our organizations to see that they take action to

---

[*] This chapter draws heavily on Van Fleet and Van Fleet (2022) and Van Fleet, White, and Van Fleet (2018).

make them less dysfunctional by hopefully eliminating both bullying and harassment. Any such change, however, must be done in a way so as to maintain the dignity and respect of everyone in the organization.

Think about baseballs and cricket balls (Van Fleet, White, and Van Fleet 2018). Both are spherical in shape, about nine in. circumference, five ounces in weight, fabricated with a cork center wrapped in yarn or string, and covered with leather strips sewn together. They are very much alike, but they are also significantly different. So, too, it is with bullying and harassment. They may be similar, but they are different forms of unacceptable behavior in the workplace. But both must be eliminated to reduce dysfunction in organizations. As you read this chapter, think about how you understand bullying and harassment and how they might be reduced or eliminated in your organization.

Something to Think About

A warehouse company provided pallet racking, shelving, and storage for numerous organizations in its several facilities in different locations throughout California. While it used material handling equipment for most of the larger packages or crates, it still employed a large number of Hispanic employees for the basic handling of packages and other items. However, those employees were not treated with respect. They were subjected to taunts and derogatory names such as *wetback, beaner, stupid Mexican,* and *Puerto Rican b-h* by their supervisors, all of whom were not Hispanic. The Hispanic workers, who were not just Mexican but also from several other Spanish-speaking countries, were not the only employees who were ridiculed; other employees also were identified with other derogatory stereotypes. Were the Hispanic employees bullied or harassed?

Bullying and harassment can take many forms from aggression, coercion, deceit, seduction, and threatening conduct, including verbal abuse, intimidation, and humiliation, to even sabotage and more (Wilson 2021; Ethics Resource Center 2013). Verbal abuse can cause feelings of shame, a loss of passion, a negative obsession with work, and increased blood pressure (Holly 2021). You may be able to expand this list based on your personal experiences and observations (for other examples, see Van Fleet and Van Fleet 2022). They may include being ridiculed in front of others, being lied about, continually being left out, or being repeatedly criticized unjustly (Kohut 2008).

Bullying comes in various forms (Indeed Editorial Team 2022):

1. The blatantly insulting bully—the perpetrator is usually a supervisor or manager and also usually yells or screams to establish dominance or control by making their employees feel smaller through harsh and belittling comments.
2. The passive–aggressive bully—the perpetrator makes comments that seem like compliments but really are not, or they may use sarcasm to insult the victim(s).
3. The scheming bully—the perpetrator gossips or spreads false rumors about the victim while being nice to them when face to face.
4. The unintentional bully—the perpetrator makes unfiltered comments without thinking about their words before speaking and may even be unaware that they are unfairly or harshly treating others.

Another classification of bullying has six categories, some of which overlap others. They include (Vinney 2021):

1. Physical bullying. This type of bullying involves an assault on a person's body, including hitting, kicking, tripping, or pushing.
2. Verbal bullying. Here bullying includes insults, name-calling, teasing, and even threats.
3. Relational bullying. This is closely related to verbal bullying and involves embarrassing the victim in public, spreading rumors, purposely leaving them out of social situations, or ostracizing them from a group.
4. Cyberbullying. This type of bullying involves computers or cell phones and includes text messages, social media, apps, or online forums and involves posting or sending harmful content, including messages and photos, and sharing personal information that causes humiliation.
5. Sexual bullying. While usually verbal, this type can include physical bullying as well and includes sexual comments or actions, including

sexual jokes and name-calling, crude gestures, spreading sexual rumors, sending sexual photos or videos, and touching or grabbing someone without permission.

6. Prejudicial bullying. This type typically is verbal and includes online or in-person bullying based on the target's race, ethnicity, religion, or sexual orientation.

Harassment, on the other hand, can be based on characteristics such as verbal, racial, sexual, sexual orientation, gender, religious, physical, ability-based, and age-based. In the United States, seven of these are protected classes by law, notably race, color, religion, sex, national origin, disability, and sexual orientation (Cotterell 2018). Other forms of harassment include (11 Types of Workplace Harassment (And How to Stop Them) 2022):

1. Personal—based on the victim's work, personality, or looks, or generalized behavior that offends the victim, such as telling an off-color joke

2. Physical—shoving or a soft punch to the shoulder or more

3. Power—from a supervisor or manager

4. Psychological—intentionally causing someone to feel put down and belittled on a personal level, a professional level, or both

5. Online/digital—cyberbullying; retaliation—the perpetrator harasses the victim to seek revenge, hoping to prevent the behavior from happening again

6. Quid pro quo—the perpetrator, often a supervisor or manager, may offer something of value in exchange for a sexual or other favor

7. Third-party—the perpetrator is someone from outside the organization: a vendor, supplier, customer, or client

Still another classification of harassment involves eight types (Swartz Swidler 2019). They are:

1. Discriminatory harassment. This type includes race, gender, religion, disability, sexual orientation, and age and includes slurs, insults, demeaning treatment, and harassing texts or e-mails.

2. Online harassment. This type involves sharing personal details about a coworker in a mass chat, spreading lies about a victim in an office chat, and sending repeated and unwelcome messages of a sexual nature to a coworker.

3. Retaliatory harassment. This type involves someone harassing a coworker or employee to get revenge on him or her for doing something.

4. Sexual harassment. This type may overlap discriminatory harassment, but it includes unwelcome sexual conduct, advances, or behavior. This type includes creating a hostile work environment and quid pro quo behavior. Examples are showing sexual pictures or pornography, displaying sexual posters, sending explicit text messages, making sexual comments or asking sexual questions, telling sexual jokes, unwanted touching, and inappropriate gestures.

5. Quid pro quo sexual harassment. This type is a form of sexual harassment and usually involves someone in a position of authority offering benefits or threatening an adverse action to another member of the organization in exchange for that person's agreeing to engage in sexual conduct.

6. Third-party harassment. This type occurs when a client, customer, contractor, or another person from outside of the organization harasses a member of the organization.

7. Workplace violence/physical harassment. This type includes threats of violence, hitting, kicking, shoving, threatening behavior, physical intimidation, destruction of property, and throwing things. (The next chapter covers workplace violence in more detail.)

8. Interestingly, this classification also includes bullying in the form of humiliation, inappropriate comments, constant criticism, offensive jokes, ostracism/isolation, intimidation, and yelling or cursing.

The Equal Employment Opportunity Commission defines harassment as unwelcomed contact that becomes "unlawful where (1) enduring the offensive conduct becomes a condition of continued employment, or (2) the conduct is severe or pervasive enough to create a work environment that a reasonable person would consider intimidating, hostile, or abusive" (EEOC 2023). While organizations should take deliberate actions to reduce and eliminate bullying and harassment, they do not always succeed. In situations where the organization fails to remedy the problem, victims may take legal action against the perpetrator and/or the organization. Generally, such legal action and enforcement is by state laws, which vary considerably (see examples at USLegal.com 2024). Regardless of issues of legality, organizations need to reduce and eliminate harassment and, for that matter, bullying to prevent the organization from becoming dysfunctional.

While bullying is often thought of in relation to schools (Straus 2011; Smokowski and Kopasz 2005; Espelage and Swearer 2003) or nursing (Berry et al. 2016; Houck and Colbert 2017), it is also common in many workplaces (Crothers and Lipinski 2014: Einarsen et al. 2011; Parzefall and Salin 2010; Rayner and Cooper 2006; Rayner and Keashley 2005). Unfortunately, bullying frequently occurs in conjunction with sexual harassment (Stein and Mennemier 2011; Stein 2003). Bullying and harassment are not just problems in the United States as they have been reported in many other countries (Saguy 2011; Rosenthal and Budjanov-canin 2011; Hoel and Einarsen 2010; Loh, Restubog, and Zagenczyk 2010; Gorman 2008; Hartill 2008; Smith et al. 2002).

Researchers have attempted to identify the traits and characteristics of perpetrators and victims (see Neuman and Baron 2003; Coyne *et al.* 2000; Heames and Harvey 2006; Hoel and Cooper 2001; Hoel *et al.* 1999; Neuman and Baron 1997, 1998) or aspects of organizations that could bring about incidents (Parzefall and Salin 2010; Matthiesen 2004; Salin 2003; Folger and Skarlicki 1998). Still, other studies examine the influence of external factors (see Cowie *et al.* 2000, for an overview). Salin (2003) suggests that social theory suggests that the relative powerlessness between members of an organization influences who and why particular individuals become perpetrators or victims.

Individuals from a variety of cultures with different beliefs, values, and attitudes must work together in very competitive, stressful situations in today's organizations. In these types of situations, managers may feel that they should be able to do whatever they feel necessary to get results. On the other hand, the *routine activities* model used in criminology (Reynald 2016; Hollis, Felson, and Welsh 2013; Cohen and Felson 1979) suggests that bullying and harassment are more likely to occur in the absence of *capable guardians*. Capable guardians would be other workers or managers who would be likely to report any incidents. So, to keep from becoming dysfunctional, organizations should ensure that everyone in the organization can and will be a capable guardian.

The Impact

Bullying and harassment obviously impact victims, but they also impact witnesses and make their organizations dysfunctional (Lutgen-Sandvik, Tracy, and Alberts 2007; Rayner et al. 2002). The effects of bullying on job satisfaction, stress, anger, and health were more serious than were the effects of sexual harassment (Lapierre et al. 2005). Bullying is a *crippling and devastating problem* (Adams and Crawford 1992, 13) that can damage a victim's self-esteem, physical health, cognitive functioning, and emotional health (Brodsky 1976; Einarsen and Mikkelsen 2003; Keashly and Harvey 2005). Victims and those who observe the incident(s) may experience depression, anxiety, and insomnia. Organizations can expect significant costs, including legal, medical, lowered productivity, emotional well-being, morale, turnover, burnout, and so on. (Gumbus and Lyons 2011; Needham 2003). These, in turn, lead to further increases in organizational dysfunction.

Something to Think About

Laila was transferred to a new group at her insurance claims company. To ensure consistency in their work, communication within the group was important. So, weekly meetings were held to keep everyone working at their highest levels. Laila's new group was mostly men, whereas her previous unit was mostly women. Despite being a high performer, Laila was publicly criticized at virtually every weekly work group meeting. She was humiliated by this and began to blame herself. After several months, she was not even notified as to when and where the meetings would be. She also received no invitation to the agency's Super Bowl party. She felt ostracized and got severely depressed. Eventually, she got medical help for her depression, but the situation at work did not improve, and her performance suffered. Finally, she was terminated due to poor performance. Was Laila bullied or harassed?

Gale and her associates (Gale et al. 2019) reported observing strong associations between all types of abuse and depression, sleep disturbances, fatigue, and workplace injuries. Roscigno (2019) found that racial/ethnic minorities experience discrimination four to six times higher than their white counterparts; women are three to four times more likely than their male peers to experience gender discrimination and sexual harassment; and workers in their 50s and 60s are more likely to experience age discrimination. Witnesses or observers were more likely to suffer the emotional and psychological consequences of the experience than those who had not seen the incident (Acquadro Maran, D., Varetto, A., and Civilotti C., 2022). Among those who had seen an incident, if they did nothing, they had "a threefold risk of becoming a victim of bullying at follow-up" (Rosander and Nielsen 2023). It is not just employees who engage in workplace sexual harassment. Sexual harassment from clients or customers also has been shown to lead to employee depressive symptoms (Friborg et al. 2017).

Recently, the first attempt to provide a global overview of individuals' own experiences of violence and harassment at work was conducted by the ILO, Lloyd's Register Foundation, and the Gallup organization (International Labor Organization 2022).[†] The survey consisted of interviews in 2021 with nearly 125,000 individuals in 121 countries with more than one in five (22.8 percent or 743 million) employed individuals having experienced at least one form of violence or harassment at work. The forms identified are physical, psychological, and sexual. Of those who had experienced workplace violence or harassment, one-third (31.8 percent) indicated that they had experienced more than one form, and 6.3 percent indicated that they had experienced all three forms. Other findings were that psychological violence or harassment was the most common form, more than three in five victims indicated that whatever form it was, it occurred multiple times, and young women were twice as likely as young men to have experienced the sexual form, while migrant women were almost twice as likely as nonmigrant women

---

[†] This paragraph is based on the Summary of Results section of the International Labor Organization report, 2022.

to report having experienced it. When asked about what might prevent them from disclosing or reporting such incidents, the respondents indicated that the most common barriers discouraging them from talking about their own experiences were that it would be a *waste of time* or it would damage their reputation.

Kuhl (2017) suggests that bullying results in more than U.S.$250 million in losses to organizations each year due to lost productivity, employee turnover, health care insurance claims, worker's compensation disputes, employee recruitment, retraining, and litigation. She also notes that organizations experience losses of U.S.$14,000 per employee in reduced performance and 18 million in lost days of work. She identifies numerous other impacts of bullying, notable that victims typically experience increased rates of:

1. Difficulty sleeping (insomnia and other sleep problems)
2. Stomach or digestive problems (gastrointestinal distress)
3. High blood pressure
4. Headaches
5. Feelings of anxiety
6. Symptoms of post-traumatic stress disorder
7. Depression or sadness
8. Pain

More recently, Kolmar (2022) reported that sexual harassment against women at work is widespread in the United States. Despite how common it is, many women choose not to report it, and of those who do, there do not seem to be any consequences for the perpetrator. Some of the specific findings were:

1. Over half of women experience sexual harassment at work.
2. Those in accommodation and food services account for 14 percent of harassment charges.
3. Fifty percent of female academic faculty and staff and between 20 and 50 percent of female students have experienced some form of sexual harassment.

4. Sexual harassment is expensive, costing companies U.S.$2.6 billion in lost productivity and another U.S.$0.9 billion in other costs (legal, added paperwork, staff to handle complaints, and the like).

5. Half of the women who reported being sexually harassed reported that it hurt their careers.

6. Only 30 percent of women strongly agree that their employer properly handles harassment complaints.

The Problem

Bullying and harassment have become increasingly significant problems in our workplaces. The widespread use and acceptance of social media and networking provide previously inconceivable opportunities for unacceptable behaviors with their own unique social, humanitarian, and productivity issues (Mainiero and Jones 2013; Lucero, Allen, and Elzweig 2013; Sewell and Barker 2006; Tabak and Smith2005). In addition to bullying and harassment, a multitude of other words may be used as labels for these behaviors—abusive management, aggressive management, dark side behaviors, emotional abuse, incivility, bullying, harassment, misbehavior, misconduct, mobbing, psychological violence, and sexual harassment, to name some of the more common ones (for a more complete set, see Vardi and Weitz 2016; Einarsen, Hoel, and Cooper 2002). Bullying, harassment, and some form of improper, abusive management seem to be the most commonly used words (Jenkins 2013; Ramsay, Troth, and Branch 2011; Notelaers et al. 2013).

Although the terms bullying and harassment are widely used, they are rarely precisely defined. This lack of precise definitions makes it difficult to distinguish between them in efforts to write policies or legislation (Carbo and Hughes 2010; Gradinger, Strohmeier, and Spiel 2010; Greenwald 2010). "The absence of a shared descriptive language for the phenomenon is doubly perplexing for employers, legislators, and other members of society who seek to address this source of psychological pain in the workplace" (Crawshaw 2009). There clearly is a need for a better understanding of the similarities and differences among the many words used to describe or identify improper behavior in general (Hollis 2016;

McGill 2016; Goldsmid and Howie 2014) and bullying and harassment in particular (Straus 2011; Straus 2016; Van Fleet and Van Fleet 2014; Miller 2012; Smolinski 2011; Rickard n.d.).

Given the lack of clarity for these terms, it is apparent that words describing them would be similar in many cases. That would indicate that the concepts actually overlap in some sense. Figure 5.1 is a hypothetical Venn diagram suggesting what those areas of overlap might look like (the sizes and the amount of overlap in the diagram are illustrative only).[‡]

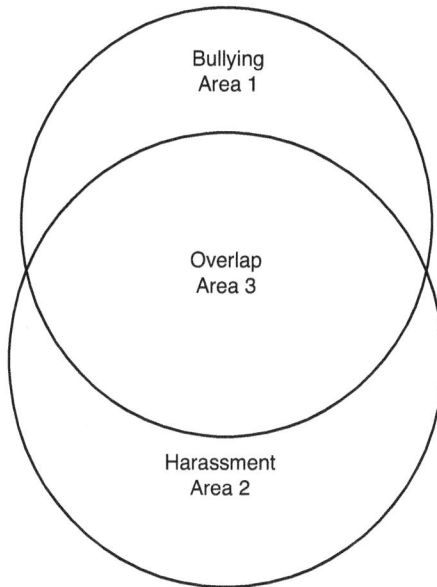

Figure 5.1 Venn diagram of possible relations between bullying and harassment (physical, psychological, and sexual)

Area 1: Words unique to Bullying;
Area 2: Words unique to Harassment;
Area 3: Words common to all three concepts

[‡] A Venn diagram *uses overlapping circles to indicate logical relationships between two or more sets of items.* The English logician John Venn popularized the diagram in the 1880s.

To try to clarify the distinctions between bullying and harassment, a survey that also included background information was constructed using SurveyMonkey, announced through social media (LinkedIn, Twitter, Facebook) groups identified as workplace violence or bullying, and made available for nearly six months. The survey was based on *bad boss* behavioral anecdotes that appeared in Van Fleet and Van Fleet (2007). The respondents could completely agree on only one specific behavior as bullying (Van Fleet and Van Fleet 2012). This indicated that researchers, policymakers, and legislators would have a difficult time trying to reach a consensus due to a lack of agreement as to the terms being employed.

A second effort to clarify our understanding of bullying and harassment used the Social Science Citation Index in 2016 to identify all articles dealing first with bullying and then with harassment. To be even more inclusive (Tepper, Moss, and Duffy 2011), articles dealing with abusive management/supervision were included. In total, 4,667 citations were obtained for bullying, 5,086 for harassment, and 392 for abusive management/supervision. Common words (e.g., articles and prepositions), numbers, proper names, and abbreviations were removed, and the remaining words were subjected to a qualitative analysis. The words were entered into Symphony Content Analysis Software (www.activejava. com/) to form word clouds.

Word or tag clouds are a technique for visually representing the most prominent words in a body of literature (Xu and Li 2013; Abulaish, Islamia, and Anwar 2013; Panke and Gaiser 2009; Viegas and Watrtenberg 2008). Word clouds graphically display the frequency of words used by participants of qualitative methods and have become "an innovative approach to quickly summarize and present information from thematic analyses" (Panke and Gaiser 2009). Visual representations help to reduce the burden of information overload (Guerra, Simonini, and Vincini 2015; Brooks et al. 2014; Helic et al. 2011). In that way, word clouds are useful as exploratory and analytical techniques to obtain visual information about a topic (Atenstaedt 2012; Cidell 2010; Hearst and Rosner 2008; Sinclair and Cardew-Hall 2008; Kaser and Lemire 2007).

In Symphony Content Analysis Software, to make the visualization clearer, only the 50 most frequent words were used (visual clarity increases as the number of displayed words decreases). The words closest to bully were behave, experience, social, victim, relate, violence, associate, age, self, and effect. The words closest to harass were behave, experience, social, sex, respond, gender, relate, and race, but male, female, and women were also close. The words closest to abusive management were behave, supervise, supervisor, time, relationship, and employee, but work, job, role, level, and effect were also close. Only the word behave was common to all three, but experience, social, and relate were common to both bullying and harassment, and effect was common to bullying and abusive management.

With only the 50 most frequent words used, the cloud for bully does not contain harass or abuse, and the cloud for abuse does not contain bully or harass, but the cloud for harass does contain both bully and abuse. Apparently, articles about bullying rarely mention harassment or abuse, and likewise, those about abusive management rarely mention bullying or harassment. Articles about harassment mention both bullying and abuse, suggesting that harassment may be the more inclusive concept. However, the clouds have other common words, suggesting that, while the concepts are different, there are areas where they are clearly related; that is to say, they overlap in some way.

Using the entire set of words yields a better understanding. There were 14,129 unique words after removing nonapplicable words (articles, prepositions, proper names, specific geographic locations) and terms associated purely with research methods (logit, intercorrelations, etc.). Referring back to Figure 5.1, Area 1 (words unique to bullying) contained 23.71 percent of the words, Area 3 (words unique to harassment) contained 32.32 percent of the words, while the remaining 43.35 percent were common to bullying and harassment. Delving even deeper, if only the words that occur four or more times are examined, Area 1 now has only 4.91 percent, Area 3 has 8.30 percent, while Area 3 has 86.79 percent. There is more in common than there is different in these concepts.

Recognizing this considerable overlap between words used with bullying and harassment, the entire set of words was used to form a final word cloud. This cloud shows bully(ing) as the central word with harass close by. Other words close by include behave, experience, victim, self, associate, and relate, but also nearby are social, sex, peer, and work. More distant words are abuse and aggressive. This, then, raises the question of how frequently are bullying and harassment used together?

Something to Think About

Sam's video editing company in New York began having most of its employees work from home. They work on a wide variety of projects, including films, movies, documentaries, TV shows, and web-based programs. Working remotely in his own apartment, Sam felt secure and happy with his job. However, a new supervisor changed all that. In Zoom meetings, the supervisor seemed to pick on him, noting the smallest issues with his work. In group e-mails, when he responded, the supervisor would immediately come back to him and would not copy the others in the response, so Sam was unsure about what others' reactions were. Despite having worked for the company for almost 10 years, Sam began to feel that this job was no longer for him. Sadly, he began looking for another position. Was the new supervisor just doing his job, was he a bully, or was he harassing Sam?

Multidimensional scaling (MDS) was used to examine that question. MDS is used in exploratory data analysis (Chabowski, Samiee, and Hult 2017; Hout, Papesh, and Goldinger 2013; Jaworska and Chupetlovska-Anastasova 2009). MDS is used in large datasets to reduce the effect of *noise* and improve information retrieval (Tzeng, Lu, and Li 2008). Further, MDS provides a way to better understand the similarity or dissimilarity of individual words in a dataset (Pinkley, Gelfand, and Duan 2005; MacCallum 1988; Shoben 1983). As it had been used to study deviant workplace behaviors (Robinson and Bennett 1995), its use seemed reasonable.

The results (see Van Fleet and Van Fleet 2018 for details as to methodology) have the words bully, harass, violence, women, and suicide clustered together, with aggressive, victim, and cyberbullying clustered nearby. Two other nearby clusters are also nearby. One consists of the words work, workplace, discriminate, and race, while the other has the words public, management, job, worker, employee, organization, and organizable. Nurse is alone but close to bully. Bully(ing) and harass(ment) are separated by the words women, violence, and suicide, suggesting that they are key terms in differentiating bullying and harassment. Other nearby words include aggressive, victim, cyberbullying, race, discriminate, and work and workplace. Again, this suggests that those terms are closely related to both concepts. As bully(ing) and harass(ment) appear close to one another, this also suggests that they frequently occur together and share many words in common.

What is learned from this? Does the similarity mean more than the differences? Improper behavior directed toward children is usually identified as bullying. Improper behavior involving sexual content is sexual harassment. Improper physical behavior is generally bullying. Name-calling or related actions are harassment. Improper managerial behavior involving public verbal criticism is bullying (Van Fleet and Van Fleet 2012). Usually, usually, usually, but not always. Therein lies the problem. Labels used by one scholar, agency, or organization are likely to be different from those used by others, confusing those impacted by the work.

Whatever label is used, repetition may be required. Is repetition a necessary aspect of either bullying or harassment? MacKinnon (1979) says, "sexual harassment may occur as a single encounter or as a series of incidents at work." Words suggesting repetition did not emerge as high-frequency words, but some were found. *Repeat* occurred 211 times in the bullying set and 104 times in the harassment set, and *persist* 122 times in each set. They were infrequent but nevertheless noteworthy. But repeated negative behavior may still be labeled differently by different persons or organizations. The labels are viewed as alike but also different.

Preventing Dysfunction

So, with all this confusion, how are organizations going to develop policies so as not to become dysfunctional? In order to develop workable, enforceable policies, organizations need definitions or at least descriptions of bullying and harassment (Carbo and Hughes 2010; Greenwald 2010; Gradinger *et al.* 2010; Yamada 2004). One study suggests that such behavior by managers has a greater impact than when done by nonmanagers (Cortina and Magley 2009; Roscigno *et al.* 2009; Tepper 2007), so it might be useful and important to recognize that in a policy statement, although doing so might not be feasible. Thus, just like baseballs and cricket balls, bullying and harassment are similar but different. How should they be differentiated? How does one separate them? Similar to the Sorites Paradox of trying to decide the precise moment when a tadpole becomes a frog (Cargile 1969)—which cannot be done—we may not know when or if harassment becomes bullying, or vice versa. Perhaps it is not necessary to separate them.

If not, one definition might be (Van Fleet and Van Fleet 2018): Unwelcome verbal or physical conduct constitutes bullying or harassment when this conduct explicitly or implicitly affects an individual's employment, unreasonably interferes with an individual's work performance, or creates an intimidating, hostile, or offensive work environment. More recently (Van Fleet and Van Fleet 2022), we suggested using a shorthand expression B≈H (pronounced simply by the letters *BH*) to note that bullying and harassment are approximately the same and may also include other similar forms of dysfunctional behavior. Using that approach, the definition becomes:

B≈H refers to verbal or physical conduct that explicitly or implicitly affects an individual's health, unreasonably interferes with an individual's work performance, or creates an intimidating, hostile, or offensive work environment.

Using this more inclusive definition in policy statements, organizations can train personnel to recognize and deal with improper behavior, thereby reducing or eliminating it in the workplace. A well-developed policy statement should at least include a general opening statement, definition or definitions used, procedures to be followed by those impacted (victim and/or observers), specifications regarding enforcement and consequences, and perhaps what, where, and how records are kept. An example opening statement might be something like this:

[NAME OF BUSINESS] is committed to providing a working environment free from B≈H (bullying, harassment, and other forms of abusive behavior). We aim to ensure that everyone in the organization is treated and treat others with dignity and respect.

The [NAME OF BUSINESS] will not permit or condone any form of B≈H. This policy covers bullying or harassment that occurs at work and out of the workplace, including business or work trips, work-related events, and social functions or events. This policy covers B≈H and applies to everyone at all levels, including employees, management, agency and casual workers, and also third parties such as independent contractors, customers, and suppliers.

A policy statement with an opening like this should go a long way to develop psychosocial working conditions and create psychological safety and reduce and eventually eliminate any and all behaviors that would cause the organization to become dysfunctional. Then, when a complaint is made based on the policy, several steps should be taken:

1. The complaint must be taken seriously.
2. The complainant must be informed that an investigation will take place.
3. An unbiased investigation should be conducted.
4. There should be careful and complete follow-through by informing the complainant and other relevant personnel of the results of the investigation.
5. Any corrections called for by the investigation should be carried out.
6. Above all, ensure that no retaliation occurs.

But bullying and harassment are not the only causes of dysfunctional organizations. The next chapter explores another.

Rethinking This Chapter

Look at the notes and definitions you wrote down at the beginning of this chapter. How might you change those now? Do you feel that it is important to treat bullying and harassment as separate topics? If so, why? With those changes in mind, respond to the following questions and actions. Managers, human resource professionals, and students should do this carefully in order to be prepared to deal with B≈H issues. Even if you are not currently employed, your responses should be made as if you are working in an organization. In a classroom setting, your responses should be shared and compared through discussion with others.

Chapter Questions

1. Have you ever experienced or witnessed bullying and harassment?
2. What specific actions could, or should, you or your organization take to reduce bullying and/or harassment?
3. What costs or impacts to you or your organization concern you the most? Identify your *top five*.

Introductory Actions

1. Draft a policy statement for your organization.
2. What information should be collected by your organization for each incident of bullying or harassment?
3. Who in the organization should keep records of bullying and harassment, for how long, and for what purpose(s)?

Case to Consider

Arrick Versus Power Company (2018)

Yvonne started working in a clerical position for Power Company, but having been a law enforcement officer for many years, she was determined to work her way up into a field engineer position, which was held almost exclusively by men. She was awarded the position two years after she started. Unfortunately, her supervisor felt that women did not belong on his field engineering team, treated her poorly, held her to different standards, and put roadblock after roadblock in her way to a second promotion. Yvonne spoke up at the two meetings about her supervisor's discrimination against women, pointing out that when the supervisor was appointed, there were four women employed, and he got rid of three of them. He did not get rid of any men. Even men who were guilty of misconduct were not discharged. She also noted several direct acts of discrimination, but no one took any action to correct her supervisor's behavior. He assigned her to handle a dispute with a contractor, expecting she would go to the job site alone and knowing that the contractor had a bad temper and a history of confrontation with field staff. She took another employee with her. However, the contractor was ferocious in their interaction. Yvonne decided that her supervisor was so determined to get rid of her that he would even place her life in danger. She quit the next day. Yvonne had taken careful factual contemporaneous notes about all of her interactions with her supervisor and stored them at her home. Those notes would likely have been admissible if the case had gone to trial and would have been determinative that she was, in fact, the victim of sex discrimination. The case did not go to trial. It was settled for a confidential amount.

(*Source*: www.roxanneconlinlaw.com/selected-case-summaries/selected-case-summaries-sexual-harassment-and-discrimination/.)

Case Questions for Discussion

1. Is the supervisor's behavior bullying or harassment?
2. If you had been Yvonne, what might you have done differently? Why?
3. The law firm, Roxanne Conlin and Associates, P.C., notes that it was settled without trial. Once again, if you had been Yvonne, would you have settled?

Chapter 5 Takeaways

- Bullying and harassment are significant problems in our workplaces, lowering morale and productivity while increasing dissatisfaction, stress, turnover, and causing fatigue. Have you experienced either in your workplace?
- Bullying and harassment may consist of aggression, coercion, deceit, seduction, and threatening conduct, including intimidation and humiliation, sabotage, and verbal abuse

that can cause feelings of shame, a loss of passion, a negative obsession with work, and increased blood pressure. Have you seen, heard about, or experienced any of these in your workplace?

- Bullying and harassment are also labeled abusive management, aggressive management, dark-side behaviors, emotional abuse, incivility, bullying, harassment, misbehavior, misconduct, mobbing, psychological violence, and sexual harassment. Have you seen, heard about, or experienced any of these in your workplace?
- Organizations need clear policy statements and training based on those policies. Does your organization have a policy statement?

Recommended Reading

In addition to the many sources used in this chapter, the following case and article could expand your understanding of the chapter's material:

Case: Harlos, K., A. Konrad, and L. Monzani. n.d. *Three Cases on Workplace Mistreatment.* https://store.hbr.org/product/three-cases-on-workplace-mistreatment/W20807.

Article: Praslova, L.N., R. Carucci, and C. Stokes. 2022. "How Bullying Manifests at Work—and How to Stop It." *Harvard Business Review Digital Article.* https://hbr.org/2022/11/how-bullying-manifests-at-work-and-how-to-stop-it.

CHAPTER 6

Violence*

As with previous chapters, make some notes of what you expect in this chapter. Write down what you feel is a definition of workplace violence. Keep that definition in mind as you read this chapter.

Introduction

As they strive to achieve success, managers increasingly have come to recognize that the resources most important to an organization's success are its human resources (Lyons and Conley 2012; Mugera 2012; Chacko, Wacker, and Asar 1997). However, one of the more threatening issues to organizations is workplace violence, which can be devastating to productivity and the quality of life of their employees (U.S. Department of Agriculture (USDA) 2001). Workplace violence refers to willful or negligent acts, including either proscribed criminal acts or coercive behavior, that occur in the course of performing any work-related duty and that lead to significant negative results, such as physical or emotional injury, diminished productivity, or property damage (Van Fleet and Van Fleet 2010, 45). This definition, unlike many others, indicates that behavior is labeled workplace violence if it is work-related and leads to negative work results, regardless of where it occurs, regardless of whether the harm is physical or emotional, and regardless of the relationship between perpetrator and victim. This definition, then, indicates that workplace violence can originate from employees toward other employees, managers, or an organization itself. Further, this definition also includes behavior from managers or outsiders toward employees (Van Fleet and Griffin 2006), and the behavior may occur off the organization's premises.

---

* This chapter draws heavily on Van Fleet (2017) and Van Fleet and Van Fleet (2010 and 2017).

Workplace violence is clearly an international phenomenon (International Labour Organization 2022) having been noted in England (Fevre et al. 2011; Buckley 2022), India (Staernose 2013), China (Lo et al. 2011), Saudi Arabia (Alyousef and Alhamidi 2022), Brazil, Bulgaria, Lebanon, Portugal, South Africa, Thailand, Australia (di Martino 2002), and elsewhere (Bowie, Fisher, and Cooper 2005; Holt-Gimenez 2015;). Even though workplace violence is not new and occurs internationally, it is difficult to predict its magnitude because research is relatively new, and most countries do not have organizations specifically focused on workplace violence (Bowie, Fisher, and Cooper 2005). Reports by the International Labor Organization (International Labor Organization 2022; International Labor Organization 2023a and 2023b) are making it clear that more needs to be done. Even when the more violent incidents (i.e., homicide) are reported, other forms of physical and psychological harm are not (Fisher and Lab 2010). In the United States, studies and statistics are more readily available.

Psychological safety to protect and develop the human capital of an organization has been suggested as a critical goal for all organizations (Edmonson 2019; Radecki et al. 2018; Shelman and Connolly 2012). Unfortunately, relatively few organizations have established effective programs to combat violence at work (International Association of Chiefs of Police 1996). In today's complex organizational settings, onshoring, offshoring, outsourcing, reorganizing, reengineering, revamping, budget-cutting, downsizing, and just-in-time delivery have increased while at the same time, morale, job security, motivation, loyalty, dedication, staffing, and esprit de corps have decreased. Everyone in any given organization may be undertitled, underutilized, underpaid, underappreciated, underemployed, and even in danger of being laid off or terminated and, hence, unemployed. If that were not enough, other factors such as lean-and-mean manufacturing, illegal immigration, and the threats of mass disaster and terrorism (often on top of increasing mortgage payments and credit card debt) can result in those in an organization feeling overworked, overstressed, overloaded, and maybe overwatched personally and electronically. So, getting organizations to focus on the value of their human capital through psychosocial and psychological safety is difficult.

Something to Think About

John was a tough manager at a local retail store. He sometimes docked employees for no reason just to keep up his reputation as a tough manager. The company had a computer-based active shooter training program that perhaps gave him the idea so that when his personal problems became too much for him, he came out shooting. He simply went into a break room and started shooting. He didn't aim at anyone in particular. He didn't care whom he shot, and before his gun ran out of ammunition, he turned it on himself. Could this have been foreseen?

In organizations today, work-life imposes more stress than support, so employees and managers can expect an increase in incidents of interpersonal conflicts and workplace violence (National Institute for Occupational Safety and Health 2006). Workplace violence—sometimes dubbed *going postal* in its most severe form—has become an unpleasant reality. It may result from a crime, a carryover from domestic or substance abuse problems, a product of the organizational changes mentioned earlier, or as a result of a dysfunctional, sick, or toxic organization. Regardless of the cause, the costs and consequences are significant and long-lasting (Paul and Townsend 1998). To reduce or eliminate those costs and to prevent your organization from becoming dysfunctional, everyone in the organization needs to be trained to recognize how stress and anger build to a *boiling point* and erupt in the form of workplace violence unless intervention occurs.

Numerous incidents, as well as costs, are sufficient to call for attention by more than OSHA. Organizational managers must pay attention and get involved. Years ago, the U.S. Department of Labor indicated that an average of more than three persons die at the workplace each and every workday of the year, and that does not count the innocent bystanders who are also affected (U.S. Department of Labor 2017). From 1992 to 2019, 17,865 persons were killed in a workplace homicide (Harrell et al. 2022). Of those, 21 percent of the victims were in sales and related occupations,

82 percent were male, and 79 percent were gun-related. From 2015 to 2019, there was an average of 1.3 million nonfatal workplace violence incidents each year, consisting of about 53,000 rapes or sexual assaults, 46,000 robberies, 186,000 aggravated assaults, and 979,000 simple assaults (Harrell et al. 2022).

Simple assaults consist of such actions as pushing or shoving, slapping, or hitting, and it has been estimated that more than two million U.S. workers suffer these sorts of attacks at work each year (Northwestern National Life Insurance Company 1993). Other examples include stopping up executive toilets so they must use the workers' bathrooms; stealing from hotel guests to embarrass the hotel; parking housecleaning carts in one location while the maids take a break in another location; intentionally damaging a part on an assembly line; intentionally dropping a washer inside a car door on the assembly line; and taking the cassettes of lobby music home to randomly record noise in sections so that the tapes are startlingly unpleasant when they are playing the next day (Mantell 1994). Individuals may incur most of the costs from these incidents, but, as noted earlier, dysfunctional organizations also incur costs—decreased productivity, medical and legal expenses, lost work time, lowered quality, and a damaged culture and public image.

Forces and Tendencies

Everyone in an organization has some potential tendency to exhibit violent behavior (Griffin and Lopez 2005 and 2004; Denenberg and Braverman 1999). Those tendencies range from very low to very high—and organizations usually have no idea of what they are for any given individual. The higher the tendency, the greater the likelihood that the individual will display violent behavior at some time, in many cases, targeted toward a supervisor or manager (Inness, Barling, and Turner 2005). If the tendency is low, rather than physical violence, the employee may resort to shouting, spreading rumors, or other aggressive but nonviolent behavior. These sorts of behaviors can escalate toward more violent behavior, and, in any case, the organization will be dysfunctional (Coleman 2004). Those in charge of organizations should remember that OSHA regulations call for all organizations to "furnish to each of his employee's employment and a place of employment which are free from recognized hazards that are causing or are likely to cause death or serious physical harm to his employees" (OSH Act of 1970).

Clearly, dysfunctional organizations have higher incidences of violence and aggression and are less effective (Johnson et al. 2013). Yet almost all organizations have some propensity for workplace violence. However, there are forces that can act to decrease that propensity. To reduce or eliminate violence, both managers and employees need to be aware of issues or situations that may cause violence to erupt. Those influences include economic, social, and political forces outside the organization; inherent characteristics and dispositions of individuals; and the organization itself—its culture and managers (Van Fleet and Van Fleet 2010 and 2014). While any one of these forces could be strong enough to result in violence, generally, workplace violence only occurs when two or more of these forces are present in an organization.

Bad economic times and changing job markets may cause so much stress that members of an organization feel that their only recourse is to resort to violence. Social factors, particularly diverse demographics, are also a significant force. Age, immigration status, and gender are especially important because of the increasingly large number of females in many businesses (Sachs et al. 2014; Van Fleet, Van Fleet, and Seperich 2014; Southern Poverty Law Center 2010). Organizations with highly diverse and stressful environments can anticipate increasing numbers of incidents of interpersonal conflicts and possible workplace violence because of miscommunication, social or cultural differences, and differences in power (National Institute for Occupational Safety and Health 2006). People in power frequently treat those with less power in parent–child relational ways. "Even protectiveness and benevolence toward the poor, toward minorities, and especially toward women have involved equating them with children" (Bateson 1989, 107). Treating women and minorities like children can lead to increases in workplace violence and is a sure way for an organization to become dysfunctional.

Workplace violence cannot be attributed solely to outside forces. "What happens here" is also influential (Griffin, Stoverink, and Gardner 2012). The organization's culture and its management (particularly frontline supervisors) can increase or decrease the potential for violence (Griffin and Lopez 2004). Organizations that treat people poorly may have employees who resort to violence to *get even* in some way (Griffin and O'Leary Kelly 2004).

Something to Think About

Monique was a transgender African-American woman who was loved by her family and friends but not by all of her coworkers at the office where she worked. They frequently talked about her, and even when she was aware of it, she kept smiling and doing her job. Nevertheless, one coworker, who didn't approve of her lifestyle, brought a gun to work and shot her to death in the parking lot of the company where they both worked. How should a company act to preclude something like this?

Individual factors also relate to workplace violence. Some individuals seem to have *short fuses*, quickly resorting to violence when things do not go their way or when they have been drinking or taking drugs. Individual factors such as hostile attributional bias, hatred based on race, religion, gender, sexual orientation, or other personal characteristics could also lead to aggression or even violence (Jacobs and Scott 2011; LeBlanc and Barling 2004). Initially, members of organizations do not resort to physical violence but rather engage in emotional forms of workplace violence, such as shouting, spreading rumors, fomenting malicious gossip, or simply being rude to others (Porath and Erez 2007, 2009). Stress and frustration can build over time, so the individual propensity for violence can escalate (Van Fleet and Van Fleet 2007). Understanding how emotions build before erupting into a violent explosion can enable others to recognize points where an individual's *boiling point* may possibly be reduced before it is too late (Van Fleet and Van Fleet 2007 and 2010).

The Violence Volcano

The metaphor of a volcano (Van Fleet and Van Fleet 2006; see also the phases of workplace violence proposed by Baron (2001) helps to conceptualize the process whereby the *boiling point* is reached and an individual *erupts*. Volcanoes tend to rumble, tremble, and even spew to give warning signs of an approaching threat. Individuals also give warning signs. The pace with which an individual moves through the sequential phases of the Violence Volcano can vary greatly, from almost immediate to hours, days, months, or even years. While exact predictions are probably impossible, successful intervention is more likely when we understand the process. There are six phases involved:

- **Reaction**. Minor annoyances (family arguments, poor performance ratings, put-downs by associates) occur that frustrate and aggravate the individual or a single, major event (e.g., rejection, divorce, or job termination) that starts the process. In this phase, the individual consciously or subconsciously sees the annoyance or event as a provocation.
- **Rejection**. The individual begins reacting in a relatively quiet way. He or she may try to hurt or annoy those believed to be the cause of his or her troubles by pretending to be forgetful, playing dumb, or slowing down. He or she rejects others by refusing to cooperate or even giving them the *cold shoulder*. Over time, the individual will become increasingly defiant.
- **Expression**. At this point, negative emotions build as the individual begins to reveal anger and frustration through verbal or behavioral expressions by spreading rumors and gossiping, making unwanted sexual comments, arguing with coworkers, customers, vendors, and management, exhibiting bullying behavior, or blaming others in an attempt to create a scapegoat. Others in the organization should become aware that something is wrong with the individual, that he or she is hurt, upset, and very angry.
- **Escalation**. The individual escalates his or her behavior. Bullying behavior may mushroom. Arguments, swearing, and yelling increase. The individual may openly defy company policies and procedures and express feelings of being victimized by management. He or she may send sexual or violent notes to coworkers or management or express a desire to hurt coworkers or management and threaten retaliation if demands are not met.
- **Intensification**. As negative emotions intensify, the individual starts to display dysfunctional behavior, to show signs of going ballistic or berserk. He or she may block the path to physically limit another person's activities as to where to go, what to do,

or with whom to talk. He or she may grab someone while
berating, threatening, or making sexually suggestive remarks
or gestures. He or she may stalk a perceived enemy or display
intense anger through abusive or threatening language,
suicidal threats, physical fights, or destruction of property.

- **Eruption**. Finally, the individual acts or reacts in a forceful,
reprehensible manner, such as sabotaging equipment or
stealing property for revenge, or using weapons to harm
others. The lives of everyone are now at stake as are company
assets. The consequences of an eruption will be costly and
long-lasting.

What to Do

Anyone in an organization should be able to use the phases of the Violence Volcano to see numerous points along the way where intervention
might impede a violent outburst by reducing the *temperature* to prevent
it from reaching the *boiling point*. More specifically, the following seem to
be particularly useful (Howard 2008; Wilkinson 2001):

- **Improve the Environment**. Remove toxic leaders who
micromanage, abuse power, demonstrate a lack of anger
management, threaten or demean others, and/or engage in
illegal/unethical behavior (Goldman 2006). The organization
should monitor the internal and external environments for
indicators or warning signs of violence and help employees
deal with stress. This would also include minimizing any
negative effects of organizational change such as substantial
layoffs, downsizing, restructuring, or reengineering. Everyone,
whether affected or not, should be notified in a caring way
and far enough in advance so that they can make adequate
plans. When layoffs are necessary, outplacement services can
be provided using either internal human resources personnel
or independent consultants. Those deemed to be at high
risk of committing violence particularly need outplacement
services to reduce their potentially violent reactions. The

same is true for those who have difficulty adjusting to change, have been laid off previously, have other family members experiencing job loss, or are emotionally fragile.

- **Have a Strong Antiviolence Policy**. There must be a policy that communicates the organization's commitment to everyone in and out of the organization. The policy may say nothing more than, "This company will not tolerate violence and aggression," or "This organization will not tolerate violence, aggression, or any other practice that abuses the dignity of our stakeholders, including our employees." An example is shown here.

Example Policy

The purpose of this Administrative Regulation is to establish a zero-tolerance policy prohibiting workplace violence to protect the health and safety of employees and the general public.

It is the policy of this organization that violence or threats of violence in the workplace, whether implied or explicit, shall not be tolerated. There is no excuse for, and there shall be no tolerance of, acts of violence or threats of violence by anyone at any level in the City, and there is no excuse for, and there shall be no tolerance of harassment, intimidation, threats, or bullying.

This policy applies to all employees of the organization.

A more comprehensive policy should also specifically mention unacceptable behaviors and the sanctions to be applied when they occur.

- **Crisis Management Team**. A crisis management team should be formed with members from several different areas of the organization such as human resources, legal, security, and facility management (Spillan 2003). Methods for contacting the team should be made available to everyone in the organization. The team should develop written plans to be followed should the volcano ever erupt or show signs of erupting. The team should also help in developing training programs for dealing with incidents and the aftermath of any incident. One way to deal with the aftermath of an incident is to use an EAP. An EAP can clearly provide a support system for employees. EAPs generally have four objectives: assisting supervisors and managers with performance deficits that are associated with personal problems; offering professional help to employees and their immediate families; educating employees about how to prevent future problems; and reducing the social stigma often associated with such personal problems (Couser, Nation and Hyde 2021; Baskar, Shinde and Srinivasan 2021; Kirk and Brown 2003; Berridge, Cooper, and Highley-Marchington 1997).

- **Identify and Prioritize Assets**. The most important assets are the members of the organization. Priority should be given to protect those most likely to be targeted by an angry employee, former employee, or outsider, and those whose duties put them in vulnerable situations. Critical facilities and equipment such as the company power plant, generators, telephone switchboard, computers, and so on should also be safeguarded. Those who will be responsible for carrying out emergency plans (senior management, supervisors, and human resource personnel) should be given a protected place (a *safe room*) and a secondary exit for escaping from the facility. Those in positions to first encounter an angry outsider (e.g., receptionists) should be protected (in extreme circumstances, having their area enclosed in bulletproof glass), and they should be provided with detailed instructions as to what to do should the occasion warrant action.

- **Assess Hazards**. Security systems should be kept up to date, but even the most sophisticated cameras, alarms, and key-card access systems can be thwarted by a determined, violent person. While those systems deter outsiders, those already inside the organization may still pose a threat. Formal needs assessments or hazards assessments should be conducted with assistance from an outside, independent consultant.

One hundred percent protection may simply be impossible; however, some basic steps can be taken, for example, a silent alarm button at the receptionist's desk, a glass partition and locked door for the receptionist, or double doors with a security guard at the building entrance where badges are checked for access. An outside consultant could also conduct attitude/climate surveys and meet with employees to identify problems and issues that need to be addressed.

- **Assess Security Risks**. The best way to handle potential incidents is to have an early detection system. Training everyone to detect and report the signs indicated by the Violence Volcano would be a first step. Pre-employment screening, if properly performed, could enable the organization to avoid hiring potentially violent employees in the first place. Supervisors could be trained to recognize potential problems or by using postemployment behavioral observation plans (BOPs) or dangerousness assessments. BOPs involve supervisors noting the behaviors of the Violence Volcano and sending those notes to an independent agency. The use of an independent agency helps to reduce confrontations between supervisors and employees and can lead to more effective referrals for counseling. Dangerousness assessments refer to formalized psychological evaluations conducted to determine if a person represents a clear and imminent threat (Johnson 1986). Performed by a licensed psychologist or psychiatrist, they are best when everyone in the organization is evaluated to determine their *fitness-for-duty* or dangerousness assessment. Organizations may hesitate to use the dangerousness assessment because they are not sure about the techniques' legitimacy, because they are afraid that it may trigger violence by an already unstable person, or because they are afraid that legal and privacy restrictions may pose more problems than they are prepared to deal with. Legal concerns can be addressed by the process performed by a licensed medical practitioner and by having carefully defined procedures regarding referral, treatment, and returning to work. Organizations are expected to provide a safe workplace without trampling on someone's rights.

- **Establish Controls**. Controls are necessary for systems to work and assets to be protected (Fleming and Harvey 2002). Some simple controls might be for the organization to require that no one works alone, especially after hours and on weekends, or that security is called to escort employees to their cars after hours, that passwords be changed frequently, or that employees wear ID badges. When discharging or terminating an individual, there should be precautions in place. It is generally a reasonable procedure to have human resources or security personnel present at the time of termination, although care must be taken not to embarrass the employee being discharged. Organizations must also make clear who is ultimately responsible for decision making and taking action during potential or actual violent events. When an individual is leaving the organization for any reason, the organization must repossess badges, keys, and other items, but those actions must be handled carefully so as not to trigger a violent reaction. Locks and security codes should be changed.

- **Reporting**. Everyone should receive instructions about the organization's policy and procedures for reporting a threat (when, how, and to whom), especially regarding how to react to angry fellow employees. Reporting can be encouraged by having a procedure in place and assuring confidentiality for the person making the report. Those in charge of the organization especially need specific procedures for intervening when a problem occurs. They need to know exactly how to observe, document, prepare for a meeting with the problem employee, confront the employee, and follow up. Generally, only issues that appear to interfere directly with the employee's ability to perform the job effectively should be reported.

- **Balance Rights.** To avoid becoming dysfunctional, organizations must do more than prevent a hostile environment; they also must balance the rights of problem employees with the rights of other employees to a safe workplace. Special care must be taken to assure anonymity when complaints are filed because, if or when the perpetrator figures out that his or her behavior has been reported, the situation may worsen.

- **Develop Contingency Plans.** The organization should develop plans to minimize the risks associated with workplace violence. As these plans are critical to dealing with workplace violence, they should include three components: (1) how to handle or what to do when violence is only a threat (a threat intervention or de-escalation plan), (2) what to do when the issue has escalated to the point where traumatic violence seems eminent (a trauma intervention or trauma prevention plan), and (3) what to do when a workplace violent incident actually erupts (a trauma plan) (Saam 2010; Fischer, Halibozek, and Walters 2019). The development of these plans is complicated and difficult (McConnell and Drennan 2006) because violent events are rare and difficult to predict. Developing plans takes time from supervisory personnel and requires coordination across organizational units.

Something to Think About

As Alvyn entered the warehouse store, he noted an Asian family coming in. He followed them until they came to an aisle with kitchen knives. He saw his opportunity and quickly picked up a large knife. He stabbed the father and the mother before turning on the two children. When an employee intervened, Alvyn also cut him. While in the custody of the police, he said he had done it because they were from the country that had started spreading COVID-19. Could the store have done anything to prevent this?

Train Everyone

Everyone in the organization needs to be cognizant of the Violence Volcano. With that awareness, it may be possible to identify potential *eruptors* before it is too late and also help keep others from aggravating the problem unintentionally (Kirk and Franklin 2003). Training helps create a safe environment and also provides employees with greater security. Training should involve three components: prediction, prevention, and reaction.

To keep the volcano from erupting, the organization should improve the environment, have a strong antiviolence policy, establish a crisis management team, identify and prioritize assets, assess hazards and security risks, establish controls, set up reporting procedures, balance the rights of those involved, and develop contingency plans.

Prediction. Everyone in the organization should be trained to be observant. Trained observers can see signals or warning signs and can then alert others or managers to be on the alert themselves. The focus of the training should be on behaviors or warning signs, rather than on personalities, and it should emphasize having tolerance for diversity in the organization.

Prevention. This aspect of training is to help everyone in the organization know how to diffuse a hostile and potentially violent situation. Many organizations focus this training on first-line supervisors, but it is better if everyone in the organization is trained.

Reaction. Finally, everyone in the organization should be trained on how to respond if a violent incident occurs, including when to attempt to intervene and when to flee the scene. The training should be conducted in a manner like that used in safety drills for fire, earthquakes, and similar catastrophic events. Procedures regarding what to do should be posted throughout the workplace along with those for fires.

Managers and supervisors exert a profound influence on their immediate surroundings and hence on the daily job experiences of those in their group, team, or department. However, at times, they may be the source of the problem. Managers who are poorly chosen or poorly trained create dysfunctional environments and, hence, contribute to an overall dysfunctional organization. They should be trained not to be abusive or authoritarian as those characteristics are sure to create dissatisfaction and hostile environments. They must know how to treat disturbed employees, as they "have special needs and don't always respond to 'normal' behaviors on your part" (Mantell and Albrecht 1994, 141).

Managers in particular need training that covers stress management, conflict resolution, communication, team building, dealing with difficult people, managing change, conducting terminations, as well as recognizing the indicators or *early warning signs* of potential violence. They should be encouraged to spend time with the members of the unit so that they are able to detect early warning signs of stress. Their training should include how to detect signs of emotional upset, not just indicators of explosiveness, and the procedures to follow when they do detect potential problems. They should learn to treat employees with respect and dignity but also to apply disciplinary actions consistently and refuse to tolerate certain behaviors.

Everyone in the organization, managers and nonmanagers, should be trained in positive work behavior to reduce the propensity for violence. They need to know how to recognize when others are feeling excess stress, and they must be trained in proper behavior (Bitsch and Olynk 2008; Bitsch et al. 2006; Van Fleet and Van Fleet 2007). It is particularly important that managers be involved (Bitsch and Yakura 2007). When correctly performed, that training will establish respect and build the trust that is necessary for the effective functioning of an organization (Barney and Hansen 1994). The training could take advantage of an organization's diversity to build effective teams based on trust, understanding, and mutual respect (Brovelli 2012).

Managing diversity is not easy, which is why training is so important. Effectively managing diversity means being flexible, bending but not breaking the rules. The organization should include the proviso that managers had the right and responsibility to grant exceptions up to a certain limit. Managers would then not have to 'bend the rules' (Veiga, Golden, and Dechant 2004, 89). When the welfare of others is involved, rule-bending may well be worth doing (Badaracco 2001).

Effectively managing diversity is easier if everyone in the organization is properly trained. Diversity training designed specifically to enable members of an organization to work together has been shown to be an effective means of minimizing conflict and, hence, violence. An excellent form of diversity training involves proversity (Graham 1997). Proversity is where the focus of the training is on what people have in common rather than on their differences. Using proversity in training, then, seeks to develop individual characteristics that can be used to bring people together.

It is important, however, to note that the effectiveness of violence prevention is not determined by manuals and training alone but rather by equipping those in the organization with "the capabilities, flexibility, and confidence to deal with sudden and unexpected problems" (Robert and Lajtha 2002). The organization must develop psychosocial working conditions and create psychological safety for its members. Doing so is a very difficult challenge, given the topic of the next chapter.

Rethinking This Chapter

Look at the notes and definition you wrote down at the beginning of this chapter. How might you change it now? Focus your thinking on the Violence Volcano as you reflect on this chapter. With any changes in mind, respond to the following questions and actions. Managers, human resource professionals, and students should do this carefully in order to be prepared to deal with violent incidents. Even if you are not currently employed, your responses should be made as if you are working in an organization. In a classroom setting, your responses should be shared and compared through discussion with others.

Chapter Questions

1. Have you ever experienced or witnessed the sort of behavior that might lead to violence?
2. Have you ever experienced or witnessed a workplace violence incident? Be prepared to discuss your observations.
3. What specific actions could, or should, you or your organization take to prevent violent incidents?

Introductory Actions

1. Draft a policy statement for your organization.
2. What specific information should be collected by your organization regarding workplace violence?
3. Who in the organization should keep records regarding workplace violence, for how long, and for what purpose(s)?

Case to Consider

Navy Yard Shooting

Aaron Alexis wasn't a stranger. He wasn't an intruder. By all appearances, he was just another employee reporting for work at the Washington Navy Yard. He parked his car and used his pass to scan in, stopping off in the bathroom before heading to his desk.

Except Alexis wasn't just another person coming to work. In his bag was a gun and ammunition. When he exited the bathroom, he began shooting indiscriminately. That day, September 16, 2013, he killed 12 people and injured four others.

There was the time he allegedly shot out the rear tires of a construction worker's car, the time he got thrown out of a nightclub for getting into an altercation, and the time his gun went off at home, going all the way through the ceiling and entering the apartment above. The victims suing his employer argued that all of this should have been flagged in background checks and should have been enough not to get him hired.

About a month before the shooting, Alexis suffered from paranoia and, while on an assignment, claimed he was being followed and that people were using microwave signals to control his movements. At the time, he was employed by a company called The Experts Inc. and was, essentially, a government contractor. Experts chose not to report his recent behavior to the Department of Defense so as to protect his privacy.

Source: Verbatim from www.marketplace.org/2019/06/26/workplace-violence-shooting-lawsuits-sue-employer/

Case Questions for Discussion

1. Would his coworkers have been aware of the problems as most occurred away from the workplace?
2. Should Experts have disclosed their information? If so, why? If not, why?
3. Peter Grenier, principal at the Grenier Law Group, agreed to take on this case. Why do you think he did so?

Chapter 6 Takeaways

- Workplace violence refers to willful or negligent acts, including either proscribed criminal acts or coercive behavior, that occur in the course of performing any work-related duty and that lead to significant negative results, such as physical or emotional injury, diminished productivity, or property damage. Have you seen, heard of, or experienced workplace violence?

- Everyone in an organization has some potential tendency to exhibit violent behavior ranging from very low to very high, and the higher the tendency, the greater the likelihood that the individual will display violent behavior at some time. How would you assess the likelihood at your organization?

- Workplace violence cannot be attributed solely to outside forces as the organization's culture. Its management (particularly frontline supervisors) can increase or decrease the potential for violence. How would you rate your frontline supervisors?

- The Violence Volcano helps to visualize the process whereby the *boiling point* is reached and an individual *erupts*. What stage of the volcano exists for your organization?

- To keep the volcano from erupting, the organization should improve the environment, have a strong antiviolence policy, establish a crisis management team, identify and prioritize assets, assess hazards and security risks, establish controls, set up reporting procedures, balance the rights of those involved, and develop contingency plans. Does your organization do or have any of these?

- Train everyone focused on prediction, prevention, and reaction. Does your organization do this type of training?

Recommended Reading

In addition to the many sources used in this chapter, the following case and article could expand your understanding of the chapter's material:

Case: Miller, S.R. and P. Paziotopoulos. n.d. *Nordstrom: The Workplace Violence Dilemma*. https://store.hbr.org/product/nordstrom-the-workplace-violence-dilemma/W17077.

Article: Dowling, M. and C. Sathya. 2022. "How U.S. Businesses Can Help Reduce Gun Violence in Their Communities." *Harvard Business Review Digital Article*. https://hbr.org/2022/09/how-u-s-businesses-can-help-reduce-gun-violence-in-their-communities.

CHAPTER 7

Terrorism*

Make some notes regarding what you expect in this chapter. Write down what you feel is a definition of terrorism. Keep it in mind as you read this chapter.

Introduction

Terrorism at the workplace had been an issue that impacted only a few organizations operating overseas that occasionally had to deal with political and criminal terrorists from foreign countries (Crenshaw 2000 and 1992; Burke and Cooper 2018; Van Fleet and Van Fleet 1998; O'Hare 1994). The complexity and diversity of many organizations, however, have resulted in a growing "collision of cultures, political ideologies, religious doctrines, economic struggles, and national-security measures" that increase the likelihood of terrorism for all organizations (Bowman 1994, xvii). Although a terrorist attack is not likely to strike your organization, it is important to be prepared mentally and emotionally. This situation, plus the fact that dysfunctional leaders can foster terrorists within their organizations (internal terrorists), makes it imperative that managers develop their knowledge of terrorism in general, as well as internal terrorists in particular (Van Fleet and Van Fleet 2006; Engene 2007; Sloan 2000 and 1986).

Terrorism has become a problem for a potentially large number of organizations (Blair et al. 2004; Van Fleet and Van Fleet 1996; O'Hare 1994) for several reasons. First, organizations may symbolize business, globalization, beliefs, or a culture that is disliked by terrorists. Second, organizations are attractive targets because they concentrate hated victims in one location. Third, massive attacks on an organization can have both

---

* This chapter draws heavily on Van Fleet and Van Fleet, 2006 and 1998.

short- and long-term economic effects, disrupting normal social, business, and governmental activities (Schouten, Callahan, and Bryant 2004). "Terrorist activities are carried out with absolute ruthlessness, by various means (psychological pressure, physical violence, the use of weapons and explosives), in the conditions of specially publicized to them and intentionally created anxiety in society" (Walek 2018, 112).

When a terrorist attacks the workplace where people spend much of their time and normally feel safe, the health consequences for those affected might be severe (Berthelsen et al. 2021). Experiencing a terrorist attack, even if an individual is uninjured physically, can have severe psychosocial effects (Nissen et al. 2019). Surviving an attack can lead to an increase in occupational stress attributable and feelings of distrust and apprehension toward those perceived to fit the stereotype of a *terrorist* (Howie 2007).

Terrorism is increasingly being studied, especially by academics, so there now is a growing body of literature, especially on international political terrorism (see, e.g., Alexander and Swetnam 2001; Alexander 1992; Cooley 1999; Hoffman 1998; Hoffman 1992; Jenkins 1978; Laqueur 1987; Merkl 1986; and Pillar 2001). The relatively newer focus on terrorism in business and similar organizations is reflected in the fact that the psychological abstracts had "no reference to terrorism or to related terms, such as 'hostages' or 'hijacking,' until the end of 1981" (Merari 1991, 91). Whereas terrorism had been studied (e.g., Gurr 1970), articles reporting research on terrorists or terrorism in journals that are indexed by the psychological abstracts did not appear with any substantial frequency until the 1980s (Merari 1991, 91).

A major reason for the lack of research on terrorism in organizations is that it is difficult to conduct research on a phenomenon that is highly diverse, very unpredictable, and relatively infrequent, even if its consequences are lasting and, in some cases, quite substantial (Merari 1991). Further, conducting field studies of actual terrorists or terrorist organizations would be very dangerous although some efforts of that sort have been made (Jamieson 1990; Soule 1989), including a study of terrorist finances (Adams 1986). Terrorism, or at least some forms of it, is very similar to workplace violence in general, but that is not true of all forms of terrorism (Reich 1990). The problem lies in part with the very definition of terrorism, which seems to be changing to encompass more forms of dysfunctional behavior (Cooper 2001).

Something to Think About

An individual, later described as a right-wing Christian extremist, planted a bomb outside of a building where he thought Hispanics were employed. Six people were killed and another 20 injured, none of whom were Hispanic. The building sustained substantial damage, making it unusable for several weeks. After setting the bomb, the man walked to a car and left the scene. Witnesses got the make and model of the car, so he was quickly apprehended. If you had been there, would you have been calm enough to get the make and model of the car?

Definition

While terrorism is ancient (Geifman 1992), the terms *terrorism* and *terrorist* are only about 200 years old (Laqueur 1987). There were "109 different definitions [of terrorism and/or terrorist] provided by various writers between 1936 and 1981" (Laqueur 1987, 143). Some definitions include anyone who attempts to further his or her views by a system of coercive intimidation (Johnson 1986, 31). Another refers to anyone who commits an act of violence, be it sabotage, murder, or kidnapping, against an organization's facilities or personnel (Scotti 1986, 5). Some definitions only refer to *politically motivated* acts of violence (Bowman 1994, 11), while others are much broader and include any act of violence or the threat of violence if the intention is to create fear (Scotti 1986, 3). "The FBI defines terrorism, domestic or international, as the unlawful use of force or violence against persons or property to intimidate or coerce a Government or civilian population in furtherance of political or social objectives" (Pomerantz 1987, 14). "Despite more than twenty years of research and an extensive body of literature produced on the topics of terrorism definitions, scholars and practitioners have not arrived at a definite conclusion on what is terrorism" (Mahon 2022).

Almost all of the definitions of terrorism refer to it being used for political ends (e.g., Schmid 2012). Additionally, as the word *terror* refers to extreme fear, virtually all definitions include coercion and/or fear. Terrorism, then, involves the use of fear to intimidate or coerce, influence, or affect the operation of organizations, and generally, although not always, will involve violent or dangerous actions. Recognizing the variations in definitions, we developed a definition focused more on acts against organizations that are mostly nonpolitical (Van Fleet and Van Fleet 1998). That definition is, then:

> Terrorism refers to intentional, premeditated, and sometimes retaliatory actions on the part of one or more individuals to create extreme stress or fear among those in an organization that lasts long enough to accomplish the purpose of furthering the perpetrator's own views.

Internal Terrorism

Internal terrorism is sometimes used as synonymous with domestic terrorism (committed by homegrown groups who have no ties or connections outside the country of origin), but that is not how it is used here. Instead, here it refers to terrorism performed by someone inside the organization as distinct from that performed by someone outside the organization. It is intended to evoke fear in others in the organization or its management in an effort to achieve the terrorist's goals. Because single, isolated incidents of criminal or aggressive behavior (workplace violence) are unlikely to create a climate of fear sufficiently long-lasting and strong enough to bring about the change necessary to accomplish the terrorist's goal, the individual resorts to terrorism.

Internal terrorism can range from acts of sabotage and vandalism to the use of chemical, biological, or radioactive weapons or, of course, the use of weapons, usually a firearm. Potential targets include:

- Other members of the organization, perhaps especially members of management
- Building lobbies or loading docks
- Computers and telephone systems

- Electrical or air-handling systems
- Water supply systems
- Storage areas for volatile materials

The Internal Terrorist

As noted in an earlier chapter, all individuals enter organizations with some potential predisposition to exhibit violent behaviors (Griffin and Lopez 2004; see also Denenberg and Braverman 1999). Those predispositions could be very low (even zero) levels, or they could range up to very high ones that could easily lead to violent behavior. Also, as noted earlier, organizations (or parts of organizations or particularly dysfunctional leaders within organizations) can create internal environments (cultures or climates) that either diminish or hold in check such predispositions or inflame them (see also Litzky et al. 2006). A 2 × 2 conceptual scheme seems to underlie their work as well as that of others. Because most of the literature focuses on workplace violence or terrorism itself, it is really focusing only on the cell consisting of individuals with a high predisposition toward violence and organizations that engender or inflame such violence or terrorism (see also Van Fleet and Griffin 2006).

A more complete understanding would involve the 3 × 2 model shown in Figure 7.1. Here the two columns represent the organizational predispositions as proposed by Griffin and Lopez (2004), and the first and third rows correspond to the individuals with low or high propensities. The difference, then, is that a middle row is added to represent individuals who, while they have a low predisposition toward violence, have a high willingness to engage in nonviolent behaviors that cause fear in others as a way of achieving their own particular goals. These are the individuals most likely to be internal terrorists. These internal terrorists typically focus on managers. They prey upon the fears of managers who are trying to cope with the ever-changing task and general environments as well as a maze of legal constraints. Typically, these terrorists are intelligent and creative individuals who understand the line between behavior that is legally permissible and that which is not (Van Fleet and Van Fleet 1998).

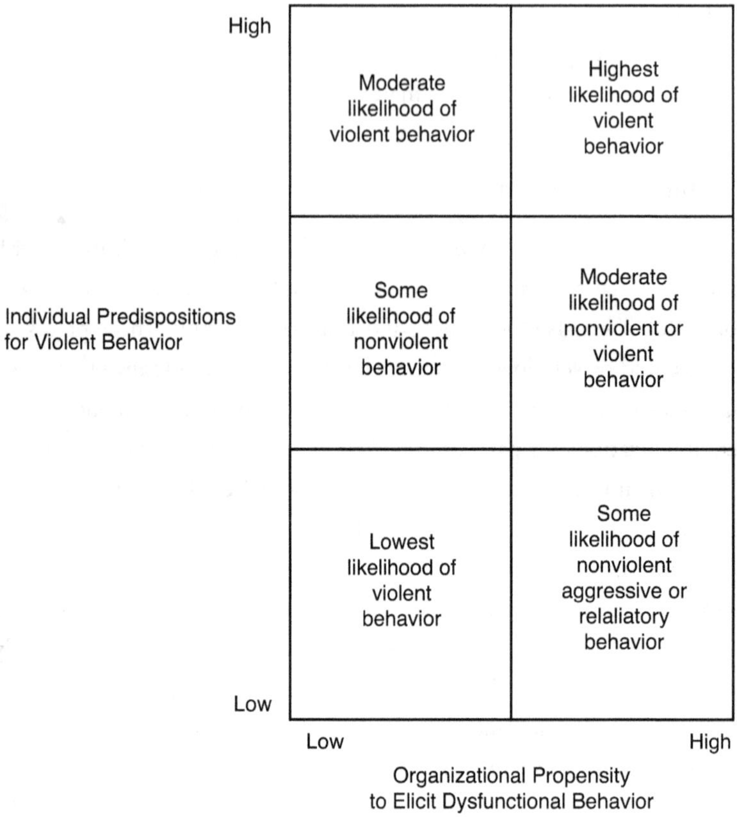

Figure 7.1 **A framework of person–situation determinants of violent behavior in organizations**

Source: Van Fleet and Van Fleet 2006; adapted from Griffin and Lopez 2004.

These terrorists use a variety of tactics. They may:

1. Have others speak up while they remain quietly behind the scenes, thus minimizing their own risk
2. Mask their real goals by hiding behind a legitimate issue that they anticipate others will follow
3. Use anonymous letters, notes, and/or memos that would lend credence to their ideas or would discredit others
4. Spread malicious gossip to discredit ideas or people
5. Do favors for others in an effort to try to coopt them and get them to support the terrorist's goals

Whichever tactic they use, their goal is personal gain, and the tactic is used in order to create a climate of fear—to terrorize the organization—albeit in a relatively low-key, nonviolent manner and without bringing undue legal attention upon themselves (Kinney 1995, 96).

Something to Think About

George was a municipal maintenance worker who had been with the city for over six years and was generally regarded as a satisfactory employee. However, during a get-together with another department, some sort of dispute occurred, and he left *in a huff* quite angrily. He later returned heavily armed. He killed 12 people and wounded 16 others before fleeing the scene. After a chase, the police confronted him, and during a shootout, he was killed. Why would one dispute have led to this response?

One example of this type of internal terrorist is the employee who threatens legal action when his or her unjustified requests are turned down. The request may be a simple one, such as a change in procedure or time off for personal business, or a much larger one demanding a change in assignment, a promotion, or a salary increase that could be construed as favoritism or reverse discrimination. Another example would be the individual who possesses vital information or company secrets that, if divulged, would significantly harm the company and uses that knowledge for personal purposes. Still, another example is the employee who attempts to discredit someone or something by intentionally spreading false or misleading information, using slander and misinformation campaigns, especially through the use of computers (Naylis 1996). There may also be a disgruntled employee who threatens to discredit the company to customers so that they will not buy the company's products or services. In any event, when the objective is to create fear in the organization and especially its management, the act is clearly terrorism. These terrorists may also be employees in powerful positions within the organization who are *bullies* and accustomed to using such tactics in all of their interpersonal interactions to *get their way*.

Organizations are becoming more difficult to control in today's complex, global world. Cell phones, e-mail, the Internet, and other forms of information and communication technology (Yunos and Sulaman 2017) are two-edged swords. Organizations can use them but so can enemies of the organizations. Bitter or disgruntled employees, customers, and suppliers can use these to bring harm to organizations. A lot of members of organizations perceive themselves as paid too little, promoted too slowly, passed over, humiliated, easily replaced, and generally not particularly well thought of or rewarded for their loyalty. These individuals perceive that they are falling short of their dreams, and they blame organizations and others in the organization, managers in particular. "Asymmetric warfare has come to the workplace—managers may sometimes have the power to hire and fire, but employees have the Internet" (Van Fleet and Van Fleet 2006, 770).

All of these acts could be accomplished by social networking. Social networking[†] can be a powerful tool for instilling fear in individuals and organizations. One or more messages or suggestions posted online can cause a public relations nightmare or worse for an organization (Horn et al. 2015). It is possible for individuals to generate, edit, and share content with large numbers of people almost immediately (Shullich 2011). With this speed, damage can be done to an organization before it even knows that something has been said. It is important, therefore, for companies to monitor social media more zealously than they monitor their physical premises. Using social networking, an internal terrorist may simply:

> Raise a question or pass along an alleged comment, for example, "I've heard that XYZ's new Product X is good on Criterion A but is severely lacking on Criterion B. Has anybody out there tried it?" Readers tend to focus on Product X's suggested weakness, posting questions and concerns at other sites (Van Fleet and Van Fleet 1998).

Another tactic, *mailbox stuffing*, *bombing*, or *spamming* can effectively shut down a company's online operations, costing it both dollars and

---

[†] Cyberterrorism is not used here as its use is so closely associated with and usually defined in terms of political activity.

goodwill. "Professional spammers can merrily bombard their victims with as many messages as they like, and they have a host of automated tools to help them expand their volume and slip past filters" (Nield 2021). This tactic is a common form of Internet revenge. In February 1997, America Online (AOL) was threatened by vindictive hackers (CNET Staff 1997). AOL customers were warned that their accounts would be canceled if they attempted to go online on February 14 (Valentine's Day). The AOL attack also included e-mail messages that warned that computer viruses would be planted and chat rooms would be paralyzed through a technique called *scrolling*, which moves the on-screen text so rapidly that it is unreadable. While this particular attempt was unsuccessful, another attack years later caused AOL to ask millions of users to change their passwords and security questions (Fontana 2014). This is a type of attack that internal terrorists could use. Yet another tactic is *doxing*. "Doxing is the intentional public release onto the Internet of personal information about an individual by a third party, often with the intent to humiliate, threaten, intimidate, or punish the identified individual" (Douglas 2016). However, doxing seems to be used mostly for revenge (Obeidat et al. 2022; Cox 2019).

Another tactic of the internal terrorist is making phone calls or leaving threatening notes implying violence, lawsuits, or other actions that could harm the organization. Organizations can use threat management and security firms and can work with mental health providers to investigate and monitor these individuals (Meloy et al. 2021: Kinney 1995, 96), but doing so may be too costly for many organizations. Concern about the negative use of social networking could cause large organizations to become more conservative, bureaucratic, and/or paranoid. They may become so concerned about maintaining a *happy workplace* that they fall behind others. On the other hand, smaller organizations may be able to take advantage of the damage to larger ones and be more successful. Customers and suppliers may feel that they are being asked to pay more or provide more or do it faster without any corresponding benefit. In those situations, they may turn to anonymous letter writing or using social media to try to harm the organization. By creating and doing so, they can satisfy their wishes through fear and intimidation— internal terrorism.

Terrorism in General

Terrorism that impacts an organization is a form of antisocial behavior. Antisocial behavior is "any behavior that brings harm, or is intended to bring harm, to an organization, its employees, or stakeholders" (Giacalone and Greenberg 1997, vii). Deviant or dysfunctional behavior is antisocial behavior. While some of these behaviors involve violence, not all of them do (e.g., alcohol use, smoking, and inappropriate tardiness). Violent behavior is a subsection of dysfunctional/antisocial behavior (see, e.g., Lopez and Griffin 2004), and terrorism is another subsection, albeit one that overlaps both violent behavior and nonviolent behavior. Terrorism is dysfunctional, but other forms of dysfunctional/antisocial behavior do not involve terrorism. No definition can eliminate all overlap among categories of such behavior, and so defining terrorism is extremely difficult (Schmid 2011; Weinberg, Pedahzur, and Hirsch-Hoefler 2004; Ruby 2002).

Aspects of Terrorism

As there is no agreed-upon definition of terrorism, it is useful to consider its varying aspects. Some of the more notable ones are:

- How much damage, how many people are negatively impacted, and/or what is the cost associated with the fear and stress that the terrorist intentionally creates? While some terrorists do not care who lives or dies or what is damaged as a result of their acts, others use only psychological warfare. While there is no physical harm to people or property, the emotional damage can be substantial and long-lasting.
- Victims—Who will be the victim(s) who are to be sacrificed to help the terrorist achieve his or her goals? The victim could be an organization that does or supports something the terrorist dislikes (e.g., Planned Parenthood, a logging company perceived to be harming a forest, or a university teaching critical race theory). The victim could be a part of an organization that the terrorist has had a problem with

(an agency, department, or bureau) or a local branch or other physical facility of an organization (an office or plant). Victim(s) could also simply be either a group of individuals (formal or informal) or a single individual thought to be pivotal or powerful and interfering with or blocking the accomplishment of the terrorist's goals. Further, victims could be one or more *innocent* bystanders with no connection to the issue at hand but who nevertheless are injured or harmed by the terrorist's actions.

- Goals—The terrorist's goals could be lofty, superordinate goals such as world peace, disarmament, ecological balance, social justice, or the betterment of social processes. On the other hand, they could be more mundane, like a promotion, a favorable transfer or assignment, the removal of a coworker, or simply money. When the goal is one of these, the terrorist will still hide the true goal by expressing the reason as helping others, although even a cursory examination will reveal the real goal.

Terrorism inside an organization is different from employee or occupational crime, which is a subset of white-collar crime, which in turn is different from corporate crime (Holtfreter 2005; Friedrichs 2002; Sutherland 1940). Corporate crime generally is meant to refer to crimes committed by members of an organization to benefit the organization. White-collar crime, on the other hand, refers to those crimes committed by higher-ranking members of an organization to benefit only themselves. Occupational or employee crime refers to those crimes committed by members of an organization. Internal terrorism and occupational crime, while sharing some characteristics, are different. Occupational crime does not involve creating fear, which is fundamental to terrorism.

Occupational crimes include (Edelhertz 1983):

- Crimes committed by persons on an individual basis. Examples include espionage, defined as the theft or unauthorized acquisition of secret or restricted information, income tax evasion, bankruptcy fraud, credit purchases or taking loans with no intention to pay, and insurance fraud.

- Crimes committed by those in the organization in violation of their duty of loyalty to the employer or client. Examples include bribery, embezzlement and pilfering, and kickbacks or payments or favors given clandestinely to decision makers in return for selecting the offender's products or services.
- Crimes incidental to the organization's operations. Examples include false or misleading advertising, food and drug violations, and prescription fraud.
- Crime as a business. Fraud of one or more of three broad types—asset misappropriation, corruption, and fraudulent statements. Examples include medical fraud, lottery fraud, mutual fund fraud, real estate fraud, charity fraud, religious fraud, and even music pirating.

Related to these are:

- Theft of services
- Sabotage, robbery, burglary, larceny
- Crimes involving or using computers

Categories of Terrorists

Based on the aforementioned, then, the following are categories of terrorists (Van Fleet and Van Fleet 2006 and 1998). It should be noted that the categories overlap (compare these to those of Martin 2017):

- Political terrorists and religious fanatics—These are probably the oldest types of terrorists. Most political terrorists have specific demands to make and believe that American companies are the root of all evil (Scotti 1986, 5). Bowman (1994, 54) has suggested that the terms *fundamentalist* and *orthodox* imply that individuals and/or organizations described by these terms could easily resort to terrorism.
- Average citizen turned terrorist—Similar to political terrorists, the ordinary citizen who becomes a terrorist typically is a member of an environmental, antinuclear, animal rights, antiabortion, antigovernment, or religious group who has

come to feel that *working within the system* is unsatisfactory, so
the only recourse is violent action.

- Criminals acting as terrorists—These are criminals who use
  political excuses to mask their criminal motivations. International
  kidnapping is usually carried out by this type of terrorist.
- Insane terrorists—These terrorists are individuals suffering
  from psychological disorders and are frequently *copycats*
  desiring attention more than making a point or seeking
  money (Scotti 1986). They act irrationally, using violent
  tactics such as shooting, bombing, or kidnapping. Their goals
  may be only remotely related to the targets they choose (or to
  the people who become the inadvertent victims).
- Internal terrorists or psycho-terrorists—These terrorists
  (also sometimes termed *organizational terrorists*, see, for
  example, McCurley and Vineyard 1998) are members, former
  members, or other constituents of an organization who use
  gossip, political tactics, harassment, intimidation, and threats
  to create a climate of fear that will enable them to further
  their own objectives within an organization (Kinney 1995,
  96). They are referred to as cancers within organizations,
  although they frequently present such a positive face to many
  that they may have many supporters.

Because this latter form of terrorism is frequently nonviolent, it gets
little attention. Nevertheless, it is a formidable and growing aspect of
organizational life with which organizations must learn to cope. To examine this category, Van Fleet and Van Fleet (2006) asked a group of subjects
if they had ever observed an individual or group attempting to use fear to
get their way in the organization and, if so, to describe the incident and
then provide some minimal (and nondisclosing)) demographic information about those involved. Some illustrative examples they found include
the following:

- A member of a country club was upset with an employee
  and demanded that the employee be fired. The club manager
  did not fire the employee, so the member threatened to
  sue the club to recover his membership fees. I observed the

confrontation between the manager and the member. It
was successful because the threat of a lawsuit got the club's
attention, and they worked out a compromise.

- I observed a bookkeeper help to get her manager to quit
  because she did not like how he was changing things. She
  did so using her connections to corporate management and
  passive–aggressive behavior. When the manager tried to
  change a procedure or practice, she continued to follow the
  old procedures, causing a loss in efficiency due to a lack of a
  uniform process. She then went absent for two weeks, leaving
  the manager to do her job as well as his own. Finally, when
  she returned, it was with the news that corporate management
  fully supported her actions.

- A coworker of mine used fear to get promoted. He
  accidentally saw one of the top managers in the company with
  a lady who was not his wife. The manager was afraid for his
  marriage, so when my coworker asked for a promotion and
  reminded him that he had seen him with another woman, the
  boss promoted him right away.

- All of the people working in my department are of the same
  race, except one lady who is of a different ethnic group.
  She is not working as hard as she is supposed to. She misses
  deadlines and leaves work early. As a result, the other people
  in the department have to work harder and do part of her
  job. When my supervisor tried to fire her, she said that the
  supervisor was racist and that she would sue him if he went
  through with it. The manager decided to let her keep her job
  because he was afraid she would win in court because she was
  the only one of a different race to work for the company.

The differences between internal terrorists and other terrorists are
significant enough to suggest that findings for other terrorists are not
likely to be true for internal terrorists. Just as Greenberg (1996) has linked
employee theft to perceived injustice, so, too, internal terrorism may be
linked to higher levels of such perceived injustice. Indeed, most, if not

all, of the forms of antisocial organizational behaviors (Giacalone and Greenberg 1997)—arson, blackmail, bribery, espionage, extortion, fraud, interpersonal violence, lying, sabotage, and theft, for example—could be forms of internal terrorism if the underlying motivation is to evoke fear in an effort to achieve the terrorist's goals. Revenge (Barash and Lipton 2011; Moreno-Jimenez 2009; Barreca 1995), *reaching the breaking point* (Bright 2012; Bies et al. 1997), and *snapping* (Conway and Siegelman 1995) could also be antisocial behavior that becomes terrorism.

What Can Organizations Do?

Dysfunctional organizations are the breeding grounds for terrorists, but even those organizations can take some actions to prevent or deter terrorists. However, whatever action is taken, the rights of the individual and those of the organization must be balanced. That balancing act is a daunting task as protecting individual rights, particularly privacy rights, is difficult. Many tools or techniques that are part of an organization's anti-terrorism efforts (e.g., cameras monitoring workplaces and locker rooms, regular reviews of e-mail, metal detectors, and searches) could also be seen as infringing upon individual rights.

The first thing an organization must do is to itemize and prioritize its assets, including human assets. The organization's computers, telephones, water, and electricity sources would clearly be highly prioritized. Senior management and receptionists or clerical personnel who would be the first to encounter a terrorist should also be highly prioritized, and they should be given detailed instructions regarding actions they should take when they observe a potential problem. To ward against kidnapping, some form of executive protection should be employed, especially for those on overseas assignments (MacDonald 2019); Kelly and Cook 1994; Korsky 1990; Kelly and Barnathan 1988). As noted in an earlier chapter, even with such protective measures, many organizations are still very vulnerable to attacks from inside or from out of the organization (Barton 1993a, 1993b; Maddox 1991).

Many of the tactics to prevent terrorism are the same as for workplace violence in general and include conducting building security checks, employing burglar alarms, monitoring the premises via closed-circuit TV, installing electronic card ID systems, and employing armed guards. However, organizations should not rely exclusively on physical security measures as even the most sophisticated cameras, alarms, and key-card access systems can be bypassed by a determined terrorist. The building(s) where the organization operates should be well-lit and landscaped so that no one can hide behind shrubs or trees near walkways, parking lots, and other buildings. To bolster physical measures, organizations should use administrative controls such as requiring that employees not work alone, that passwords be changed often, that employees accompany one another or obtain escorts to their cars after hours, and that employees wear specially coded ID badges.

As noted in Chapter 4, a formal *needs assessment* should be done, usually with assistance from an outside, independent consultant. Existing programs, policies, and personnel should be evaluated and trained as necessary to promote a positive, nonviolent culture in the organization. BOPs or behavior-based safety programs (BBS) are also useful in documenting behaviors that could lead to someone becoming an internal terrorist (Spigener, Lyon, and McSween 2022).

To reduce the element of surprise counted on by terrorists, the organization should establish a terrorism prevention team (Vaisman-Tzachor 1997, 1991). The team would develop a surveillance awareness plan so that terrorists are not able to conduct surveillance (Haney and Lutters 2020; Scotti 1986, 43–46). If leaders in the organization are fearful of a terrorist attack or kidnapping, they should become unpredictable in terms of their schedules—not arriving and leaving work at the same time. Driving and walking routes should be examined to determine which are the most vulnerable and then use alternative ones to the extent possible.

Something to Think About

On a quiet summer day, a 39-year-old man armed with a handgun began shooting in the parking lot outside a Muslim mosque. Fortunately, only two were injured and not fatally, but he then entered the building and continued shooting. Eight people were killed, and another six were badly injured. Upon arrival, the police established a perimeter and demanded that the shooter surrender. Rather than surrendering, the shooter turned his gun on himself and committed suicide. Why do you think shooters like this commit suicide?

Training and Communication

Training should not just be for key personnel, but rather everyone should be trained in utilizing defensive strategies and how to cope with emergencies. When properly trained, they will be able to see signals that would otherwise be overlooked or ignored so they can alert others and be on the alert themselves. Organizations should use different forms of communication (e-mail, bulletin boards, memos, announcements, etc.) and be sure that the communication is honest and two-way. Appropriate personnel should be trained in the handling of ransom calls. They can help if they know how to keep the caller on the line, how to listen to the caller's voice, what background noises to listen for, and whether this is the time to attempt to initiate the release of the person kidnapped. Training and communication of this nature should help create a safe environment, give employees security, and show them that the organization cares about them. The organization will not return to normal immediately after employees have experienced a terrorist attack. Everyone will find it difficult to do their jobs, so the leaders in the organizations should be empathic and helpful and only gradually ease things back to normal.

Again, as noted in Chapter 4, the organization should have an EAP. EAPs reduce the likelihood that employees who are highly stressed would become terrorists. Many companies already have EAPs to deal with substance abuse, rising health, safety costs, and increased stress in the workplace (Bouzikos et al. 2022; EASNA 2009; Martin 1989). An organization should have its EAP include terrorism for several reasons. First, members of the organization would already be familiar with the EAP. Second, the EAP infrastructure would already be in place. Third, EAPs have been shown to be helpful in other types of worker assistance. Expanding the role of EAPs to include terrorism prevention should prove beneficial to organizations.

Ransomware

Related to the ransom of a person, ransomware attacks are also usually but not always about money. The Small Business Administration (SBA) reports that it is the fastest-growing malware threat (Goriel 2017). Ransomware is a form of malicious software that infects and restricts access to a computer until a ransom is paid. However, the SBA suggests 14 ways in which to protect your organization (adapted from Goriel 2017; please see the original for details).

1. Implement an awareness training program. Everyone in the organization should be aware of the threat of ransomware and how it is delivered.
2. Strengthen computers. Use strong spam filters to keep phishing e-mails from reaching those in the organization and authenticate inbound e-mail using available technologies to prevent e-mail spoofing.
3. Scan all e-mails. Scan both incoming and outgoing e-mails to detect threats and to keep executable files from reaching members of the organization.
4. Configure firewalls. The organization's firewall should block access to known malicious IP addresses.
5. Consider using a centralized patch management system. Patch all operating systems, software, and firmware on all devices used by those in the organization.
6. Scan computers automatically. Configure antivirus and antimalware programs to regularly scan the organization's computers automatically.
7. Manage the use of privileged accounts. No one in the organization should be provided with administrative access unless it is absolutely needed, and those accounts should only be used when necessary.
8. Configure access controls. Files, directory, and network share permissions should only be made available to those who need to read-specific files, and they should not have write access to those files, directories, or shares.
9. Disable macro scripts. Macro scripts are toolbar buttons and keyboard shortcuts from office files transmitted via e-mail. Organizations

should use special software to open e-mail files rather than the full office suite.

10. Implement software restriction policies (SRP). Set controls to prevent programs from executing from common ransomware locations, such as temporary folders supporting popular Internet browsers or compression/decompression programs.

11. Consider disabling the remote desktop protocol (RDP). If it is not being used, get rid of it.

12. Use application whitelisting. Only allows systems to execute programs known and permitted by the organization's security policy.

13. Execute operating system environments or specific programs in a virtualized environment.[‡] Categorize data. Prioritize information based on organizational value and then physically separate networks and data.

Bomb Threats

Bomb threats should be taken seriously, so everyone needs to be trained to react as they would to a fire alarm. Phones should have emergency numbers to facilitate quick action by notifying security. Those who normally answer the phone(s) for the organization need to be trained in a way similar to that for ransom calls—requesting information from the caller, listening for background noises, activating a call recording/tracing system if one is available, sounding appropriate alarms, and notifying appropriate personnel. Everyone should know exactly where and how to evacuate, where to meet outside the premises, and how and when to return to their workplaces. The organization should, of course, make every possible effort to prevent the planting of a bomb on company premises. Closed-circuit TV cameras with backups should be installed, and those who normally handle the mail should be taught to be on the lookout for suspicious-looking mail or packages.

[‡] For more on a virtualized environment, see https://en.wikipedia.org/wiki/Virtualization.

Plan for Afterward

It is all well and good to try to prevent terrorism, but it may happen anyway. If it does, the organization should have a plan for dealing with the consequences. A postevent plan should have numerous elements, starting with a prearranged distress signal. There should be procedures for calling security, emergency teams, and/or law enforcement agencies. Everyone should know where to report immediately and where they actually will be safe. They should understand that pay and benefits policies remain in force. After an attack, it is important to get key people back into facilities to assure others that it is safe (obviously, the structural integrity of the facility must be assured first).

The best way to prevent or at least deter terrorism in your organization is by developing psychosocial working conditions and creating psychological safety. That is the topic for the final chapter.

Rethinking This Chapter

Look at the notes and definition you wrote down at the beginning of this chapter. How might you change it now? Think about the framework in Figure 7.1 and the different categories of terrorism presented in the chapter as you reflect on the material. With any changes in mind, respond to the following questions and actions. Do this carefully in order to be prepared to deal with terrorism. Make your responses as if you are working in an organization, even if you are not currently employed. In a classroom setting, your responses should be shared and compared through discussion with others.

Chapter Questions

1. Have you ever experienced or witnessed the sort of behavior that might lead to terrorism?
2. Have you ever experienced or witnessed a terrorist event? Be prepared to discuss your observations.
3. What specific actions could, or should, you or your organization take to prevent terrorism?

Introductory Actions

1. Draft a policy statement for your organization.
2. What specific information should be collected by your organization regarding terrorism?
3. Who in the organization is or should be in charge of terrorism planning?

Case to Consider

Domestic Terrorism

Frost and Cook met in an online chat group where Frost shared the idea of attacking the power grid. Soon the two began to recruit others. Part of the recruitment process involved a booklist of readings that promoted the ideology of white supremacy and neo-Nazism. Sawall, a friend of Cook's, joined the conspiracy, and each was assigned a substation in a different region of the United States. The plan was to attack the substations with powerful rifles. They believed actions would cost the government millions of dollars and cause unrest for Americans in the region.

They met in Ohio to discuss the plot. Frost provided Cook with an AR-47 and the two trained at a shooting range. Frost also provided Cook and Sawall with suicide necklaces that were filled with fentanyl and were to be ingested if and when the defendants were caught by law enforcement. Both Cook and Sawall expressed their commitment to dying in furtherance of their mission.

Sawall and Cook purchased spray paint and painted a swastika flag under a bridge with the caption, "Join the Front." They had additional propaganda plans but were derailed during a traffic stop. Sawall swallowed his suicide pill but survived. Cook and Frost drove to Texas in March 2020, where Cook stayed in different cities with juveniles he was attempting to recruit for their plot.

(*Source*: Department of Justice, U.S. Attorney's Office, Southern District of Ohio at: www.justice.gov/usao-sdoh/pr/3-men-plead-guilty-domestic-terrorism-crime-related-p)

Case Questions for Discussion

1. Would any of the coworkers of Frost, Cook, or Sawall have been aware of their plan?
2. How might anyone interacting with one of the three have seen the warning signs?
3. The defendants face a maximum penalty of 15 years in prison. Do you feel that is just?

Chapter 7 Takeaways

- Terrorism has become a problem for some organizations because it may symbolize business, globalization, beliefs, or a culture that is disliked by terrorists. They concentrate hated victims in one location, or massive attacks on the organization can have both short- and long-term economic effects. How aware are you of the possibility of terrorism in general?

- Terrorism refers to intentional, premeditated, and sometimes retaliatory actions on the part of one or more individuals to create extreme stress or fear among those in an organization that lasts long enough to accomplish the purpose of furthering the perpetrator's own views. How aware are you of the possibility of terrorism at your organization?

- Internal terrorism is carried out by someone inside the organization to evoke fear in others in the organization or its management. Again, how aware are you of the possibility of terrorism in your organization?

- Tactics used include posting messages or suggestions online, *mailbox stuffing, bombing,* or *spamming* to shut down a company's online operations or making phone calls or leaving threatening notes implying violence, lawsuits, or other actions that could harm the organization. Have you seen, heard of, or experienced any of these tactics?

- Terrorism inside an organization is different from employee or occupational crime, which is a subset of white-collar crime, which in turn is different from corporate crime. How would you differentiate internal terrorism from occupational crime?

- Types of terrorists are political terrorists, religious fanatics, average citizens turned terrorists, criminals acting as terrorists, insane terrorists, psycho-terrorists, and organizational terrorists. Have you seen, heard of, or experienced any of these?
- Preparations include increasing security measures, training, preparing for ransomware and bomb threats, and planning for how to recover from an event. Is your organization prepared for any possible terrorism?

Recommended Reading

In addition to the many sources used in this chapter, the following case and article could expand your understanding of the chapter's material:

Case: Huang, Y. n.d. "Perspectives on Terrorism." https://store.hbr.org/product/perspectives-on-terrorism/702026.

Article: Abrahms, M. 2015. "Why People Keep Saying: "That's What the Terrorists Want." *Harvard Business Review Digital Article*. https://hbr.org/2015/11/why-people-keep-saying-thats-what-the-terrorists-want.

CHAPTER 8

Psychological and Psychosocial Safety

As with previous chapters, make some notes of what you expect in this chapter. Write down what you feel are definitions of both psychological safety and psychosocial safety. Keep those definitions in mind as you read this chapter.

Previous Chapters

In several of the previous chapters, there have been suggestions on steps that could be taken to prevent or cope with dysfunctional individuals or a dysfunctional organization. Following the framework from the Introduction, these are ones focused on people or culture.

- Assure that no retaliation occurs after an incident.
- Be creative—develop new routines and work habits to overcome monotony at work.
- Commit (in or out)—if you believe in your organization's goals, work to help accomplish them; if you don't, it is time to move on.
- Control what you can; don't worry about what you can't.
- Develop clarity—in assignments and how to respond to extreme behavior.
- Develop collaboration between leaders and others in the organization.
- Develop programs to increase everyone's safety awareness.
- Do the work; don't be a target—perform well so that there is no reason to pick on you.
- Don't derail your career—bite your tongue and do your best to follow the orders.

- Don't get drawn in—be polite and honest; keep your distance from those who complain.
- Don't gossip—do not get involved.
- Encourage individuals to voice their concerns about safety issues.
- Establish best practices for safe operations.
- Everyone in the organization needs to be cognizant of the Violence Volcano.
- Have a zero-tolerance policy for dysfunctional behaviors.
- Have firm and systematic penalties.
- Identify potential *eruptors* before it is too late.
- Obtain feedback from those in the organization.
- Return to normal as quickly as possible.
- Situations may not be forever.
- Train—provide training about the Violence Volcano, safety, and active shooters; training should be based on prediction, prevention, and reaction.
- Provide a safe working environment.
- Developing psychosocial working conditions.
- Creating psychological safety.

The last two points of developing psychosocial working conditions and creating psychological safety to prevent, deter, or correct dysfunctions in organizations were noted throughout previous chapters and merit expansion as they may be the ways with which to deal with dysfunctional cultures, individuals, and organizations.

Definitions

"Psychological safety is a condition in which you feel (1) included, (2) safe to learn, (3) safe to contribute, and (4) safe to challenge the status quo—all without fear of being embarrassed, marginalized, or punished in some way" (Clark 2020).

Psychological safety is the belief that you won't be punished or humiliated for speaking up with ideas, questions, concerns, or mistakes. At work, it's a shared expectation held by members of a team that teammates will not embarrass, reject, or punish them for sharing ideas, taking risks, or soliciting feedback (Center for Creative Leadership 2023).

"Team psychological safety is a shared belief held by members of a team that it's OK to take risks, to express their ideas and concerns, to speak up with questions, and to admit mistakes—all without fear of negative consequences" (Gallo 2023).

Something to Think About

Sarah recently joined this charitable organization because she wanted to make a difference. She has been observing and listening to learn how she can best fit in. She is making friends and starting to feel comfortable with the various projects being offered by the organization. The amount of paperwork surprises her, but she is learning that it is necessary for the organization to maintain its nonprofit status. But last week, she noticed that their group leader may have made a mistake when processing some documents. If the mistake goes unnoticed, it could cause problems when it is time to file tax documents. Because it is important that no mistakes are made, she calls this to the attention of the leader. When she does, the leader rather curtly says, "I've been working for this organization for over ten years, so I think I know what I'm doing. You just do your job and let me do mine." What do you think she will do if she ever notices him making a mistake again?

"The term 'sociological safety' doesn't currently exist in the social sciences as its parallel form does in psychology" (Jones 2022). However, psychosocial refers to the interaction of social, cultural, and environmental influences on individuals' thinking and behavior (https://dictionary.apa.org/psychosocial). "The psychosocial approach looks at individuals in the context of the combined influence that psychological factors and the surrounding social environment have on their physical and mental wellness and their ability to function" (https://en.wikipedia.org/wiki/Psychosocial). Psychosocial safety "refers to the shared belief held by workers that their psychological health and safety is protected and supported by senior management" (https://en.wikipedia.org/wiki/Psychosocial_safety_climate).

Origins

Rogers (1954) first used the term in discussing conditions necessary for creativity. He suggested that psychological safety could be established by three associated processes: (1) unconditional acceptance of an individual, (2) providing a climate with no external evaluation, and (3) entering into or psychologically identifying with the emotions, thoughts, or attitudes of others and where they can see you and what you are feeling and doing from your point of view and still accept you (Rogers 1970, 148). Bonner (1961, 269) then mentioned psychological safety in reference to providing security for individual beliefs. Schein and Bennis (1965) later use the term to describe "an atmosphere where one can take chances" (pp. 4445). Psychological safety then became associated with elements of social systems that created more or less nonthreatening, predictable, and consistent social situations in which to engage (Kahn 1990). More recently, psychological safety has been used extensively in the work by Edmondson (2003, 1999) and her colleagues (Edmondson and Bransby 2023; Edmonson and Hugander 2021; Jung et al. 2021; Harvey et al. 1019; Swendiman, Edmondson, and Mahmoud 2019; Edmondson et al. 2016; Edmondson and Lei 2014; Nembhard and Edmondson 2006; Edmondson and Roloff 2009; Edmondson and Mogelof 2006), especially in regards to teams and teamwork. Now the concept is being applied organizationally and not just to teams (Edmondson 2019).

Psychosocial effects were noted by Karasek (1979) and are generally related to safety in terms of the climate or environment (e.g., Derdowski and Mathisen 2023; Sjöblom, Mäkiniemi, and Mäkikangas 2022; Rodriguez 2020; Dollard, Dormann, and Idris 2019; also see https://tinyurl.com/289cjju9). Slavich (2020) proposed what he termed a new framework called the social safety theory. Volume 10, Issue 2 of the *Nouvelle Revue de Psychosociologie* (2010) was entitled "'Psychosocial Risks,' a New Social Category?" A psychosocial safety climate (PSC) is defined as one in which the organizational policies, practices, and procedures are designed for the protection of workers' psychological health and safety (Dollard and Bakker 2010). So, psychological safety predates psychosocial safety, although they overlap in terms of the types of behaviors involved, their impacts on organizations and individuals, and their importance to organizations.

Stages

Psychological and psychosocial safety seem to follow a progression based on the development of those in the organization, particularly the leaders. That progression has been characterized as involving four somewhat overlapping stages (the following is based on Clark 2020). Those stages are as follows.

Stage 1: Inclusion Safety

At this early stage, leaders set the tone by genuinely inviting others to participate. They must encourage others to learn and grow and support them even when they lack confidence or make mistakes. They need to learn people's names, look at them face-to-face, and look them in the eyes (Clark n.d., 3). The leaders need to demonstrate that the views of others are being heard and that they are paying attention to what is being said. Being ignored is painful and can lead to dysfunctional or even destructive behavior, so it is important that openness is demonstrated so that everyone knows that they are included in the decision processes of the organization. Leaders should prohibit personal attacks, including comments or behaviors that show disrespect (Clark n.d., 6). Be sure to express gratitude and appreciation when someone does well and make sure you say hello and thank you every day (Clark n.d., 7).

Stage 2: Learner Safety

This stage involves asking questions. Members of the organization are encouraged to be no longer passive participants but rather to get involved and ask questions. Learning is a process of acquiring new knowledge and skills by observing and questioning those who already possess the information or skills being sought. Leaders should share the learning goals for themselves and others (Clark n.d., 10). Based on having developed in the inclusion stage, those being asked questions will welcome the questions and, in a sense, become teachers. In this way, everyone in the organization learns and feels safe while learning. When you don't know the answer, admit it and seek help from others (Clark n.d., 12). Cheer the learning of others and help to build their confidence in the learning process (Clark n.d., 14).

Something to Think About

IntegrityCo is a major provider of health care. It offers a range of services, including acute care, outpatient, short-term hospitalization, and public health programs. IntegrityCo has over 2,000 unionized and nonunionized employees. IntegrityCo is a relatively new organization, resulting from the combination of three other health care organizations. It was hoped that this would lead to efficiencies in patient care. However, combining three into one was difficult as it required the introduction of two new unions, integration of differing patient records and IT systems, and a restructuring of the management team. As a health care organization, IntegrityCo strives to ensure good patient care. However, recruitment and retention of staff are problematic as many employees feel that their contributions are not valued. This is especially important, given the reality of its aging workforce and increasing health-related disability rates among its staff. How should IntegrityCo go about trying to develop a psychosocial safe environment?

(*Source*: adapted from Case Study Research Project Findings, 2017)

Stage 3: Contributor Safety

As those in the organization learn more and develop more skills, they advance in the organization. That advancement may be formal (new title, position, or authority), or it may be informal (more respect and deference by others). Leaders should help others by having them conduct meetings (Clark n.d., 16). As individuals advance successfully in the organization, their contributions grow, and they help others also to become contributors so that the whole organization benefits from these developments. Leaders should share the vision for where the organization should be and explain the why for what needs to be done (Clark n.d., 19). Leaders need to report their own mistakes and ask others about their thoughts (Clark n.d., 21).

Stage 4: Challenger Safety

Now psychological and psychosocial safety emerge as those in the organization are able to challenge the status quo without retribution, reprisal, or any risk of damaging their personal standing or reputation. When someone sees something or even just feels that something needs to be done or could be better, they are confident that they can raise questions, make suggestions, or be creative without fear of being put down or punished in any way. Leaders should prohibit interruptions to protect others, which is especially important in diverse organizations (Clark n.d., 25). Everyone should respect local knowledge and ask disruptive questions (Clark n.d., 29). At this stage, psychological safety "must become institutionalized and systematized" to ensure its longevity (Edmondson 2019a, 82).

Yet another view of stages is that of Tuckman (1965), as modified by Tuckman and Jensen (1977). They suggest five stages: forming, storming, norming, performing, and adjourning.

Forming

Similar to Clark's inclusion stage, this is when people get to know each other and seek to establish a purpose. The leader is in charge, and members tend to be polite and avoid controversy as they receive guidance and instruction from the leader.

Storming

Now the members of the organization get to learn one another's strengths and weaknesses. Arguments and conflicts arise as leadership starts to become shared. Gradually, positions are established, and the members move on to the next stage.

Norming

Members reach some sort of consensus regarding roles, behavior, and communication. Collaboration becomes more frequent, and everyone becomes more comfortable with one another. As they continue to develop, the next stage is achieved.

Performing

Roles are clear, leadership is shared, and the organization becomes fully functional. Psychological safety is achieved, and real accomplishments occur, leading to the final stage.

Adjourning

Members evaluate and celebrate their success and document everything for the future.

Value

In the final stages, psychological safety becomes a reality. "Psychological safety is not a nice-to-have. It's actually a prerequisite to any high-performing organization" (Pindar 2023). It increases employee confidence, improves diversity, decreases turnover, enhances the organization's brand, and, most importantly, it increases productivity and performance (TandemHR 2022). "A 2017 Gallup report found that if organizations increase psychological safety, it makes employees more engaged in their work and can lead to a 12 percent increase in productivity" (Stieg 2020). So, not only do members of the organization feel better in psychologically safe environments, but the organization benefits from increased productivity and performance. Psychosocial work environments have been shown to be related to mental health, which in turn impacts performance (Madsen and Rugulies 2021; Shahidi et al. 2021; Chirico 2017; Widerszal-Bazyl and Cieślak 2000). So, you have to ask yourself, is my organization psychologically safe and psychosocially safe, and, if not, how much must be done in order for it to become safe?

How Close Are You?

If you wonder how close to psychological safety your current workplace is, Martin (2021) suggests that you ask these questions:

- What is the degree to which it is permissible to make mistakes?
- To what degree can difficult and sensitive topics be discussed openly?
- How much are people willing to help each other?
- To what degree can you be yourself and be welcomed for it?

Then ask:

- What can we count on each other for?
- What is our team's purpose?
- What is the reputation we aspire to have?
- What do we need to do differently to achieve that reputation and fulfill our purpose?

Edmondson (2019b, 181–182) poses a similar set of questions for leaders. Her questions (modified) involve:

- Framing the work—What is the nature of the work? To what extent is the work complex and interdependent? How uncertain is the situation? Have I spoken of failures in the right way, given the nature of the work?
- Emphasizing purpose—Have I made clear why our work matters and for whom? How often do I talk about the importance of our work?
- Situational humility—Have I made it clear that I don't have all the answers? Have I emphasized that we can always learn more?
- Proactive inquiry—How often do I ask questions rather than just express my perspectives? Do I demonstrate questions that are broad and deep?

- Systems and structures—Have I created a structure to elicit
  ideas and concerns? Are the structures designed to ensure a
  safe environment for open dialogue?
- Express appreciation—Have I listened and made it clear that
  I am hearing what matters? Do I acknowledge or thank others
  for bringing up matters or questioning me?
- Destigmatize failure—Have I destigmatized failures? What
  else could I do? When someone brings bad news, how do
  I make it a positive experience? Do I offer help or support?
- Sanction clear violations—Have I made boundaries clear?
  Do people know what is blameworthy? Do I respond to clear
  violations in an appropriately tough manner?

If you find that your workplace is not yet psychologically or psycho-socially safe or even physically safe, you need to take action to get there.

Getting There (V-REEL)

Numerous suggestions have been made on specific steps or procedures for advancing through these four stages. The V-REEL framework will help get you there. The V-REEL framework was originally developed by Flint (2018) as a practical guide for entrepreneurs and other organizations to think through what they know (and need to know) about their resources and capabilities in order to assess their potential for creating value in their respective environments. The framework is applicable to any and all organizations—profit and nonprofit, large and small. It is used here with Dr. Flint's endorsement in a way similar to its use in strategy, where the letters are interpreted as follows:

- *V* indicates value. In this case, it is the value of having a
  psychologically, psychosocially, and physically safe workplace.
  This would be a high value to be sought.
- *R* indicates the rareness of that value. Few organizations have
  truly achieved completely safe workplaces across all dimensions.
- *E* the first E indicates factors, forces, or behaviors that might
  erode or chip away at your ability to create value, that is,
  psychologically, psychosocially, and physically safe workplaces.

- *E* the second E indicates factors, forces, or behaviors that enable or help to create that value.
- *L* indicates longevity or how long you have to obtain the value before it is too late.

Value and Rareness

The value of psychologically, psychosocially, and physically safe workplaces has clearly been established. Psychological safety impacts employee well-being, retention rates, creativity, employee engagement, and team collaboration (Cooper 2023). A psychosocial safety climate has positively impacted work engagement and job performance (Idris, Dollard, and Tuckey 2015). It has also been shown to reduce presenteeism (Mansour et al. 2022). Both psychological and psychosocial safety are needed at work (Lennox 2021). Physical safety can result in reduced absenteeism, higher-quality production, more motivated and competent workers, as well as reductions in replacement and training costs (Thiede and Thiede 2015). According to a recent survey, companies receive a return on investment of U.S.$3 or more for each U.S.$1 they invest in improving workplace safety (Mlynek 2021). Unfortunately, despite the benefits, these forms of safety at work are not all that common (Scorza 2018).

Eroding Factors

Numerous eroding factors have been identified throughout the book. A few of them are:

- Arguing
- *Bigotry*
- Dictatorial leadership
- Empire-building
- *Gossiping*
- Inconsistent messaging
- Lack of collaboration
- *Preferential treatment*
- Saying one thing, meaning another
- *Spreading rumors*
- Backstabbing
- Bullying
- Drinking
- *Favoritism*
- Harassment
- Lack of accountability
- Poor customer service
- *Prejudice*
- Sexual comments
- *Swearing*

- Taking drugs
- *Turf wars*
- Leader refuses to take responsibility for errors

- Toxic culture
- *Yelling*
- Overemphasis on the leader's personal success

Something to Think About

The SuperStor warehouse was large and had storage racks that, in some instances, were essentially two stories tall. Joe, Sam, and Harry were told to rearrange the items stored on the top of one such shelf unit. To reach the items to rearrange them, the three of them climbed up onto the unit. The weight of the three of them proved too much for the shelf, and it gave way underneath them. All three fell, but Joe hit his head on the metal shelf unit before landing on the floor. Part of the shelf unit fell from a height of about 11 feet, hitting Joe on the back of the head and shoulders. He was taken to an emergency room for treatment. He suffered soft tissue damage to his right shoulder, requiring physical therapy for several months, during which time he was unable to work. Their supervisor had not warned them about the risks associated with working at height nor were the three workers aware of the dangers associated with climbing on the shelves. What should SuperStor have done to prevent this incident?

(*Source*: adapted from Case Study #5, 2018)

Enabling Forces

Various suggestions have been made as to what would contribute to psychological or psychosocial safety and, hence, be enabling forces. Wegner (n.d.) suggests that the leaders of the organization should:

- Establish an open and respectful communication culture
- Be transparent in order to build trust
- Set clear expectations
- Reframe failure and mistakes as opportunities for learning and growth
- Take a supportive and consultative approach to leadership

Edmonson and Hugander (2021), on the other hand, feel that leaders should:

- Focus on performance
- Train both individuals and teams
- Incorporate visualization
- Normalize vulnerability related to work

Barnett (n.d.) advises leaders to:

- Show your team you're engaged
- Let your team see that you understand
- Avoid blaming to build trust
- Be self-aware—and demand the same from your team
- Nip negativity in the bud
- Include your team in decision making
- Be open to feedback
- Champion your team

Bosler (2021) feels that psychological safety is a key component of diversity, equity, and inclusion efforts on the part of the organization, and so suggests that leaders should:

- Promote self-awareness
- Demonstrate concern for team members as people
- Actively solicit questions
- Promote positive dialogue and discussion
- Be precise with information, expectations, and commitments
- Provide multiple ways for employees to share their thoughts
- Show value and appreciation for ideas
- Explain reasons for change
- Own up to mistakes

Attfield (2019) has a slightly different set of suggestions. She suggests that leaders should:

- Break the *Golden Rule*
- Welcome curiosity

- Promote healthy conflict
- Give employees a voice
- Earn and extend trust
- Promote effectiveness, not efficiency
- Think differently about creativity

The National Association of Safety Professionals (NASP 2023) suggests that organizations take these steps:

- Create a positive and supportive culture
- Prioritize training and onboarding
- Have clear policies for bullying and harassment
- Adjust employee workspaces
- Foster supportive leadership through training
- Construct strong lines of communication
- Facilitate career development
- Provide staff with psychosocial safety training
- Host team-building events

NASP also suggests that leaders must create and communicate actionable policies and manage risk by taking these steps:

- Identify psychosocial hazards
- Assess the risks and prioritize
- Implement risk control measures
- Monitor and review

Ravishankar (2022), in a *Harvard Business Review* article, states that organizational leaders should:

- Not fixate on building a *perfect* team
- Allow the team to make mistakes
- Avoid placing blame when things go wrong
- Recognize and reward people when things go right
- Encourage diversity, equity, and inclusion

- Understand and support diversity
- Check their own biases
- Build cultural competence
- Communicate with care
- Be vulnerable
- Show empathy

Tiwari and Lenka (2016) have a somewhat different set of recommendations. They suggest that organizations:

- Provide opportunities for members to share their ideas by having regular meetings, brainstorming sessions, and a database available to everyone.
- Encourage employees to raise concerns and express appreciation when they do.
- Encourage employees to contribute their thoughts and expertise.
- Develop a program for continuous learning by organizing workshops, conferences, and seminars and by encouraging members to accept challenging assignments and to furnish the necessary infrastructure, resources, and financial support to accomplish this.
- Provide opportunities for members to take risks and be intrapreneurs by providing flextime and allowing failures while they attempt risky projects.

O'Donohoe and Kleinschmit (2022) feel that leaders should:

- Evaluate and set explicit norms and expectations
- Model vulnerability
- Remember, everyone has a unique perspective
- Be a transparent communicator
- Create a culture of appreciation
- Get to know your team

There appear to be 17 *themes* among these enabling factors, although there is still overlap among them. Those *themes* and the underlying factors are:

1. Blame—Avoid blaming to build trust; avoid placing blame when things go wrong; earn and extend trust; nip negativity in the bud.
2. Clarity—Set clear expectations; have clear policies for bullying and harassment; be precise with information, expectations, and commitments; incorporate visualization.
3. Communication—Communicate with care; construct strong lines of communication; establish an open and respectful communication culture; explain reasons for change.
4. Concern—Demonstrate concern for team members as people; let your team see you understand; adjust employee workspaces.
5. Discussion—Promote positive dialogue and discussion; promote healthy conflict; monitor and review.
6. Diversity—Encourage diversity, equity, and inclusion; understand and support diversity.
7. Innovation—Welcome curiosity; think differently about creativity.
8. Involvement—Actively solicit questions; be open to feedback; encourage employees to contribute their thoughts and expertise; encourage employees to raise concerns and express appreciation when they do; give employees a voice; provide opportunities for members to share their ideas by having regular meetings, brainstorming sessions, and a database available to everyone; provide multiple ways for employees to share their thoughts, include your team in decision making.
9. Learning/training—Train both individuals and teams; prioritize training and onboarding; develop a program for continuous learning by organizing workshops, conferences, and seminars and by encouraging members to accept challenging assignments and to furnish the necessary infrastructure, resources, and financial support to accomplish this; facilitate career development; host team-building events; provide staff with psychosocial safety training; build cultural competence.
10. Mistakes—Allow the team to make mistakes; reframe failure and mistakes as opportunities for learning and growth; own up to mistakes.

11. Performance—Focus on performance; promote effectiveness not efficiency; evaluate and set explicit norms and expectations.

12. Risk—Assess the risks and prioritize; implement risk control measures; provide opportunities for members to take risks and be intrapreneurs by providing flextime and allowing failures while they attempt risky projects.

13. Self-awareness—Be self-aware—and demand the same from your team; check your own biases; promote self-awareness.

14. Support—Create a positive and supportive culture; foster supportive leadership through training; take a supportive and consultative approach to leadership; create a culture of appreciation; champion your team; recognize and reward people when things go right; show value and appreciation for ideas.

15. Transparency—Be a transparent communicator; be transparent in order to build trust.

16. Understanding—Get to know your team; remember everyone has a unique perspective; show empathy; show your team you're engaged.

17. Vulnerability—Be vulnerable; model vulnerability; normalize vulnerability related to work.

Longevity

Organizations striving to prevent or correct dysfunctions should adopt each and every one of these *themes*, although it may be useful to prioritize them as once some are implemented, it will be easier to implement others. Once all are in place, the organization will be in Stage 4 and will likely remain functional for a long period of time. However, with turnover, new members may not avoid one or more of the eroding factors, and changes in the environment could also lead some to fall back on those factors. As noted earlier, the enabling factors "must become institutionalized and systematized" to ensure its longevity (Edmondson 2019b, 82). You should expect that members' perceptions will not all align, so as a leader, you need to recognize, acknowledge, and address each and every team member so that they bring their own thoughts, perceptions, and experiences to the organization and then use different steps to bolster, rebuild, or reinforce psychological safety within your unit (Loignon and Wormington 2022, 15).

Final Results

A careful and detailed use of the V-REEL framework will help your organization to achieve Edmundson's State 4. However, as Edmondson (2019b) suggests, Stage 4 is "a never-ending and dynamic journey" (103).

> Psychological safety at work *doesn't* mean that everybody is nice to each other all the time. It means that people feel free to "brainstorm" out loud, voice half-finished thoughts, openly challenge the status quo, share feedback, and work through disagreements together—knowing that leaders value honesty, candor, and truth-telling and that team members will have one another's backs (Center for Creative Leadership 2023).

"Psychological safety isn't about being nice. Nor is it about constantly agreeing with one another for the sake of avoiding hurt feelings" (Anonymous 2020). Casabianca (2022) indicates that psychological safety is not:

- Guaranteed applause for everything people have to say at work
- Saying what you think the other person wants to hear
- Lack of accountability
- Tolerance of toxic behaviors
- Praising without any reason or purpose
- Dialing back performance standards
- Promoting the *comfort zone*
- Becoming friends with your direct reports or colleagues

In a psychologically safe environment, members of the organization share the belief that:

> They will not be exposed to interpersonal or social threats to their self or identity, their status or standing, and to their career or employment when engaging in learning behaviors such as asking for help, seeking feedback, admitting errors or lack of knowledge, trying something new or voicing work-related dissenting views (Kaloudis 2019).

Interpersonal or social threats consist of rejection, disrespect, and intimidation, including being labeled unfavorably or receiving a punishment that impacts the person's identity, status, and/or career (Qualls and the CultureAlly Team 2022).

Psychological safety is not equal to trust, although, in a psychologically safe environment, members of the organization trust one another (Lumanta 2021). Edmondson is noted in a *Harvard Business Review* article (Gallo 2023) as saying a psychologically safe environment isn't about being *nice,* nor is it *comfortable* because "Anything hard to achieve requires being uncomfortable along the way." "It is an absence of interpersonal fear. In a work environment, psychological safety supports the belief that taking appropriate risks regarding your behaviors in a group context is safe" (Buckley 2022).

Amy Gallo (2023) also relates an anecdote that conveys the essence of a psychologically safe environment. After having spent a lot of time, energy, and money on a project that failed to recoup the investment, when she sat down with her manager to discuss the failure, she expected her manager to be "frustrated or even angry and I expected her to at least ask 'What went wrong?' or 'How could we have prevented this?' Instead, she asked a simple question:

> What did you learn?" Instead of fear of failure, it was regarded as a
> learning experience. "The Fearless Organization is not only a better
> place for employees, it's also a place where innovation, growth, and
> performance take hold" (Edmondson 2019a, p. 19).

Rethinking This Chapter

Look at the notes and what you wrote down at the beginning of this chapter. How might you change those now? With those changes in mind, respond to the following questions and actions. Managers, human resource professionals, and students should do this carefully in order to be prepared to deal with health and safety issues. Even if you are not currently employed, your responses should be made as if you are working in an organization. In a classroom setting, your responses should be shared and compared through discussion with others.

Chapter Questions

1. Have you ever experienced or witnessed any of the eroding factors in your organization? Which ones?
2. Have you ever experienced or witnessed any of the enabling factors in your organization? Which ones?
3. How close is your organization to being psychologically safe?

Introductory Actions

1. Outline a plan for introducing enabling factors to your organization.
2. What information should be collected by your organization to move toward becoming psychologically safe?
3. Who in the organization should be responsible for moving toward becoming psychologically safe?

Case to Consider

Company Inaction

The human resources manager for the organization receives a visit from a female employee. Later, as the employee leaves for lunch, she finds her car in the office parking lot, damaged by numerous dents on all four doors. It is evident from clear impressions of muddy boot soles on parts of the damaged areas that someone had been kicking the car. The woman had recently been the victim of serious long-term sexual harassment that had been investigated by the organization. The result had been the firing, two days earlier, of the senior manager who had coerced the woman into a sexual relationship. The human resources manager had met that morning with the fired manager to complete certain required separation paperwork.

The woman employee said that she remembered once hearing the former manager boasting of damaging the car of someone who had cut him off in traffic after he had pulled an elderly driver from the car and slapped him around. The woman employee is afraid that the former manager is responsible for the damage to her car and also fears that he will harm her as well. The woman says that when she first brought the matter to her present supervisor, she was told that there was nothing about the situation that the organization could do, and that there was no connection to the workplace. Besides, says her manager, because no articulated threat had been made, she should call a body shop and not the incident response team.

The woman, remembering a briefing on workplace violence to all employees, did not accept this response and went to the human resources manager. She says that she thinks she is being retaliated against for providing a truthful statement in the company's sexual harassment investigation and is primarily concerned for her safety.

The human resources manager speaks to other employees formerly supervised by the fired manager. They confirm that he had frequently spoken of angry confrontations he had initiated when subordinates had frustrated him. Two of the employees reported that he had threatened to *teach them a lesson* if they ever crossed him. Both reported that they felt physically threatened by his words and menacing manner.

(*Source*: *Workplace Violence: Prevention, Intervention, and Recovery*. Hawaii Workplace Violence Working Group Committee, 2001)

Case Questions for Discussion

1. Do you agree or disagree with the supervisor's handling of this situation?
2. Do you think the position of the woman's current manager is appropriate for your organization: short of incontrovertible proof of direct connection, the organization should do nothing to make an employee feel more secure.
3. What else do you think the organization should have done in this situation?
4. Does your organization conduct thorough background checks of prospective employees?
5. Does your organization stress safety with all managers and promote upward reporting of employee safety and security concerns to the attention of responsible executives?

Chapter 8 Takeaways

- Psychological safety is the belief that you won't be punished or humiliated for speaking up with ideas, questions, concerns, or mistakes, whereas psychosocial safety refers to the shared belief held by workers that their psychological health and safety are protected and supported by senior management. Are you psychologically safe at your organization?
- Stages are inclusion, learner, contributor, and challenger. What stage are you in?
- There are questions to ask yourself to determine how close your organization is to being psychologically safe. Have you asked those questions?
- The V-REEL framework will help reduce any organizational dysfunction: value, rareness, eroding factors, enabling factors, and longevity. What eroding and enabling factors exist in your organization?
- Psychologically safe organizations are good places to work, and they are also places where innovation, growth, and performance occur. Is your organization currently psychologically safe? If not, what can you do about it?

Recommended Reading

In addition to the many sources used in this chapter, the following case and article could expand your understanding of the chapter's material:

Case: Teckchandani, A. n.d. "PeopleFirst Inc: A Star Employee but a Terrible Manager." https://hbsp.harvard.edu/product/W20780-PDF-ENG.

Article: Gallo, A. 2023. "What Is Psychological Safety?" *Harvard Business Review Digital Article.* https://hbr.org/2023/02/what-is-psychological-safety.

Is It Working?

Have you used the V-REEL framework to understand better how and why certain behaviors are associated with dysfunctional organizations? I would love to hear from you. Send comments to:

Dr. David D. Van Fleet, comments
dr.vanfleet@gmail.com

Bibliography

11 Types of Workplace Harassment (And How to Stop Them). 2022. *I-Sight*. www.i-sight.com/resources/11-types-of-workplace-harassment-and-how-to-stop-them.

Abulaish, M., J.M. Islamia, and T. Anwar. 2013. "A Keyphrase-Based Tag Cloud Generation Framework to Conceptualize Textual Data." *International Journal of Adaptive, Resilient and Autonomic Systems* 4, pp. 7291. https://doi.org/10.4018/jaras.2013040104.

Ackerman, G.A. and M. Burnham. 2021. "Towards a Definition of Terrorist Ideology." *Terrorism and Political Violence* 33, no. 6, pp. 1160–1190. https://doi.org/10.1080/09546553.2019.1599862.

Acquadro, M.D., A. Varetto, and C. Civilotti. 2022. "Sexual Harassment in the Workplace: Consequences and Perceived Self-Efficacy in Women and Men Witnesses and Non-Witnesses." *Behavioral Sciences* 12, no. 9, p. 326. https://doi.org/10.3390/bs12090326.

Adams, A. and N. Crawford. 1992. *Bullying at Work: How to Confront and Overcome It*. London, UK: Virago Press.

Adams, J. 1986. *The Financing of Terror*. New York, NY: Simon & Schuster.

Akella, D. 2016. Workplace Bullying: Not a Manager's Right. *Journal of Workplace Rights*, SAGE Open 6, no. 1. https://doi.org/10.1177/2158244016629394.

Alemu, D.S. 2016. Dysfunctional Organization: The Leadership Factor. *Open Journal of Leadership* 5, pp. 1–7.

Alexander, Y. and M.S. Swetnam. 2001. *Usama Bin Laden's Al-Qaida: Profile of a Terrorist Network*. Ardsley, NY: Transnational Publishers.

Alexander, Y., ed. 1992. *International Terrorism: Political and Legal Documents*, Boston, MA: M. Nijhoff, Dordrecht.

Alpass, F., N. Long, K. Chamberlain, and C. MacDonald. 1997. "Job Satisfaction Differences Between Military and Ex-Military Personnel: The Role of Demographic and Organizational Variables." *Military Psychology* 9, pp. 227–249.

Alyousef, S.M. and S.A. Alhamidi. 2022. "Exploring Experiences of Workplace Violence and Attempts to Address Violence Among Mental Health Nurses in the Kingdom of Saudi Arabia." *SAGE Open Nursing* 8. https://doi.org/10.1177/23779608221142716. PMID: 36533256; PMCID: PMC9755545.

Anjum, A., X. Ming, A.F. Siddiqi, and S.F. Rasool. 2018. "An Empirical Study Analyzing Job Productivity in Toxic Workplace Environments." *International Journal of Environmental Research and Public Health* 15, no. 5, p. 1035. https://doi.org/10.3390/ijerph15051035. PMID: 29883424; PMCID: PMC5982074.

Anonymous. 2020. "How Important Is Psychological Safety, Really?" *Kudos*. www.kudos.com/blog/how-important-is-psychological-safety-really.

Anonymous. 2023. "What Are the Determinants of Organizational Culture?" *Angola Transparency*. https://angolatransparency.blog/en/what-are-the-determinants-of-organizational-culture/.

Aquino, K. 2000. "Structural and Individual Determinants of Workplace Victimization: The Effects of Hierarchical Status and Conflict Management Style." *Journal of Management* 26, no. 2, pp. 171–193.

Association of Certified Fraud Examiners. 2020. *Report to the Nations*. Association of Certified Fraud Examiners: Austin, TX, USA, 2020.

Atenstaedt, R. 2012. Word Cloud Analysis of the BJGP. *British Journal of General Practice* 62, p. 148. https://doi.org/10.3399/bjgp12X630142.

Attfield, B. 2019. "7 Ways to Create Psychological Safety at Work." *Jostle Blog*. https://blog.jostle.me/blog/psychological-safety-at-work.

Badaracco, J.L., Jr. 2001. "We Don't Need Another Hero." *Harvard Business Review* 79, no. 8, pp. 120–126.

Bailey, A.A. 2006. "Retail Employee Theft: A Theory of Planned Behavior Perspective." *International Journal of Retail & Distribution Management* 34, no. 11, pp. 802–816. https://doi.org/10.1108/09590550610710219.

Baker, W. 2020. "How to Overcome Your Reluctance to Ask for Help at Work." *Greater Good Magazine*. https://greatergood.berkeley.edu/article/item/how_to_overcome_your_reluctance_to_ask_for_help_at_work.

Banks, A. n.d. "The 5 Characteristics of Dysfunctional Teams." *The Predictive Index*. www.predictiveindex.com/blog/dysfunctional-teams-the-5-characteristics/.

Barash, D.P. and J.E. Lipton. 2011. *Payback: Why We Retaliate, Redirect Aggression, And Take Revenge*. NY: Oxford University Press.

Barnett, G. n.d. "8 Ways to Create Psychological Safety in the Workplace." *The Predictive Index*. www.predictiveindex.com/blog/psychological-safety-in-the-workplace/.

Barney, J.B. and M.H. Hansen. 1994. "Trustworthiness as a Source of Competitive Advantage." *Strategic Management Journal* 15, pp. 175–190. http://www.jstor.org/stable/2486817.

Baron, A. 2001. *Violence in the Workplace*. San Francisco, CA: Pathfinder Publishing.

Barreca, R. 1995. *Sweet Revenge: The Wicked Delights of Getting Even*. New York, NY: Harmony Press,.

Barton, L. 1993a. *Crisis in Organizations*. Cincinnati: South-Western College Publishing.

Barton, L. 1993b. "Why Business Must Prepare a Strategic Response to Corporate Sabotage." *Industrial Management* 35, no. 2, pp. 16–19.

Baskar, K., E.M.B. Shinde, and D.A. Srinivasan. 2021. "Promoting Mental Well-Being Through Employee Assistance Programmes." *NHRD Network Journal* 14, no. 1, pp. 64–82.

Bateson, M.C. 1989. *Composing a Life*. New York, NY: Grove Press.

Battaglia, M. 2015. "How to Be a Functional Employee in a Dysfunctional Organization." *Biz417*. www.biz417.com/blog/how-to-be-a-functional-employee-in-a-dysfunctional-organization/.

Bauer, M. 2023. "What Is a Dysfunctional Employee?" *The Nest*. https://woman.thenest.com/dysfunctional-employee-10884.html.

Baumert, J., B. Schneider, K. Lukaschek, R.T. Emeny, C. Meisinger, N. Erazo, N. Dragano,. and K.H. Ladwig. October 2014. "Adverse Conditions at the Workplace Are Associated With Increased Suicide Risk." *Journal of Psychiatric Research* 57, pp. 90–95. https://doi.org/10.1016/j.jpsychires.2014.06.007.

Bennett, R.J. and S.L. Robinson. 2000. "Development of a Measure of Workplace Deviance." *Journal of Applied Psychology* 85, no. 3, pp. 349–360.

Bennett, R.J. and S.L. Robinson. 2003. "The Past, Present, and Future of Workplace Deviance Research." In *Organizational Behavior: The State of the Science*, ed. J. Greenberg, 247–281. 2nd ed. Mahwah, NJ: Lawrence Erlbaum Associates.

Berridge, J., C. Cooper, and C. Highley-Marchington. 1997. *Employee Assistance Programs and Workplace Counselling*. Chichester, England: John Wiley.

Berry, L.L. and K. Seiders. 2008. "Serving Unfair Customers." *Business Horizons* 51, no. 1, pp. 29–37.

Berry, P.A., G.L. Gillespie, B.S. Fisher, D. Gormley, and J.T. Haynes. 2016. "Psychological Distress and Workplace Bullying Among Registered Nurses." *Online Journal of Issues in Nursing* 21, no. 3, p. 8. https://doi.org/10.3912/OJIN.Vol21No03PPT41. PMID: 27857181; PMCID: PMC8941490.

Berthelsen, M., M.B. Hansen, A. Nissen, M.B. Nielsen, S. Knardahl, and T. Heir. 2021. "The Impact of a Workplace Terrorist Attack on the Psychosocial Work Environment: A Longitudinal Study From Pre- to Post-Disaster." *Frontiers in Public Health* 9. https:doi.org/10.3389/fpubh.2021.708260.

Bies, R.J. and T.M. Tripp. 1995. "Beyond Distrust: Getting Even and the Need for Revenge." In *Trust in organizations*, eds. R.M. Kramer and T.R. Tyler, 246–260. Newbury Park: Sage.

Bies, R.J., T.M. Tripp, and R.M. Kramer. 1997. "At the Breaking Point: Cognitive and Social Dynamics of Revenge in Organizations." In *Antisocial Behavior in Organizations*, eds. R.A. Giacalone and J. Greenberg, 18–36. Thousand Oaks, CA: Sage Publications.

Bilsker, D. 2006. "Mental Health Care and the Workplace." *The Canadian Journal of Psychiatry* 51, no. 2, pp. 61–62.

Bird, D. 2020. "How to Deal With a Toxic Boss: 7 Tips." *The Enterprisers Project.* https://enterprisersproject.com/article/2020/9/how-deal-toxic-boss.

Bitsch, V. and E.K. Yakura. 2007. "Middle Management in Agriculture: Roles, Functions, and Practices." *International Food and Agribusiness Management Review* 10, no. 2, pp. 1–28.

Bitsch, V. and N.J. Olynk. 2008. "Risk-Increasing and Risk-Reducing Practices in Human Resource Management: Focus Group Discussions With Livestock Managers." *Journal of Agricultural and Applied Economics* 40, no. I, pp. 185–120.

Bitsch, V., G.A. Kassa, S.B. Harsh, and A.W. Mugera. 2006. "Human Resource Management Risks: Sources and Control Strategies Based on Dairy Farmer Focus Groups." *Journal of Agricultural and Applied Economics* 38, no. 1, pp. 123–136.

Blair, J.D., M.D. Fottler, and A.C. Zapanta. 2004. *Bioterrorism, Preparedness, Attack and Response.* Amsterdam: Elsevier.

Blanchard J., Y. Li, S.K. Bentley, M.D. Lall, A.M. Messman, Y.T. Liu, D.B. Diercks, R. Merritt-Recchia, R. Sorge, J.M. Warchol, C. Greene, J. Griffith, R.A. Manfredi, and M. McCarthy. 2022. "The Perceived Work Environment and Well-Being: A Survey of Emergency Health Care Workers During the COVID-19 Pandemic." *Academy of Emergency Medicine* 29, no. 7, pp. 851–861.

Boddy, C.R. 2017. "Psychopathic Leadership a Case Study of a Corporate Psychopath CEO." *Journal of Business Ethics* 145, no. 1, pp. 141–156. www.jstor.org/stable/45022207.

Bonner, H. 1961. *Psychology of Personality.* New York, NY: The Ronald Press Company.

Boogaard, K. 2022. "The 4 Types of Company Culture, Explained." *Work Life.* www.atlassian.com/blog/teamwork/types-of-corporate-culture#:~:text=They%20identified%204%20types%20of,that%20helps%20your%20team%20flourish.

Bosler, S. 2021. "9 Strategies to Create Psychological Safety at Work." *Quantum Workplace.* www.quantumworkplace.com/future-of-work/create-psychological-safety-in-the-workplace.

Bouzikos, S., A. Afsharian, M. Dollard, and O. Brecht. April 21, 2022. "Contextualising the Effectiveness of an Employee Assistance Program Intervention on Psychological Health: The Role of Corporate Climate." *International Journal of Environmental Research and Public Health* 19, no. 9, p. 5067. https://doi.org/10.3390/ijerph19095067.

Bowie, V., B.S. Fisher, and C. Cooper. 2005. *Workplace Violence.* New York, NY: Routledge.

Bowman, S. 1994. *When the Eagle Screams,* New York, NY: Birch Lane Press Book/Carol Publishing Group.

Brahm, F. and J. Poblete. 2022. "Cultural Evolution Theory and Organizations." *Organization Theory* 3, no. 1. https://doi.org/10.1177/26317877211069141.

Bright, J. 2012. Securitization, Terror and Control: Towards a Theory of the Breaking Point. *Review of International Studies* 38, no. 4, pp. 861–879.

Brodsky, C.M. 1976. *The Harassed Worker*. Toronto, Ontario, Canada: Lexington Books, DC Heath.

Brooks, B.J., D.M. Gilbuena, S.J. Krause, and M.D. Koretsky. 2014. "Using Word Clouds for Fast, Formative Assessment of Students' Short Written Responses." *Chemical Engineering Education* 48, pp. 190–198.

Brovelli, E. 2012. "Powerful Diversity: Fueling Excellence Through Ethnically Diverse Teams." *International Food and Agribusiness Management Review* 15, no. Special Issue A, pp. 57–60.

Buckley, R. 2022. "Psychological Safety in the Workplace Is More Than Being Nice." *Entrepreneur*. www.entrepreneur.com/leadership/9-steps-to-create-a-psychologically-safe-workplace/441076.

Burke, R.J. and C.L. Cooper. 2018. *Violence and Abuse in and Around Organisations*. London, England: Routledge.

Burke, R.J. and T. McAteer. 2007."Work Hours and Work Addiction: Work Now, Pay Later." In *Research Companion to the Dysfunctional Workplace*, ed. C.L. Cooper, 152–167. Northampton, MA: Edward Elgar Publishing, Inc.

Burton, J. 2002. "The Leadership Factor: Management Practices Can Make Employees Sick." *Accident Prevention*, pp. 22–26.

Butler, R.J., N. Kleinman, and H.H. Gardner. 2014. "I Don't Like Mondays: Explaining Monday Work Injury Claims." *Industrial & Labor Relations Review* 67, pp. 762–783.

Cano, R. 2019. "Dysfunctional Leadership and Organizations." *Linkedin*. www.linkedin.com/pulse/dysfunctional-leadership-organizations-raymond-cano/.

Carbo, J. and A. Hughes. 2010. "Workplace Bullying: Developing a Human Rights Definition From the Perspective and Experiences of Targets." *WorkingUSA* 13, no. 3, pp. 387–403.

Career Contessa. n.d. *10 Signs You're in a Toxic Work Environment*. www.careercontessa.com/advice/toxic-work-environment/.

Cargile, J. 1969. "The Sorites Paradox." *The British Journal for the Philosophy of Science* 20, pp. 193–202. https://doi.org/10.1093/bjps/20.3.193.

Carroll, C.E., ed. 2016.*The SAGE Encyclopedia of Corporate Reputation,* Vol. 12. SAGE Publications, Inc. https://doi.org/10.4135/9781483376493.

Casabianca, S.S. 2022. "How to Create Psychological Safety at Work and Why It Makes a Difference." *PsychCentral*. https://psychcentral.com/health/psychological-safety-at-work.

Case Study #5. 2018. *Safety Pal*. https://yoursafetypal.com/case_studies/case-study-5/.

Case Study Research Project Findings. 2017. *Mental Health Commission of Canada*. Ottawa, ON: Mental Health Commission of Canada. www.mentalhealthcommission.ca.

Center for Creative Leadership. 2023. "What Is Psychological Safety at Work? How Leaders Can Build Psychologically Safe Workplaces." *CCL*. https://www.ccl.org/articles/leading-effectively-articles/what-is-psychological-safety-at-work/#:~:text=Psychological%20safety%20is%20the%20belief,taking%20risks%2C%20or%20soliciting%20feedback.

Chabowski, B.R., S. Samiee, and G.T.M. Hult. 2017. "Cross-National Research and International Business: An Interdisciplinary Path." *International Business Review* 26, pp. 89–101. https://doi.org/10.1016/j.ibusrev.2016.05.008.

Chacko, T.I., J.G. Wacker, and M.M. Asar. 1997. "Technological and Human Resource Management Practices in Addressing Perceived Competitiveness in Agribusiness Firms." *Agribusiness* 13, pp. 93–105.

Chappell, D. and V. Di Martino. 1998. *Violence at Work*. Geneva: International Labour Office.

Chen, H. n.d. *Seven Signs of Ineffective Compliance Programs–Expanded*. https://huichenethics.com/2018/04/11/seven-signs-of-ineffective-compliance-programs-expanded/.

Chew, S.B. 2019. "Why Employees Don't Speak Up for Safety—The Importance of Psychological Safety." *Linkedin*. www.linkedin.com/pulse/why-employees-dont-speak-up-safetythe-importance-safety-boon-chew/.

Chirico, F. 2017. "The Forgotten Realm of the New and Emerging Psychosocial Risk Factors." *Journal of Occupational Health* 59, no. 5, pp. 433–435.

Chirimbu, S. 2014. "Challenges of Leadership in Modern Organizations: Knowledge, Vision, Values." *Annals of Spiru Haret University, Economic Series, Universitatea Spiru Haret* 5, no. 3, pp. 39–47.

Ciby, M. and R.P. Raya. 2015. "Workplace Bullying: A Review of the Defining Features, Measurement Methods and Prevalence Across Continents." *IIM Kozhikode Society & Management Review* 4, no. 1, pp. 38–47.

Cidell, J. 2010. "Content Clouds as Exploratory Qualitative Data Analysis." *AREA* 42, pp. 514–523. https://doi.org/10.1111/j.1475-4762.2010.00952.x.

Clark, C.M. and K. Ritter. 2018. "Policy to Foster Civility and Support a Healthy Academic Work Environment." *Journal of Nursing Education* 57, no. 6, pp. 325–331.

Clark, T.R. 2020. *The 4 Stages of Psychological Safety*. Oakland: Berret-Koehler Publishers, Inc.

Clark, T.R. n.d. *The 4 Stages of Psychological Safety: Behavioral Guide*. Lehi, UT: Leader Factor. www.leaderfactor.com/resources/the-4-stages-behavioral-guide.

CNET Staff. 1997. http://news.com.com/2100-1023-270979.html?legacy=cnet.

Cohen, A., M. Smith, and H.H. Cohen. 1975. *Safety Program Practices in High Versus Low Accident Rate Companies—an Interim Report*. Cincinnati: U.S. Department of Health and Human Services.

Cohen, L.E. and M. Felson. 1979. "Social Change and Crime Rate Trends: A Routine Activities Approach." *American Sociological Review* 44, no. 4, pp. 588–608.

Coleman, P.T. 2004. "Implicit Theories of Organizational Power and Priming Effects on Managerial Power Sharing Decisions: An Experimental Study." *Journal of Applied Social Psychology* 34, no. 2, pp. 297–321.

Conchie, S.M., S. Moon, and M. Duncan. 2013. "Supervisors' Engagement in Safety Leadership: Factors That Help and Hinder." *Safety Science* 51, pp. 109–117. https://doi.org/10.1016/j.ssci.2012.05.020.

Conway, F. and J. Siegelman. 1995. *Snapping.* 2nd ed. New York, NY: Stillpoint Press.

Cooley, J.K. 1999. *Unholy Wars: Afghanistan, America and International Terrorism.* Pluto Press, London.

Cooper, H. 2001. "Terrorism: the Problem of Definition Revisited." *American Behavioral Scientist* 44, no. 6, pp. 881–893.

Cooper, L. 2023. "The Relationship Between Performance and Psychological Safety." *Training Industry.* https://trainingindustry.com/articles/performance-management/the-relationship-between-performance-and-psychological-safety/.

Corey, D. 2021. *A Guide to Building and Maintaining Your Culture Garden.* 17. Xoxoday Culture Ebook. https://tinyurl.com/yckmhhrt.

Cortina, L.M. and V.J. Magley. 2009. "Patterns and Profiles of Response to Incivility in the Workplace." *Journal of Occupational Health Psychology* 14, no. 3, pp. 272–288.

Cortina, L.M., V.J. Magley, J.H. Williams, and R.D. Langhout. 2001. "Incivility in the Workplace: Incidence and Impact." *Journal of Occupational Health Psychology* 6, no. 1, pp. 64–80.

Cotterell, T. 2018. "Understanding Title VII: What Organizations Need to Know About Employees in Protected Classes." Forbes.com. www.forbes.com/sites/forbeshumanresourcescouncil/2018/08/22/understanding-title-vii-what-organizations-need-to-know-about-employees-in-protected-classes/?sh=5b720cf53a32 (accessed October 20, 2021).

Counterpart. 2022. *The High Cost of Employee Theft in the Workplace.* https://yourcounterpart.com/blog/the-high-cost-of-employee-theft-in-the-workplace/#:~:text=Employee%20theft%20affects%20a%20whopping,supplies%20to%20committing%20serious%20fraud.

Couser, G.P., J.L. Nation, and M.A. Hyde. 2021. "Employee Assistance Program Response and Evolution in Light of COVID-19 Pandemic." *Journal of Workplace Behavioral Health* 36, no. 3, pp. 197–212.

Couzzo, S. September 13, 2018. "This NYC Priest's Dramatic Downfall Was Just the Beginning of Perv-Priest Scandals." *New York Post.* https://nypost.com/2018/09/13/this-nyc-priests-dramatic-downfall-was-just-the-beginning-of-perv-priest-scandals/.

Cowie, H., P. Naylor, I. Rivers, P. Smith, and B. Pereira. 2000. "Measuring Workplace Bullying." *Aggression and Violent Behavior* 7, no. 1, pp. 33–51.

Cox, G. 2019. "People Use 'Doxing' to Get Revenge Online." *The Spectrum*. www .thespectrum.com/story/news/local/mesquite/2019/05/20/p-c-periodicals-people-use-doxing-get-revenge-online/3740799002/.

Coyne, I., E. Seigne, and P. Randall. 2000. "Predicting Workplace Victim Status From Personality." *European Journal of Work and Organizational Psychology* 9, no. 3, pp. 335–349.

Crawshaw, L. 2009. "Workplace Bullying? Mobbing? Harassment? Distraction by a Thousand Definitions." *Consulting Psychology Journal: Practice and Research* 61, no. 3, pp. 263–267.

Crenshaw, M. 1992. "Current Research on Terrorism: The Academic Perspective." *Studies in Conflict and Terrorism* 15, pp. 111.

Crenshaw, M. 2000. "The Psychology of Terrorism: An Agenda for the 21st Century." *Political Psychology*, 21 no. 2, pp. 405-20.

Czerwonka, E. 2022. "Reasons 'The Customer Is Always Right' Is Wrong." *Buddy Punch*. https://buddypunch.com/blog/reasons-the-customer-is-always-right-is-wrong/.

Dalpes, K. 2023. "5 Reasons Why the Customer Is Always Right." *Zendesk Blog*. https://tinyurl.com/ycyuyfhc.

Dandira, M. 2012. "Dysfunctional Leadership: Organizational Cancer." *Business Strategy Series* 13. https://doi.org/10.1108/17515631211246267.

Das, T.K. and B.S. Tang. 2000. "Instabilities of Strategic Alliances: An Internal Tensions Perspective." *Organization Science: A Journal of the Institute of Management Sciences* 11, no. 1, pp. 77–101.

Daskal, L. 2016. "50 Forms of Dysfunction in the Workplace." *Inc.* www.inc .com/lolly-daskal/50-forms-of-dysfunction-in-the-workplace.html.

Davis-Sramek, B., B.S. Fugate, and A. Omar. 2007. "Functional/Dysfunctional Supply Chain Exchanges." *International Journal of Physical Distribution & Logistics Management* 37, no. 1, pp. 43–63.

de Bruijn, A.L. 2021. "Organizational Factors and Workplace Deviance: Influences of Abusive Supervision, Dysfunctional Employees, and Toxic Work Environments." In The Cambridge Handbook of Compliance, eds. B. van Rooij and D.D. Sokol, 639–661. Cambridge, UK: Cambridge University Press.

De Cremer, D. January/February 2014. "Why Ethics Is Often Grey and Not White: Business Ethics Challenges in a Global World." *World Financial Review*, pp. 23–25.

De la Garza, C. and E. Fadier. 2005. "Towards Proactive Safety in Design: A Comparison of Safety Integration Approaches in Two Design Processes." *Cognition, Technology & Work* 7, no. 1, pp. 51–62.

Deal, T. and A. Kennedy. 2000. *Corporate Cultures: The Rites and Rituals of Corporate Life*. New York, NY: Perseus Books Publishing.

Demerouti, E., L.M.A. Soyer, M. Vakola, and D. Xanthopoulou. 2020. "The Effects of a Job Crafting Intervention on the Success of an Organizational Change Effort in a Blue-Collar Work Environment." *Journal of Occupational and Organizational Psychology* 94, no. 2, pp. 374–399.

Denenberg, R.V. and M. Braverman. 1999. *The Violence Prone Workplace*. Ithaca, NY: Cornell University Press.

Derdowski, L.A. and G.E. Mathisen. 2023. "Psychosocial Factors and Safety in High-Risk Industries: A Systematic Literature Review." *Safety Science* 157, p. 105948. https://doi.org/10.1016/j.ssci.2022.105948.

Dey, S. n.d. "What Are the Eight Important Characteristics of Culture?" *Preserve Articles*. www.preservearticles.com/social-science/what-are-the-eight-important-characteristics-of-culture/13438.

di Martino, V. 2002. *Workplace Violence in the Health Sector : Country Case Studies, Brazil, Bulgaria, Lebanon, Portugal, South Africa, Thailand and an Additional Australian Study: Synthesis Report*. Geneva: ILO.

DiGangi, C. 2016. *7 Scandals From the Nonprofit World*. www.yahoo.com/entertainment/7-scandals-nonprofit-world-120046834.html.

Dobrilova, T. 2021. "15 Disturbing Workplace Violence Statistics for 2023." *Techjury*. https://techjury.net/blog/workplace-violence-statistics/#gref.

Dollard, M., C. Dormann, and M.A. Idris. 2019. *Psychosocial Safety Climate a New Work Stress Theory: A New Work Stress Theory*. Cham, Switzerland: Springer Nature Switzerland AG.

Dollard, M.F. and A.B. Bakker. 2010. "Psychosocial Safety Climate as a Precursor to Conducive Work Environments, Psychological Health Problems, and Employee Engagement." *Journal of Occupational and Organizational Psychology* 83, no. 3, pp. 579–599.

Dombeck, M. 2020. *The Long-Term Effects of Bullying*. Miller Place, New York, NY: American Academy of Experts in Traumatic Stress. www.aaets.org/traumatic-stress-library/the-long-term-effects-of-bullying.

Douglas, D.M. 2016. "Doxing: A Conceptual Analysis." *Ethics and Information Technology* 18, pp. 199–210. https://doi.org/10.1007/s10676-016-9406-0.

Dranitsaris, A. 2021. "The Cost of Tolerating Dysfunctional Leadership Behavior." *Linkedin*. www.linkedin.com/pulse/cost-tolerating-dysfunctional-leadership-behavior-dranitsaris-ph-d-/.

Drydakis, N. 2022. "Adverse Working Conditions and Immigrants' Physical Health and Depression Outcomes: A Longitudinal Study in Greece." *International Archives of Occupational and Environmental Health* 95, pp. 539–556.

Duffy, M.K., D.C. Ganster, and M. Pagon. 2002. "Social Undermining in the Workplace." *Academy of Management Journal* 45, no. 2, pp. 331–351.

Dunlop, P.D. and K. Lee. 2004. "Workplace Deviance, Organizational Citizenship Behavior, and Business Unit Performance: The Bad Apples Do Spoil the Whole Barrel." *Journal of Organizational Behavior* 25, no. 1, pp. 67–80.

EASNA. 2009. *Selecting and Strengthening Employee Assistance Programs: A Purchaser's Guide.* Arlington, VA: Employee Assistance Society of North America.

Eddleston, K.A. 2008. "Commentary: The Prequel to Family Firm Culture and Stewardship: The Leadership Perspective of the Founder." *Entrepreneurship Theory and Practice* 32, no. 6, pp. 1055–1061.

Edelhertz, H. 1983. "White-Collar and Professional Crime." *American Behavioral Scientist* 27, no. 1, pp. 109–128.

Edmondson, A.C. 1999. "Psychological Safety and Learning Behavior in Work Teams." *Administrative Science Quarterly* 44, no. 2, pp. 350–383.

Edmondson, A.C. 2003. "Managing the Risk of Learning: Psychological Safety in Work Teams." In *International Handbook of Organizational Teamwork and Cooperative Working*, eds. M.A. West, D. Tjosvold, and K.G. Smith, 255–275. West Sussex, England.

Edmondson A.C. 2019a. "The Role of Psychological Safety." *Leader to Leader*, pp. 13–19.

Edmondson, A.C. 2019b. "The Fearless Organization." *Creating Psychological Safety in the Workplace for Learning, Innovation, and Growth* pp. 181–182. Hoboken, NJ, New Jersey: John Wiley & Sons, Inc.

Edmondson, A.C. and D.P. Bransby. 2023. "Psychological Safety Comes of Age: Observed Themes in an Established Literature." *Annual Review of Organizational Psychology and Organizational Behavior* 10, pp. 55–78.

Edmondson, A.C. and J.P. Mogelof. 2006. "Explaining Psychological Safety in Innovation Teams." In *Creativity and Innovation in Organizations*, eds. L. Thompson and H. Choi, 109–136. Mahwah, NJ: Erlbaum.

Edmondson, A.C. and K. Roloff. 2009. "Leveraging Diversity Through Psychological Safety." *Rotman Magazine*, pp. 47–51.

Edmondson, A.C. and M.A. Roberta. 2022 "Executive Decision Making at Zola." https://hbsp.harvard.edu/product/622074-PDF-ENG.

Edmondson, A.C. and P. Hugander. 2021. "4 Steps to Boost Psychological Safety at Your Workplace." *Harvard Business Review.* https://hbr.org/2021/06/4-steps-to-boost-psychological-safety-at-your-workplace.

Edmondson, A.C. and Z. Lei. 2014. "Psychological Safety: The History, Renaissance, and Future of an Interpersonal Construct." *Annual Review of Organizational Psychology and Organizational Behavior* 1, no. 1, pp. 23–43.

Edmondson, A.C., M. Higgins, S. Singer, and J. Weiner. 2016. "Understanding Psychological Safety in Health Care and Education Organizations:

A Comparative Perspective." *Research in Human Development* 13, no. 1, pp. 65–83.

Edmondson, M. 2017. *Success: Theory and Practice.* New York, NY: Business Expert Press.

Edmondson, M. 2020. *Agility: Management Principles for a Volatile World.* New York, NY: Business Expert Press.

EEOC.2023. *Equal Employment Opportunity Commission.* www.eeoc.gov/harassment.

Einarsen, S. 1999. "The Nature and Causes of Bullying at Work." *International Journal of Manpower* 20, pp. 16–27.

Einarsen, S. 2000. "Harassment and Bullying at Work: A Review of the Scandinavian Approach." *Aggression and Violent Behavior: A Review Journal* 4, no. 5, pp. 371–401.

Einarsen, S. 2005. "The Nature, Causes and Consequences of Bullying at Work: The Norwegian Experience." *Perspectives Interdisciplinaires Sur Le Travail et la Santé.* https://doi.org/10.4000/pistes.3156.

Einarsen, S. and E.G. Mikkelsen. 2003. "Individual Effects of Exposure to Bullying at Work." In *Bullying and emotional abuse in the workplace. International perspectives in research and practice, eds.* S. Einarsen, H. Hoel, D. Zapf, and C.L. Cooper, 127–144. London: Taylor & Francis.

Einarsen, S., H. Hoel, and C.L. Cooper. 2002. *Bullying and Emotional Abuse in the Workplace.* London, UK: CRCV Press.

Einarsen, S., H. Hoel, D. Zapf, and C.L. Cooper. eds. 2011. *Bullying and Harassment in the Workplace: Development in Theory and Practice.* 2nd ed. Boca Raton, Fla: Taylor and Francis.

Elliott, M. February 4, 2002. "The Incredible Shrinking Business." *Time*, p. 26.

Elshaer, I.A., M. Ghanem, and A.M.S. Azazz. 2022. "An Unethical Organizational Behavior for the Sake of the Family: Perceived Risk of Job Insecurity, Family Motivation and Financial Pressures." *International Journal of Environmental Research and Public Health* 19, no. 11, pp. 6541. https://doi.org/10.3390/ijerph19116541.

Emmerich, R. 2004. *Top 10 Workplace Dysfunctions—And How to TERMINATE Them.* www.thankgoditsmonday.com/pdf/top_10_workplace_dysfunctions_and_how_to_terminate_them_1500.pdf.

Engene, J.O. 2007. "Five Decades of Terrorism in Europe: The TWEED Dataset." *Journal of Peace Research 44, no.* 1, pp. 109–121.

Espelage, D.L. and S.M. Swearer. 2003. "Research on School Bullying and Targetization: What Have We Learned and Where Do We Go From Here?" *School Psychology Review* 32, no. 3, pp. 365383.

Ethics Resource Center. 2013. National Business Ethics Survey. Virginia, VA: Arlington.

Fargnoli, M. 2021. "Design for Safety and Human Factors in Industrial Engineering: A Review Towards a Unified Framework." *Proceedings of the 11th Annual International Conference on Industrial Engineering and Operations Management*, Singapore.

Fasanya, B., ed. 2020. *Safety and Health for Workers*. London, UK: IntechOpen.

Ferris, D.L., H. Lian, D.J. Brown, and R. Morrison. 2015. "Ostracism, Self-Esteem, and Job Performance: When Do We Self-Verify and When Do We Self-Enhance?" *Academy of Management Journal* 58, no. 1, pp. 279–297. https://doi.org/10.5465/ amj.2011.0347.

Fevre, R., D. Lewis, A. Robinson, and T. Jones. 2011. *Insight Into I/I-Treatment in the Workplace: Patterns, Causes and Solutions*. Wales, UK: Economic and Social Research Council.

Finkle, L. 2018. "6 Signs You May Be a Dysfunctional Company (or Leader)." *Linkedin*. www.linkedin.com/pulse/6-signs-you-may-dysfunctional-company-leader-linda-finkle/.

Fischer, R.J., E.P. Halibozek, and D.C. Walters. 2019. "Contingency Planning Emergency Response and Safety." *Introduction to Security*, pp. 249–268.

Fisher, B.S. and S.P. Lab, eds. 2010. *Encyclopedia of Victimology and Crime Prevention.*, Vol. 1. Thousand Oaks, Calif.: Sage Publications, Inc.

Fleming, P. and H.D. Harvey. 2002. "Strategy Development in Dealing With Violence Against Employees in the Workplace." *Journal of the Royal Society for the Promotion of Health* 122, no. 4, pp. 226–232. https://doi.org/10.1177/146642400212200409.

Flint, D. 2018. *Think Beyond Value—Building Strategy to Win*. New York, NY: Morgan James Publishing.

Folger, R. and D.P. Skarlicki. 1998. "When Tough Times Make Tough Bosses: Managerial Distancing as a Function of Layoff Blame." *Academy of Management Journal* 41, no. 1, pp. 79–87.

Fontana, J. 2014. "AOL Asking Users to Change Passwords After Discovering Breach." *ZDNET*. www.zdnet.com/article/theres-been-a-big-rise-in-phishing-attacks-this-one-worked/.

Foote, A.R. and A. Barash. 2021. *Bullying in the Workplace: A Harbinger of Serious Problems*. https://news.bloomberglaw.com/daily-labor-report/bullying-in-the-workplace-a-harbinger-of-serious-problems.

Fors Brandebo, M. and A. Alvinius, eds. 2019. *Dark Sides of Organizational Behavior and Leadership*. https://doi.org/10.5772/intechopen.71976.

Forsey, C. 2022. *18 Core Company Values That Will Shape Your Culture & Inspire Your Employees*. https://blog.hubspot.com/marketing/company-values.

Friborg, M.K., J.V. Hansen, P.T. Aldrich, A.P. Folker, S. KJær, M.B.D. Nielsen, R. Rugulies, and I.E. Madsen. 2017. "Workplace Sexual Harassment and Depressive Symptoms: A Cross-Sectional Multilevel Analysis Comparing

Harassment From Clients or Customers to Harassment From Other Employees Amongst 7603 Danish Employees From 1041 Organizations." *BMC Public Health* 17, p. 675. https://doi.org/10.1186/s12889-017-4669-x.

Friedrichs, D.O. 2002. "Occupational Crime, Occupational Deviance, and Workplace Crime." *Criminal Justice* 2, no. 3, pp. 243–256.

Fugas, C.S., S.A. Silva, and J.L. Meliá. 2012. "Another Look at Safety Climate and Safety Behavior: Deepening the Cognitive and Social Mediator Mechanisms." *Accident Analysis & Prevention* 45, pp. 468–477. https://doi.org/10.1016/j.aap.2011.08.013.

Furnham, A. 2007. "Personality Disorders and Derailment at Work: The Paradoxical Positive Influence of Pathology in the Workplace." In *Research Companion to the Dysfunctional Workplace*, ed. C.L. Cooper, 22–39. Northampton, MA: Edward Elgar Publishing, Inc.

Gale, S., I. Mordukhovich, S. Newlan, and E. McNeely. 2019. "The Impact of Workplace Harassment on Health in a Working Cohort." *Frontiers in Psychology* 10, no. 1181. https://doi.org/10.3389/fpsyg.2019.01181.

Gallo, A. 2023. "What Is Psychological Safety?" *Harvard Business Review*. https://hbr.org/2023/02/what-is-psychological-safety.

Gallup. 2018. *Gallup's Approach to Culture Building a Culture That Drives Performance*. Washington DC: Gallup, Inc.

Geifman, A. 1992. "Aspects of Early Twentieth-Century Russian Terrorism: The Socialist-Revolutionary Combat Organization." *Terrorism and Political Violence* 4, Summer, p. 223.

Georgiev, D. 2023. *18 Shocking Workplace Injury Statistics to Know in 2023*. https://techjury.net/blog/work-related-injury-statistics/#gref.

Gephart, R.P., Jr. 1987. "Organization Design for Hazardous Chemical Accidents." *The Columbia Journal of World Business* 22, pp. 51–58.

Gerwing, C. 2016. "Meaning of Change Agents Within Organizational Change." *Journal of Applied Leadership and Management* 4, pp. 21–30.

Giacalone, R.A. and J. Greenberg. 1997. *Antisocial Behavior in Organizations*. Thousand Oaks, CA: Sage Publications.

Goldman, A. 2006. "Personality Disorders in Leaders: Implications of the *DSM IV-TR* in Assessing Dysfunctional Organizations." *Journal of Managerial Psychology* 21, no. 5, pp. 392–414. https://doi.org/10.1108/02683940610673942.

Goldman, A. 2008. "Company on the Couch: Unveiling Toxic Behavior in Dysfunctional Organizations." *Journal of Management Inquiry* 17, no. 3, pp. 226–238.

Goldman, A. 2009. *Transforming Toxic Leaders*. Stanford, CA: Stanford University Press.

Goldman, A. 2010. *Destructive Leaders and Dysfunctional Organizations: A Therapeutic Perspective*. Cambridge, UK: Cambridge University Press.

Goldsmid, S. and P. Howie. 2014. "Bullying by Definition: An Examination of Definitional Components of Bullying." *Emotional and Behavioural Difficulties* 19, pp. 210–225. https://doi.org/10.1080/13632752.2013.844414.

Goleman, D. 2000. "Leadership That Gets Results." *Harvard Business Review* 78, no. 2, pp. 78–90.

Gordon, G.G. 1991. "Industry Determinants of Organizational Culture." *The Academy of Management Review* 16, no. 2, pp. 396–415.

Goriel, N. 2017. "14 Tips to Protect Your Business From Ransomware Attacks." *SBA News and Views*. www.sba.gov/blog/14-tips-protect-your-business-ransomware-attacks.

Gorman, E. 2008. "The Politics of Sexual Harassment: A Comparative Study of the United States, the European Union, and Germany." *Gender & Society* 22, pp. 828–830. https://doi.org/10.1177/0891243208320252.

Goth, G. 2021. "Post-Pandemic, Should Employers Still Subsidize Fitness at Home?" *SHRM*. www.shrm.org/resourcesandtools/hr-topics/benefits/pages/post-pandemic-should-employers-still-subsidize-fitness-at-home.aspx.

Gottfredson, R. 2018. "4 Mindsets That Drive Dysfunctional Leadership." *Association for Talent Development*. www.td.org/insights/4-mindsets-that-drive-dysfunctional-leadership/.

Gradinger, P., D. Strohmeier, and C. Spiel. 2010. "Definition and Measurement of cyberbullying." *Cyberpsychology: Journal of Psychosocial Research on Cyberspace* 4, no. 2. www.cyberpsychology.eu/view.php?cisloclanku02010112301.

Graham, L.O. 1997. *Proversity.* Hoboken, NJ: John Wiley and Sons.

Greenberg, J. 1996. *The Quest for Justice on the Job,* Thousand Oaks, CA: Sage Publications.

Greenberg, J. 2002. "Who Stole the Money, and When? Individual and Situational Determinants of Employee Theft." *Organizational Behavior and Human Decision Processes* 89, no. (1), pp. 985–1003.

Greenwald, J. 2010. *Broad Definition of Bullying Poses Problem for Firms.* www.businessinsurance.com/article/20100613/ISSUE01/306139987.

Griffin, R.W. and A.M. O'Leary-Kelly, eds. 2004. *The Dark Side of Organizational Behavior.* San Francisco: Jossey-Bass.

Griffin, R.W. and Y.P. Lopez. 2004. "Toward a Model of the Person-Situation Determinants of Deviant Behavior in Organizations." Paper presented at the 64th Annual Meeting of the Academy of Management, New Orleans, LA.

Griffin, R.W. and Y.P. Lopez. 2005. "Bad Behavior in Organizations: A Review and Typology for Future Research." *Journal of Management* 31, pp. 988–1005.

Griffin, R.W., A. Stoverink, and R. Gardner. 2012. "Negative Co-Worker Exchanges." In *Personal Relationships: The Effect on Employee Attitudes, Behavior, and Wellbeing, SIOP Organizational Frontiers Series,* eds. L.T. Eby and T.D. Allen, 131–156. New York, NY: Taylor and Francis Group.

Griffin, R.W., A.M. O'Leary-Kelly, and J.M. Collins, eds. 1998. *Dysfunctional Behavior in Organizations: Violent and Deviant Behavior.* Stamford, CN: JAI Press.

Guerra, F., G. Simonini, and M. Vincini. 2015. "Supporting Image Search With Tag Clouds: A Preliminary Approach." *Advances in Multimedia* 2015, no. 439020. https://doi.org/10.1155/2015/439020.

Gulati, R., P.R. Lawrence, and P. Puranam. 2005. "Adaptation in Vertical Relationships: Beyond Incentive Conflict." *Strategic Management Journal* 26, no. 5, pp. 415–440.

Gumbus, A. and B.M. Lyons. 2011. "Workplace Harassment: The Social Costs of Bullying." *Journal of Leadership, Accountability, and Ethics 8*, pp. 72–90.

Gunderman, R.B. and E.M.Z. Sechrist. 2018. "How Neglect Fosters Workplace Toxicity." *Journal of the American College of Radiology* 16, no. 2, pp. 252–254.

Gurchiek, K. 2005. "Bullying: It's Not Just on the Playground; Bosses Report Being Targeted in the Workplace." *HR Magazine.* findarticles.corn/p/articles/mi_m3495/is_6_50/ai_n13826260.

Gurr, T.T. 1970. *Why Men Rebel.* Princeton, NJ: Princeton University Press.

Haas, E.J. 2020. "The Role of Supervisory Support on Workers' Health and Safety Performance." *Health Communication* 35, no. 3, pp. 364–374.

Hakim, D. and J. Ewing. 2015. "Volkswagen's Software Was 'Illegal Defeat Device,' German Regulator Says." *The New York Times.* www.nytimes.com/2015/12/02/business/international/volkswagens-software-use-was-illegal-german-regulator-rules.html.

Haney, J. and W. Lutters. 2020. "Security Awareness Training for the Workforce: Moving Beyond Check-the-Box Compliance." *Computer* 53, no (10), p. 10.1109/mc.2020.3001959. Long Beach, CA. doi: 10.1109/mc.2020.3001959.

Hansen, A.M., A. Hogh, R. Persson, B. Karlson, A.H. Garde, and P. Ørbæk. 2006. "Bullying at Work, Health Outcomes, and Physiological Stress Response." *Journal of Psychosomatic Research* 60, no. 1, pp. 63–72.

Harrell, E., J. Petosa, N. Dangermond, S. Derk, D. Hartley, and A.A. Reichard. 2022. "Highlights From a New Report on Indicators of Workplace Violence." *NIOSH Science Blog, Centers for Disease Control and Prevention.* https://blogs.cdc.gov/niosh-science-blog/2022/09/07/workplace-violence-indicators/#:~:text=The%20average%20annual%20rate%20of,nonfatal%20workplace%20violence%20(64%25).

Harris, L. and K. Daunt. 2004. "Jaycustomer Behavior: An Exploration of Types and Motives in the Hospitality Industry." *Journal of Services Marketing* 18, no. 5, pp. 339–357. https://doi.org/10.1108/08876040410548276.

Harris, L.C. and K.L. Reynolds. 2003. "The Consequences of Dysfunctional Customer Behavior." *Journal of Service Research* 6, no. 2, pp. 144–161. https://doi.org/10.1177/1094670503257044.

Harthill, S. 2008. "Bullying in the Workplace: Lessons From the United Kingdom." *Minnesota Journal of International Law* 17, pp. 247–302.

Harvey, J., K.J. Johnson, K.S. Roloff, and A.C. Edmondson. 2019. From Orientation to Behavior: The Interplay Between Learning Orientation, Open-Mindedness, and Psychological Safety in Team Learning." *Human Relations* 72, pp. 1726–1751.

Harvey, P., M.J. Martinko, and S.C. Douglas. 2006. "Causal Reasoning in Dysfunctional Leader-Member Interactions." *Journal of Managerial Psychology* 21, pp. 747–762.

Hayes, J. 2008. "Foreword. Workplace Conflict and How Businesses Can Harness It to Thrive." *CPP Global Human Capital Report*. Sunnyvale, CA, The Myers-Briggs Company.

Heames, J. and M. Harvey. 2006. "Workplace Bullying: A Cross-Level Assessment." *Management Decision* 44, no. 9, pp. 1214–1230.

Hearst, M.A. and D. Rosner. January 22, 2008. Tag Clouds: Data Analysis Tool or Social Signaler?" In *Proceedings of the 41st Annual Hawaii International Conference on System Sciences (HICSS 2008)*, p. 160. Washington DC, US. https://doi.org/10.1109/HICSS.2008.422.

Heinonen, N., T. Lallukka, J. Lahti, O. Pietiläinen, H. Nordquist, M. Mänty, A. Katainen, and A. Kouvonen. 2022. "Working Conditions and Long-Term Sickness Absence Due to Mental Disorders: A Prospective Record Linkage Cohort Study Among 19- to 39-Year-Old Female Municipal Employees." *Journal of Occupational and Environmental Medicine* 64, no. 2, pp. 105–114.

Helbig, K. and M. Norman. 2023. In *Psychological Safety Playbook*. Las Vegas, Neavda, NV: pagetwo.

Helic, D., C. Trattner, M. Strohmaier, and K. Andrews. 2011. "Are Tag Clouds Useful for Navigation? A Network-Theoretic Analysis." *International Journal of Social Computing and Cyber-Physical Systems* 1, pp. 33–55. https://doi .org/10.1504/IJSCCPS.2011.043603

Hemraj, M.B. 2001. "Guarding the Company Against Dishonest Employees." *Journal of Financial Crime* 9, no. 1, pp. 90–99.

Hoel, H. and C.L. Cooper. 2001. "Origins of Bullying: Theoretical Frameworks for Explaining Workplace Bullying." In *Building a culture of respect: Managing bullying at work*, ed. N. Tehrani, 3–19. London: Taylor & Francis.

Hoel, H. and S. Einarsen. 2010. "The Effectiveness of Anti-Bullying Regulations: The Case of Sweden." *European Journal of Work and Organizational Psychology* 19, pp. 30–50. https://doi.org/10.1080/13594320802643665

Hoel, H., C. Rayner, and C.L. Cooper. 1999. "Workplace Bullying." In *International Review of Industrial and Organizational Psychology*, eds. C.L. Cooper and I.T. Robertson, Vol. 14, 195–230. London: Wiley.

Hoffman, B. 1992. "Current Research on Terrorism and Low-Intensity Conflict." *Studies in Conflict and Terrorism* 15, pp. 25–37.

Hoffman, B. 1998. *Inside Terrorism.* New York, NY: Columbia University Press.

Hogh, A., V. Borg, and K.L. Mikkelsen. 2003. "Work-related Violence as a Predictor of Fatigue: A 5-Year Follow-up of the Danish Work Environment Cohort Study." *Work & Stress 17*, no. 2, pp. 182–194. https://doi.org/10.1080/0267837031000156876.

Holland, P. 2020. "The Impact of a Dysfunctional Leader on the Workplace: A New Challenge for HRM." *Personnel Review 49*, no. 4, pp. 1039–1052. https://doi.org/10.1108/PR-03-2019-0134.

Hollinger, R.C. December 17, 2017. "Research Findings From Employee Theft Articles." *Loss Prevention Magazine.* https://losspreventionmedia.com/research-findings-on-employee-theft-research/.

Hollis, L.P. 2016. "Socially Dominated: The Racialized and Gendered Positionality of Those Precluded From Bullying." In *The Coercive Community College: Bullying and Its Costly Impact on the Mission to Serve Underrepresented Populations*, ed. L.P. Hollis, 103–112. Emerald Group Publishing.

Hollis, M., M. Felson, and B. Welsh. 2013. "The Capable Guardian in Routine Activities Theory: A Theoretical and Conceptual Reappraisal." *Crime Prevention and Community Safety* 15, pp. 65–79.

Holly, K. December 17, 2021. "Dealing With Verbal Abuse at Work." *HealthyPlace.* www.healthyplace.com/abuse/verbal-abuse/dealing-with-verbal-abuse-at-work (accessed February 19, 2023).

Holtfreter, K. 2005. "Employee Crimes." In *Encyclopedia of White-Collar & Corporate Crime*, ed. L.M. Salinger, Vol. 1, 284–288. Thousand Oaks, CA: Sage.

Holt-Gimenez, E. 2015. "Racism and Capitalism: Dual Challenges for the Food Movement." *Journal of Agriculture, Food Systems* & *Community Development* 5, no. 2, pp. 23–25.

Horberry, T. and R. Burgess-Limerick. 2015. "Applying a Human-Centered Process to Re-Design Equipment and Work Environments." *Safety* 1, no. 1, pp. 7–15.

Horn, I., T. Taros, S. Dirkes, L. Hüer, M. Rose, R. Tietmeyer, and E. Constantinides. 2015. "Business Reputation and Social Media: A Primer on Threats and Responses." *Journal of Direct, Data and Digital Marketing Practice* 16, pp. 193–208. https://doi.org/10.1057/dddmp.2015.1.

Houck, N.M. and A.M. Colbert. 2017. "Patient Safety and Workplace Bullying: An Integrative Review." *Journal of Nursing Care Quality* 32, no. 2, pp. 164–171. https://doi.org/10.1097/NCQ.0000000000000209.

Hout, M.C., M.H. Papesh, and S.D. Goldinger. 2013. "Multidimensional Scaling." *Wiley Interdisciplinary Reviews: Cognitive Science* 4, pp. 93–103.

Howard, J. 2008. "Prevention Through Design—Introduction." *Journal of Safety Research* 39, no. 2, p. 113. https://doi.org/10.1016/j.jsr.2008.02.022.

Howie, L. 2007. "The Terrorism Threat and Managing Workplaces." *Disaster Prevention and Management* 16, no. 1, pp. 70–78.

Hsieh, T. 2010. *Delivering Happiness: A Path to Profits, Passion, and Purpose.* New York, NY: Grand Central Publishing.

Hueffner, E. 2022. "The Customer Is Not Always Right: 5 Reasons Why & What You Can Do When They're Wrong." *Zendesk Blog.* www.zendesk.com/blog/customer-is-not-always-right/.

Hurt, K. and D. Dye. n.d. "LetsGrowLeaders.com." https://letsgrowleaders.com/psychological-safety-why-people-dont-speak-up-at-work/.

Hwang, J., Y. Yoo, and I. Kim. 2021. "Dysfunctional Customer Behavior, Employee Service Sabotage, and Sustainability: Can Social Support Make a Difference?" *International Journal of Environmental Research and Public Health* 18, no. 7, p. 3628. https://doi.org/10.3390/ijerph18073628.

Idris, M.A., M.F. Dollard, and M.R. Tuckey. 2015. "Psychosocial Safety Climate as a Management Tool for Employee Engagement and Performance: A Multilevel Analysis." *International Journal of Stress Management* 22, no. 2, pp. 183–206. https://doi.org/10.1037/a0038986.

Indeed Editorial Team. 2022. *How To Manage Workplace Bullying (With Examples).* www.indeed.com/career-advice/career-development/workplace-bully.

Inness, M., J. Barling, and N. Turner. 2005. "Understanding Supervisor-Targeted Aggression: A Within-Person, Between-Jobs Design." *Journal of Applied Psychology 90*, no. 4, pp. 731–739. https://doi.org/10.1037/0021-9010.90.4.731.

International Association of Chiefs of Police. 1996. *Combating Workplace Violence, Guidelines for Employees and Law Enforcement.* Alexandria, VA: International Association of Chiefs of Police.

International Labor Organization. 2023a. "Workplace Violence and Harassment Remain Widespread as Victims Fear Speaking Up." *Safety+Health.* www.safetyandhealthmagazine.com/articles/23405-workplace-violence-and-harassment-remain-widespread-as-victims-fear-speaking-up-survey.

International Labor Organization. 2023b. *The Value of Essential Work.* www.ilo.org/digitalguides/en-gb/story/weso2023-key-workers#home.

International Labour Organization. 2022. *Experiences of Violence and Harassment at Work: A Global First Survey.* Geneva, Switzerland: International Labour Organization.

Irwin, B. 2020. "The Staggering Cost of Organizational Dysfunction." *Linkedin.* www.linkedin.com/pulse/staggering-cost-organizational-dysfunction-brian-irwin/.

Ivcevic, Z., J.I. Menger, and A. Miller. 2020. "How Common Is Unethical Behavior in U.S. Organizations." *Harvard Business Review*. https://hbr .org/2020/03/how-common-is-unethical-behavior-in-u-s-organizations.

Jacobs, J.L. and C.L. Scott. 2011. "Hate Crimes as One Aspect of Workplace Violence: Recommendations for HRD." *Advances in Developing Human Resources* 13, no. 1, pp. 85–98.

Jamieson, A. 1990. "Identity and Morality in the Italian Red Brigades." *Terrorism and Political Violence* 2, no. 4, pp. 508–520.

Jaworska, N. and A. Chupetlovska-Anastasova. 2009. "A Review of Multidimensional Scaling (MDS) and Its Utility in Various Psychological Domains." *Tutorials in Quantitative Methods for Psychology* 5, pp. 1–10. https://doi.org/10.20982/tqmp.05.1.p001

Jenkins, B. 1978. *International Terrorism: Trends and Potentialities*. Santa Monica, CA: The Rand Corporation.

Jenkins, M. 2013. *Preventing and Managing Workplace Bullying and Harassment: A Risk Management Approach*. Queensland, AU: Australian Academic Press.

Jiang, L., Y. Zhang, and L. Feng. 2019. "A Multilevel Model of Autonomous Safety Motivation and Safety Performance." *Advances in Psychological Science* 27, no. 7, pp. 1141–1152.

Johnson, A., H. Hong, M. Groth, A. Bove, J. Crisp, and L. White. 2013. "Effect of Violence in Organizations on Organizational Effectiveness: The Role of Engagement." *Academy of Management Proceedings*, no. I, p. 12117.

Johnson, P. 1986. "The Cancer of Terrorism." In Terrorism: How the West Can Win, ed. B. Netanyahu, 31–37. NY: Straus Giroux, Farrar.

Joly, H. 2020. "How to Re-Engineer Your Business for Safety." *Harvard Business Review Digital Article*. https://hbr.org/2020/06/how-to-re-engineer-your-business-for-safety.

Jones R.D. 2022. *A Hole in Science—Grammar of the Sociological Problem*. IngoodCompany LLC. Kindle Edition. www.amazon.com/Hole-Science-Sociological-Reintroduction-SafetyTM-ebook/dp/B0B3BC6NMT.

Jones, T. 2019. "Overcoming Workplace Dysfunction and Restoring Functionality." *Association for Talent Development*. www.td.org/insights/overcoming-workplace-dysfunction-and-restoring-functionality.

Jung, O.S., P. Kundu, A.C. Edmondson, J. Hegde, N. Agazaryan, M. Steinberg, and A. Raldow. 2021. "Resilience vs. Vulnerability: Psychological Safety and Reporting of Near Misses With Varying Proximity to Harm in Radiation Oncology." *Joint Commission Journal on Quality and Patient Safety* 47, no. 1, pp. 15–22.

Jurkiewicz, C.L. and R.A. Giacalone. 2016. "Organizational Determinants of Ethical Dysfunctionality." *Journal of Business Ethics* 136, no. 1, pp. 1–12.

Kahn, W.A. 1990. "Psychological Conditions of Personal Engagement and Disengagement at Work." *Academy of Management Journal* 33, no. 4, pp. 692–724.

Kaloudis, H. 2019. "Psychological Safety at Work: What Do Psychologically Safe Teams Look Like." *Medium*. https://medium.com/@Harri_Kaloudis/psychological-safety-at-work-what-do-psychologically-safe-work-teams-look-like-5585ab0f2df4.

Kanter, R.M. 1983. *The Change Masters: Innovation for Productivity in the American Corporation*. New York, NY: Simon & Schuster.

Karasek, R.A. 1979. "Job Demands, Job Decision Latitude, and Mental Strain: Implications for Job Redesign." *Administrative Science Quarterly* 24, no. 2, pp. 285–308.

Karkoulian, S., G. Assaker, and R. Hallak. 2016. "An Empirical Study of 360-Degree Feedback, Organizational Justice, and Firm Sustainability." *Journal of Business Research* 69, no. 5, pp. 1862–1867.

Kaser, O. and D. Lemire. 2007. *Tag-Cloud Drawing: Algorithms for Cloud Visualization*. Canada: Banff. https://pdfs.semanticscholar.org/8dd0/06b45f14e8f5574170943fa6c85c39045f5c.pdf.

Keashly, L. 1998. "Emotional Abuse in the Workplace: Conceptual and Empirical Issues." *Journal of Emotional Abuse* 1, no. 1, pp. 85–117.

Keashly, L. and S. Harvey. 2005. "Emotional Abuse in the Workplace." In *Counterproductive Work Behavior: Investigations of Actors and Target*, eds. S. Fox and P.E. Spector, 201–235. American Psychological Association. https://doi.org/10.1037/10893-009.

Kelly, R.J. and J. Barnathan. 1988. "Out on a Limb: Executives Abroad." *Security Management* 32, no. 11, pp. 117–127.

Kelly, R.J. and W.J. Cook. 1994. "Experience in International Travel and Aversion to Terrorism." *Journal of Police and Criminal Psychology* 10, pp. 62–76.

Kendrick, M., K. Kendrick, P. Morton, N.F. Taylor, and S.G. Leggat. 2020. "Hospital Staff Report It Is Not Burnout, But a Normal Stress Reaction to an Uncongenial Work Environment: Findings From a Qualitative Study." *International Journal of Environmental Research and Public Health* 17, no. 11, p. 4107. https://doi.org/10.3390/ijerph17114107.

Kets de Vries, M.F.R. and C. Rook. January 10, 2018. "Coaching Challenging Executives." In *Mastering Executive Coaching*, eds. J. Passmore and B. Underhill. Routledge, INSEAD Working Paper No. 2018/01/EFE. https://ssrn.com/abstract=3099368.

Kim, J.S. and J.S. Kim. 2022. "Association of Job Crafting and Perception of Patient Safety Culture With Patient Safety Management Activities Among Hospital Nurses." *Journal of Korean Academy of Nursing Administration* 28, no. 4, pp. 382–392.

King, M.M. 2019. *Strategies to Identify and Reduce Workplace Bullying to Increase Productivity* [Doctoral Study]. Walden University. www03.core.ac.uk/download/pdf/226775577.pdf.

Kinney, J.A. 1995. *Violence at Work*. Englewood Cliffs, NJ: Prentice-Hall.

Kirk, A.K. and D.F. Brown. 2003. "Employee Assistance Programs: A Review of the Management of Stress and Wellbeing Through Workplace Counselling and Consulting." *Australian Psychologist 38*, no. 2, pp. 138–143. https://doi.org/10.1080/00050060310001707137.

Kirk, D.J. and G.M. Franklin. 2003. "Violence in the Workplace: Guidance and Training Advice for Business Owners and Managers." *Business and Society Review* 108, no. 4, pp. 523–537.

Klein, G. and Z. Shtudiner. 2021. "Judging Severity of Unethical Workplace Behavior: Attractiveness and Gender as Status Characteristics." *BRQ Business Research Quarterly* 24, no. 1, pp. 19–33.

Kleinpeter, M. 2019. *The Right Way: Providing a Common Definition, Setting Expectations, and Establishing Roles and Responsibilities*. Lubbock, TX: Chaplain Publishing, LLC.

Kohut, M.R. 2008. *Understanding, Controlling, and Stopping Bullies & Bullying at Work*. Ocala: Atlantic Publishing Group.

Kolko, J. 2015. "Dysfunctional Products Come From Dysfunctional Organizations." *Harvard Business Review*. https://hbr.org/2015/01/dysfunctional-products-come-from-dysfunctional-organizations.

Kolmar, C. November 2, 2022. "17 Distressing Sexual Harassment Statistics [2023]: Sexual Harassment." In *The Workplace*. Zippia.com. www.zippia.com/advice/sexual-harassment-workplace-statistics/

Kompella, S. 2022. "Persisting Menace: A Case-Based Study of Remote Workplace Bullying in India." *International Journal of Bullying Prevention*. https://doi.org/10.1007/s42380-022-00152-8.

Korsky, S. 1990. "Terrorism: The New Corporate Threat." *Management Review* 79, no. 10, pp. 39–43.

Kozdrój-Schmidt, A. and D.D. Van Fleet. 1995. "Learning From Mismanagement in Polish Organizations." In *Transformation Management: Organizational Reforms in Post-Communist Countries*, eds. R. Culpan and B. Nino Kumar, 29–46. Westport, CT: Greenwood Publishing Group.

Krasnovsky T. and R.C. Lane. 1998. "Shoplifting: A Review of the Literature." *Aggression and Violent Behavior* 3, no. 3, pp. 219–235. https://doi.org/10.1016/S1359-1789(97)00022-0.

Kuhl, E.A. 2017. *Workplace Bullying Is Costly*. https://workplacementalhealth.org/mental-health-topics/bullying.

Kwantes, C.T. and C.A. Boglarsky. 2007. "Perceptions of Organizational Culture, Leadership Effectiveness and Personal Effectiveness Across Six Countries." *Journal of International Management* 13, no. 2, pp. 204–230.

Kyrios, M., M. Nedeljkovic, R. Moulding, and G. Doron. 2007. "Problems of Employees With Personality Disorders: The Exemplar of Obsessive-Compulsive Personality Disorder (OCPD)." In *Research Companion to the Dysfunctional Workplace*, ed. C.L. Cooper, 40–57. Northampton, MA: Edward Elgar Publishing, Inc.

Lagios, N., F. Nguyen, F. Stinglhamber, and G. Caesens. 2022. "Dysfunctional Rules in Organizations: The Mediating Role of Organizational Dehumanization in the Relationship Between Red Tape and Employees' Outcomes." *European Management Journal*, in press. www.sciencedirect.com/science/article/abs/pii/S0263237322000858.

Langan-Fox, J. and M. Sankey. 2007. "Tyrants and Workplace Bullying." In *Research Companion to the Dysfunctional Workplace*, ed. C.L. Cooper, 58–74. Northampton, MA: Edward Elgar Publishing, Inc.

Langner, D. 2010. *Employee Theft: Determinants of Motive and Proactive Solutions* [UNLV Theses], p. 543. Dissertations, Professional Papers, and Capstones. http://dx.doi.org/10.34917/1701642

Lapierre, L.M., T.D. Allen, P.E. Spector, M.P. O'Driscoll, C.L. Cooper, S. Poelmans, and J.I. Sanchez. 2005. "Further validation of Carlson, Kacmar, and Williams' (2000) Work–Family Conflict Measure." In *2005 conference best paper proceedings of the Academy of Management*, Vol. 65 [CD]. Briarcliff Manor, NY: Academy of Management.

Laqueur, W. 1987. *The Age of Terrorism*. Boston, MA: Little, Brown and Company.

Larsson, G., A.K. Berglund, and A. Ohlsson. 2016. "Daily Hassles, Their Antecedents and Outcomes Among Professional First Responders: A Systematic Literature Review." *Scandinavian Journal of Psychology* 57, no. 4, pp. 359–367.

Le, T. N. (n.d.). Inside Microsoft Company Culture: Intriguing and Functional. Available at: https://blog.grovehr.com/microsoft-company-culture

LeBlanc, M.M. and J. Barling. 2004. "Workplace Aggression." *Current Directions in Psychological Science* 13, no. 1, pp. 9–12.

Lee, J.Y. 2022. "How Does Psychological Safety Foster Employee Performance? A Serial Multiple Mediation of Job Crafting and Thriving." *International Journal of Organization Theory & Behavior* 25, no. 3/4, pp. 98–112.

Lennox, E. 2021. "Do We Need Psychological Safety or Psychosocial Safety? What's the Difference?" *Linkedin*. www.linkedin.com/pulse/do-we-need-psychological-safety-psychosocial-whats-elena-lennox/?trk=pulse-article_more-articles_related-content-card.

Lewis, D. 2004. "Bullying at Work: The Impact of Shame Among University and College Lecturers." *British Journal of Guidance & Counseling* 32, no. 3, pp. 281–299.

Lipinski, J. and L.M. Crouthers. 2014. *Bullying in the Workplace: Causes, Symptoms, and Remedies*. New York, NY: Routledge.

Lipman, M. and W.R. McGraw. 1988. "Employee Theft: A $40 Billion Industry." *The ANNALS of the American Academy of Political and Social Science* 498, no. 1, pp. 51–59.

Litzky, B.E., K.A. Eddleston, and D.L. Kidder. 2006. "The Good, the Bad, and the Misguided: How Managers Inadvertently Encourage Deviant Behaviors." *The Academy of Management Perspectives* 20, no. 1, pp. 91–103.

Liu, C. 2020. "Workplace Ostracism: People's Psychological Attributions and Coping Strategies." *News@Hofstra*. https://news.hofstra.edu/2020/05/21/workplace-ostracism-peoples-psychological-attributions-coping-strategies/.

Liu, H. and H. Xia. 2016. "Workplace Ostracism: A Review and Directions for Future Research." *Journal of Human Resource and Sustainability Studies* 4, no. 3, pp. 197–201. https://doi.org/10.4236/jhrss.2016.43022.

Lo, T.W., D. Chappell, S. Kwok, and J. Wu. 2011. "Workplace Violence in Hong Kong, China: Nature, Impact, and Preparedness." *International Journal of Offender Therapy and Comparative Criminology* 56, no. 6, pp. 955–975.

Loh, J., S.L.D. Restubog, and T.J. Zagenczyk. 2010. "Consequences of Workplace Bullying on Employee Identification and Satisfaction Among Australian and Singaporeans." *Journal of Cross-Cultural Psychology* 41, no. 2, pp. 236–252.

Summarized by Sidle, S. D. 2010. "Eye of the Beholder: Does Culture Shape Perceptions of Workplace Bullying?" *Academy of Management Perspectives* 24, no. 3, pp. 100–101.

Loignon, A. and S. Wormington. 2022. *Psychologically Safe for Some, But Not All?* Center for Creative Leadership. https://cclinnovation.org/wp-content/uploads/2022/05/psychologicallysafe.pdf?webSyncID=4a6283cb-bae2-894a-c5dd-4d9cd70c102e&sessionGUID=834e2ea5-7576-2d62-95b3-b7102ee168aa. DOI: https://doi.org/10.35613/ccl.2022.204.

Lombardi, D.A., S.K. Verma, M.J. Brennan, and M.J. Perry. 2009. "Factors Influencing Worker Use of Personal Protective Eyewear." *Accident Analysis & Prevention* 41, no. 4, pp. 755–762.

Lopez, Y.P. and R.W. Griffin. 2004. "A Person-Situation Model of Organizational Violence." In *Proceedings of the Southern Management Association, San Antonio*, pp. 3–8.

Lovelock, C.H. 1994. *Product Plus: How product+ Service = Competitive Advantage*. New York, NY: McGraw-Hill.

Lucero, M.A., R.E. Allen, and B. Elzweig. 2013. "Managing Employee Social Networking: Evolving Views From the National Labor Relations Board." *Employee Responsibilities and Rights Journal* 25, pp. 143–158.

Lumanta, K. 2021. "Psychological Safety Is Not Just Another Word for 'Trust.'" *Michael Page*. www.michaelpage.com.au/advice/management-advice/leadership/psychological-safety-not-just-another-word-trust.

Lutgen-Sandvik, P., S.J. Tracy, and J.K. Alberts. 2007. "Burned by Bullying in the American Workplace: Prevalence, Perception, Degree and Impact." *Journal of Management Studies* 44, no. 6, pp. 837–862.

Lyons, T.P. and A.J. Connolly. 2012. "The People Question: Creating Global Advantage Through Global Talent Initiatives." *International Food and Agribusiness Management Review* 15, no. Special Issue A, pp. 19–24.

MacCallum, R. 1988. "Multidimensional Scaling." In *Handbook of Multivariate Experimental Psychology*, eds. R.B. Cattell and J.R. Nesselroade, 421–445. Boston, MA: Springer. https://doi.org/10.1007/978-1-4613-0893-5_13.

MacDonald, T. 2019. "How to Keep Executives Safe From Malicious Actors With an Executive Protection Program." *Cosive*. www.cosive.com/blog/executive-protection-program.

MacKinnon, C.A. 1979. *Sexual Harassment of Working Women*. New Haven: Yale University Press.

Maddox, R.C. 1991, Summer. "Terrorism: The Current Corporate Response." *SAM Advanced Management Journal* 56, no. 3, pp. 1821.

Madsen, I.E. and R. Rugulies. 2021. "Understanding the Impact of Psychosocial Working Conditions on Workers' Health: We Have Come a Long Way, But Are We There Yet?" *Scandinavian Journal of Work Environment & Health* 47, no. 7, pp. 483–487.

Mahon, A. 2022. "Defining Terrorism: How Ambiguous Definitions and Vague Classifications Open Doors for Power Acquisition." *Journal of Global Strategic Studies* 2, no. 1, pp. 84–97.

Maine Department of Labor. 2013. *Managing Safety and Health*. www.safetyworksmaine.gov/safe_workplace/safety_management/.

Mainiero, L.A. and K.J. Jones. 2013. "Sexual Harassment Versus Workplace Romance: Social Media Spillover and Textual Harassment in the Workplace." *The Academy of Management Perspectives 27*, no. 3, pp. 187–203. https://doi.org/10.5465/amp.2012.0031.

Maki, N., S. Moore, L. Grunberg, and E. Greenberg. 2005. "The Responses of Male and Female Managers to Workplace Stress and Downsizing." *North American Journal of Psychology 7*, no. 2, pp. 295–312.

Manning, K. 2021. *The Empathetic Workplace: 5 Steps to a Compassionate, Calm, and Confident Response to Trauma on the Job*. Nashville, TN: Harper Collins Leadership.

Mansour, S., M. Faisal Azeem, M. Dollard, and R. Potter. 2022. "How Psychosocial Safety Climate Helped Alleviate Work Intensification Effects on Presenteeism During the COVID-19 Crisis? A Moderated Mediation

Model." *International Journal of Environmental Research and Public Health* 19, no. 20, p. 13673. https://doi.org/10.3390/ijerph192013673.

Mantell, M.R. and S. Albrecht. 1994. *Ticking Bombs: Defusing Violence in the Workplace*. Burr Ridge IL: Irwin Professional Publishing.

Martin, G. 2017. "Types of Terrorism." In *Developing Next-Generation Countermeasures for Homeland Security Threat Prevention*, eds. M. Dawson, D.R. Kisku, P. Gupta, J.K. Sing, and W. Li, 1–16. Hershey, PA: IGI Global.

Martin, M. 2021. "Fostering Psychological Safety in the Workplace." *Forbes*. www.forbes.com/sites/forbescoachescouncil/2021/05/28/fostering-psychological-safety-in-the-workplace/?sh=4a49d8c84773.

Martin, R.A. 1989. "Humour and the Mastery of Living: Using Humour to Cope With the Daily Stresses of Growing Up." In *Humour and Children's Development: A Guide to Practical Applications*, ed. P.E. McGhee, 135–154. New York, NY: Haworth Press.

Matthiesen, S.B. 2004. "When Whistleblowing Leads to Bullying at Work." *Occupational Health Psychologist* 1, no. 1, p. 3.

McCann, D. 2017. "Two CFOs Tell a Tale of Fraud at HealthSouth." *CFO*. www.cfo.com/accounting-tax/2017/03/two-cfos-tell-tale-fraud-healthsouth/#:~:text=The%20infamous%20%242.8%20billion%20accounting,number%20of%20other%20company%20officials.

McCarthy, P. and C. Mayhew, eds. 2004. *Safeguarding the Organisation Against Violence and Bullying: An International Perspective*. London: Palgrave Macmillan.

McConkie, M.L. 1980. "Organizational Stories and the Practice of OD." *Southern Review of Public Administration* 4, no. 2, pp. 211–228.

McConnell, A. and L. Drennan. 2006. "Mission Impossible? Planning and Preparing for Crisis." *Journal of Contingencies and Crisis Management 14*, no. 2, pp. 59–70. https://doi.org/10.1111/j.1468-5973.2006.00482.x.

McCrum, D. 2019. "Wire Card's Suspect Accounting Practices Revealed." *Financial Times*. www.ft.com/content/19c6be2a-ee67-11e9-bfa4-b25f11f42901.

McCurley, S. and S. Vineyard. 1998. *Handling Problem Volunteers*. Downers Grove, IL: Heritage Arts Publishing/VMSystems.

McGill, N. 2016. "More Research Needed to Prevent, Understand Bullying, Report Finds." *The Nation's Health*. www.thenationshealth.org/content/46/6/E30.

Mehraein, V., F. Visintin, and D. Pittion. 2023. "The Dark Side of Leadership: A Systematic Review of Creativity and Innovation." *International Journal of Management Reviews*. https://onlinelibrary.wiley.com/doi/full/10.1111/ijmr.12334.

Meleen, M. 2020. "Facts About Past United Way Corruption and Scandals." *Love to Know*. https://charity.lovetoknow.com/charitable-organizations/facts-about-past-united-way-corruption-scandals.

Meloy, J.R., J. Hoffmann, E.R.D. Deisinger, and S.D. Hart. 2021. "Threat Assessment and Threat Management." In *International handbook of threat assessment,* eds. J.R. Meloy and J. Hoffmann, 3–21. Oxford University Press. https://doi.org/10.1093/med-psych/9780190940164.003.0001/.

Memon, M. 2022. "Organizational Culture Change: The Complete Guide." *Howspace.* https://howspace.com/blog/changing-organizational-culture-complete-guide/.

Merari, A. 1991. "Academic Research and Government Policy on Terrorism." *Terrorism and Political Violence* 3, no. 1, pp. 88–102.

Merkl, P. 1986. *Political Violence and Terror.* Berkeley, CA: University of California Press.

Meswani, H.R. 2008. "Safety and Occupational Health: Challenges and Opportunities in Emerging Economies." *Indian Journal of Occupational and Environmental Medicine* 12, no. 1, pp. 3–9. https://doi.org/10.4103/0019-5278.40808.

Mikkelsen, E. G. and S. Einarsen. 2002a. "Relationships Between Exposure to Bullying at Work and Psychological and Psychosomatic Health Complaints: The Role of State Negative Affectivity and Generalized Self-efficacy." *Scandinavian Journal of Psychology 43, no. 5,* pp. 397–405. https://doi.org/10.1111/1467-9450.00307.

Mikkelsen, E. G. and S. Einarsen. 2002b. "Basic Assumptions and Symptoms of Post-Traumatic Stress Among Victims of Bullying at Work." *European Journal of Work and Organizational Psychology 11, no.* 1, pp. 87–111. https://doi.org/10.1080/13594320143000861.

Miller, D. 2019. *Electrical Safety Case Studies.* https://blog.ehssoftware.io/safetyinsiderblog/electrical-safety-case-studies.

Miller, E.M. 2012. "Sexual Harassment and Bullying: Similar, But Not the Same. What School Officials Need to Know." *Clearing House: A Journal of Educational Strategies, Issues and Ideas* 90, pp. 191–197.

Miller, L. 2008. *From Difficult to Disturbed: Understanding and Managing Dysfunctional Employees.* New York, NY: AMACOM.

Misch, M. April 2015. "Safety Leadership: The Supervisor's Role." *Iron & Steel Technology* pp. 44–45.

Mlynek, J. 2021. "Investing in Safety—Every Dollar Spent Saves Company $3 to $5." *Grainnet Safety.* www.grainnetsafety.com/article/232910/investing-in-safety-every-dollar-spent-saves-a-company-3-to-5.

Montgomery, A. 2016. *Dysfunctional Organization: Definition and Cure.* www.intelligentmanagement.ws/dysfunctional-organization-definition-and-cure/#:~:text=The%20word%20dysfunctional%20contains%20the,goal%20it's%20supposed%20to%20pursue.

Moore, J.T., K.P. Cigularov, J.M. Sampson, J.C. Rosecrance, and P.Y. Chen. 2013. "Construction Workers' Reasons for Not Reporting Work-Related Injuries: An Exploratory Study." *International Journal of Occupational Safety and Ergonomics* 19, no. 1, pp. 97–105. https://doi.org/10.1080/10803548 .2013.11076969.

Moore, W. 2015. "A Tough Talk: Identifying Dysfunction to Clear the Way for New Ideas." *MyPurchasingCenter*. https://buyersmeetingpoint.com/ leadership-collaboration/entry/a-tough-talk-identifying-dysfunction-to-clear-the-way-for-new-ideas?format=amp.

Moreno-Jimenez, B., A. Rodriguez-Munoz, J.C. Pastor, A.I. Sanz-Vergel, and E. Garrosa. 2009. "The Moderating Effects of Psychological Detachment and Thoughts of Revenge in Workplace Bullying." *Personality and Individual Differences* 46, pp. 359–364.

Morley, D.D. and P. Shockley-Zalabak. 1991. "Setting the Rules: An Examination of the Influence of Organizational Founders' Values." *Management Communication Quarterly* 4, no. 4, pp. 422–449.

Morrison, K.W. 2016. "7 Common Workplace Safety Hazards." *Safety+Health*. www.safetyandhealthmagazine.com/articles/14054-common-workplace-safety-hazards.

Mugera, A.W. 2012. "Sustained Competitive Advantage in Agribusiness: Applying the Resource-Based Theory to Human Resources." *International Food and Agribusiness Management Review* 15, no. 4, pp. 27–48.

Murphy, K. 2012. "Re-Engineering Patient Safety Through EHR, Health IT." *Adoption & Implementation News, Xtelligent Healthcare Media*. https:// ehrintelligence.com/news/re-engineering-patient-safety-through-ehr-health-it.

Nahrgang, J.D., F.P. Morgeson, and D.A. Hofmann. 2011. "Safety at Work: A Meta-Analytic Investigation of the Link Between Job Demands, Job Resources, Burnout, Engagement, and Safety Outcomes." *Journal of Applied Psychology 96*, no. 1, pp. 71–94.

Naikal, A. and S. Chandra. 2013. "Organisational Culture: A Case Study." *International Journal of Knowledge Management and Practices* [S.l.], pp. 1724, ISSN 2320-7523. www.i-scholar.in/index.php/ijkmp/article/view/45315.

Nakase, B. 2019. "7 Tips on Toxic Work Environment Lawsuit." *Nakase Law Firm*. https://nakaselawfirm.com/7-tips-on-toxic-work-environment-lawsuit/.

Namie, G. 2021b. *2021 WBI U.S. Workplace Bullying Survey*. Workplace Bullying Institute. p. 5. www.workplacebullying.org (accessed May 2, 2023).

Nappo, N. 2019. "Is There an Association Between Working Conditions and Health? An analysis of the Sixth European Working Conditions Survey Data." *PLoS ONE* 14, no. 2, p. e0211294. https://doi.org/10.1371/journal .pone.0211294.

Nascimento, L.G.P., A.M.C. da Silva, E. Stedefeldt, and D.T. da Cunha. 2022. "Job Crafting and Burnout as Predictors of Food Safety Behaviors in the Foodservice Industry." *Foods* 11, no. 17, p. 2671. https://doi.org/10.3390/foods11172671.

Naseer, S., D. Bouckenooghe, F. Syed, A.K. Khan, and S. Qazi. 2020. "The Malevolent Side of Organizational Identification: Unraveling the Impact of Psychological Entitlement and Manipulative Personality on Unethical Work Behaviors." *Journal of Business and Psychology 35*, no. 3, pp. 333–346. https://doi.org/10.1007/s10869-019-09623-0.

NASP. 2023. "Guide to Psychosocial Safety." *NASP Blogger*. https://naspweb.com/blog/guide-to-psychosocial-safety/.

Nater, F., D.D. Van Fleet, and E.W. Van Fleet. 2023. *Combatting Workplace Violence: Creating and Maintaining Safe Work Environments*. Charlotte, NC: Information Age Publishing.

National Institute for Occupational Safety and Health. 2006. *Workplace Violence Prevention Strategies and Research Needs*. Cincinnati, Ohio: Department of Health and Human Services, National Institute for Occupational Safety and Health Publication Number 2006-144.

Naylis, G.J. 1996. "Corporate Terrorism: Managing the Threat." *Risk Management* 43, no. 6, pp. 24–48.

Needham, A.W. 2003. *Workplace Bullying: The Costly Business Secret*. Auckland, New Zealand: Penguin Books.

Nembhard, I.M. and A.C. Edmondson. 2006. "Making It Safe: The Effects of Leader Inclusiveness and Professional Status on Psychological Safety and Improvement Efforts in Health Care Teams." *Journal of Organizational Behavior* 27, no. 7, pp. 941–966.

Neuman, J.H. and R.A. Baron. 1997. "Aggression in the Workplace." In *Antisocial Behavior in Organizations*, eds. R. Giacalone and J. Greenberg, 37–67. Thousand Oaks: Sage.

Neuman, J.H. and R.A. Baron. 1998. "Workplace Violence and Workplace Aggression: Evidence Concerning Specific Forms, Potential Causes, and Preferred Targets." *Journal of Management* 24, pp. 391–419.

Neuman, J.H. and R.A. Baron. 2003. "Social Antecedents of Bullying. A Social Interactionist Perspective." In *Bullying and Emotional Abuse in the Workplace*, eds. S. Einarsen, H. Hoel, D. Zapf, and C.L. Cooper, 185–202. 1st ed. *International Perspectives in Research and Practice*. London: Taylor and Francis.

Newman, D. 2012. "Lookout: 8 Signs of Dysfunctional Management." *Future of Work*. https://fowmedia.com/lookout-8-signs-dysfunctional-management/.

Nguyen, V.T., S. Siengthai, F. Swierczek, and U.K. Bamel. 2019. "The Effects of Organizational Culture and Commitment on Employee Innovation: Evidence From Vietnam's IT Industry." *Journal of Asia Business Studies* 13, no. 4, pp. 719–742. https://doi.org/10.1108/JABS-09-2018-0253.

Nield, D. 2021. "How to Stop Spam Emails From Destroying Your Inbox: Thine Commercial Emails Shall Not Pass!" *Popular Science*. www.popsci.com/stop-spam-emails/.

Nielsen, M.B., L. Glasø, and S. Einarsen. 2017. "Exposure to Workplace Harassment and the Five-Factor Model of Personality: A Meta-Analysis." *Personality and Individual Differences* 104, pp. 195–206.

Nissen, A., M.B. Hansen, M.B. Nielsen, S. Knardahl, and T. Heir. 2019. "Employee Safety Perception Following Workplace Terrorism: A Longitudinal Study." *European Journal of Psychotraumatology* 10, no. 1, p. 1478584. https://doi.org/10.1080/20008198.2018.1478584.

Northwestern National Life Insurance Company. 1993. "Fear and Violence in the Workplace." *Research report*. Minneapolis, MN.

Notelaers, G., E. Baillien, H. De Witte, S. Einarsen, and J. Vermunt. 2013. "Testing the Strain Hypothesis of the Demand Control Model to Explain Severe Bullying at Work." *Economic and Industrial Democracy* 34, pp. 69–87.

Nunn, N. 2012. "Culture and the Historical Process." *Economic History of Developing Regions* 27, no. S1, pp. S108–S126. https://doi.org/10.1080/20780389.2012.664864.

Nussbaum, R. 2019. "Making Explicit Your Organization's Values, Norms, and Culture." *Puget Sound Chapter*. https://tinyurl.com/4f5v94hb.

O'Donohoe, J. and K. Kleinschmit. 2022. "Setting the Stage for Psychological Safety: 6 Steps for Leaders." *Health University of Utah*. https://accelerate.uofuhealth.utah.edu/resilience/setting-the-stage-for-psychological-safety-6-steps-for-leaders.

O'Hare, D. 1994. "The Rise of Kidnap and Ransom Risk." *Risk Management* 41, no. 7, pp. 83–90.

O'Leary-Kelly, A.M., R.W. Griffin, and D.J. Glew. 1996. "Organization-Motivated Aggression: A Research Framework." *Academy of Management Review* 21, no. 1, pp. 225–253.

O'Reilly, C.A. and J.A. Chatman. 2020. "Transformational Leader or Narcissist? How Grandiose Narcissists Can Create and Destroy Organizations and Institutions." *California Management Review* 62, no. 3, pp. 5–27. https://doi.org/10.1177/0008125620914989.

Obeidat, Z.M., A.A. Alalwan, A.M. Baabdullah, A.M. Obeidat, and Y.K. Dwivedi. 2022. "The Other Customer Online Revenge: A Moderated Mediation Model of Avenger Expertise and Message Trustworthiness." *Journal of Innovation & Knowledge* 7, no. 4. https://doi.org/10.1016/j.jik.2022.100230.

OSH Act of 1970. n.d. www.osha.gov/laws-regs/oshact/section5-duties.

OSHA: 3148-06R 2016. 2016. *Guidelines for Preventing Workplace Violence for Healthcare and Social Service Workers*. Washington DC: U.S. Department of Labor Occupational Safety and Health Administration.

Ouchi, W.G. 1981. *Theory Z: How American Business Can Meet the Japanese Challenge*. Boston, MA: Addison-Wesley.

Ouimet, G. 2010. "Dynamics of Narcissistic Leadership in Organizations: Towards an Integrated Research Model." *Journal of Managerial Psychology* 25, pp. 713–726.

Packard, D. 1995. *The HP Way: How Bill Hewlett and I Built Our Company*. New York, NY: Harper Business.

Panke, S. and B. Gaiser. 2009. "With My Head Up in the Clouds. Using Social Tagging to Organize Knowledge." *Journal of Business and Technical Communication* 23, pp. 318–349. https://doi.org/10.1177/1050651909333275.

Partridge, M. 2019. "Great Frauds in History: John Rigas and Adelphia." *MoneyWeek*. https://moneyweek.com/519832/great-frauds-in-history-john-rigas-and-adelphia.

Parzefall, M. and D. Salin. 2010. "Perceptions of and Reactions to Workplace Bullying: A Social Exchange Perspective." *Human Relations* 63, no. 6, pp. 761–780.

Paul, J., C.A. Strbiak, and N.E. Landrum. 2002. "Psychoanalytic Diagnosis of Top Management Team Dysfunction." *Journal of Managerial Psychology* 17, no. 5, pp. 381–393.

Paul, R.J. and J.B. Townsend. 1998. "Violence in the Workplace—A Review With Recommendations." *Employee Responsibilities and Rights Journal* 11, pp. 1–14. https://doi.org/10.1023/A:1027367831655.

Peters, T.J. and R.H. Waterman. 1982. *In Search of Excellence: Lessons From America's Best-Run Companies*. New York, NY: Harper and Row.

Peterson, D. 1980. *Analyzing Safety Performance*. New York, NY: Garland STPM Press.

Petrick, J.A. and F. Rinefort. 2004. "The Challenge of Managing China's Workplace Safety." *Business & Society Review 109*, no. 2, pp. 171–181.

Petrick, J.A. and F.C. Rinefort. 2006. "The Challenge of Managing Mexican Workplace Safety." *Business & Society Review 111*, no. 2, pp. 223–234.

Petrick, J.A., F. Rinefort, and V. Yen. 2008. "The Ongoing Challenge and Promise of Managing China's Workplace Safety." *Global Business and Finance Review 13*, no. 1, pp. 47–57.

Picincu, A. 2020. "5 Most Common Ways Employee Theft Occurs." *CHRON*. https://smallbusiness.chron.com/list-three-crimes-affect-businesses-64360.html.

Piercy, N.F. and N. Lane. 2006. "Ethical and Moral Dilemmas Associated With Strategic Relationships Between Business-to-Business Buyers and Sellers." *Journal of Business Ethics* 72, no. 1, pp. 87–102.

Piff, P.K., D.M. Stancato, S. Côté, R. Mendoza-Denton, and D. Keltner. 2012. "Higher Social Class Predicts Increased Unethical Behavior." *PNAS Proceedings of the National Academy of Sciences of the United States of America 109*, no. 11, pp. 4086–4091. https://doi.org/10.1073/pnas.1118373109.

Pillar, P.R. 2001. *Terrorism and US Foreign Policy*. Washington DC: Brookings Institution Press.

Pindar, J. 2023. "What Is Psychological Safety at Work?" *Champion Health*. https://championhealth.co.uk/insights/psychological-safety-at-work/.

Pinkley, R.L., M.J. Gelfand, and L. Duan. 2005. "When, Where and How: The Use of Multidimensional Scaling Methods in the Study of Negotiation and Social Conflict." *International Negotiation* 10, pp. 79–96. https://doi.org/10.1163/1571806054741056.

Plomp, J., M. Tims, S.V. Khapova, P.G.W. Jansen, and A.B. Bakker. 2019. "Psychological Safety, Job Crafting, and Employability: A Comparison Between Permanent and Temporary Workers." *Organizational Psychology* p. 10. https://doi.org/10.3389/fpsyg.2019.00974.

Pomerantz, S.L. 1987. "FBI and Terrorism." *FBI Law Enforcement Bulletin* 56, no. 11, pp. 14–17.

Porath, C. and C. Pearson. 2013. "The Price of Incivility." *Harvard Business Review* 91, no. 1–2, pp. 114–121, 146.

Porath, C.L. and A. Erez. 2007. "Does Rudeness Matter? The Effects of Rude Behavior on Task Performance and Helpfulness." *Academy of Management Journal* 50, no. 5, pp. 1181–1197.

Porath, C.L. and A. Erez. 2009. "Overlooked But Not Untouched: How Incivility Reduces Onlookers' Performance on Routine and Creative Tasks." *Organizational Behavior and Human Decision Processes* 109, no. 1, pp. 29–44.

Post, J.M. 1990. "Terrorist Psycho-Logic: Terrorist Behaviour as a Product of Psychological Forces." In *Origins of Terrorism: Psychologies, Ideologies, Theologies, States of Mind*, ed. W. Reich, 25–40. New York, NY: Cambridge University Press.

Prest, R. 2020. "The Supervisor's Crucial Role in Safety Performance." *Occupational Health & Safety*. https://ohsonline.com/Articles/2020/10/01/The-Supervisors-Crucial-Role-in-Safety-Performance.aspx.

Prince, M., D. Palihawadana, M.A.P. Davies, and R.D. Winsor. 2016. "An Integrative Framework of Buyer-Supplier Negative Relationship Quality and Dysfunctional Interfirm Conflict." *Journal of Business-to-Business Marketing* 23, no. 3, pp. 221–234.

Proce, J. n.d. *The 7 Habits of Highly Dysfunctional Leaders*. Texas: The City of Anna. https://nctcog.org/getmedia/6dbb3336-f7f7-4882-ba6e-bac2a1cb8c12/APWA-7-Habits-NCTCOG.pdf.

Prosser, T.F. 2008. "Dysfunctional Organizations Are Like Dysfunctional Families." *Musings on Effective Management*. https://oneffectivemanagement.wordpress.com/2008/06/12/dysfunctional-organizations-are-like-dysfunctional-families/.

Proyer, M.G., J.D. Oyler, and R.Y. Odom. 2013. "Out-of-Control Executives: What Trumps Smart?" *Journal of Management Policy and Practice* 14, pp. 11–18.

Psychogios, A., M. Nyfoudi, N. Theodorakopoulos, L.T. Szamosi, and R. Prouska. 2019. "Many Hands Lighter Work? Deciphering the Relationship Between Adverse Working Conditions and Organization Citizenship Behaviours in Small and Medium-sized Enterprises During a Severe Economic Crisis." *British Journal of Management* 30, no. 3, pp. 519–537.

Qualls, M. and the CultureAlly Team. 2022. "What Is Psychological Safety?" *CultureAlly.* www.cultureally.com/blog/whatispsychologicalsafety.

Radecki, D., L. Hull, J. McCusker, and C. Ancona. 2018. *Psychological Safety: Managing the Hidden Drivers of Individual Behavior and Team Success.* San Francisco, CA: Academy of Brain-based Leadership.

Ramsay S., A. Troth, and S. Branch. 2011. "Work-place Bullying: A Group Processes Framework." *Journal of Occupational and Organizational Psychology* 84, pp. 799–816.

Rao, K.S. 2022. "Consequences of Organisational Culture." *The Hans India.* www.thehansindia.com/hans/young-hans/business-communication-as-a-career-775846?infinitescroll=1.

Rasool, S.F., M. Wang, M. Tang, A. Saeed, and J. Iqbal. 2021. "How Toxic Workplace Environment Effects the Employee Engagement: The Mediating Role of Organizational Support and Employee Wellbeing." *International Journal of Environmental Research and Public Health* 18, no. 5, p. 2294. https://doi.org/10.3390/ijerph18052294.

Raver, J. L. 2013. "Counter Productive Work Behavior and Conflict: Merging Complementary Domains." *Negotiation and Conflict Management Research* 6, no. 3, pp. 151–159.

Ravishankar, R.A. 2022. "A Guide to Building Psychological Safety on Your Team." *Harvard Business Review.* https://hbr.org/2022/12/a-guide-to-building-psychological-safety-on-your-team.

Rayner, C. 2002. "*Round Two! Redefining Bullying at Work.*" Paper presented at The Academy of Management Meeting, Denver, CO.

Rayner, C. and C.L. Cooper. 2006. "Workplace Bullying." In *Handbook of Workplace Violence*, eds. E.K. Kelloway, J. Barling, and J.J. Hurrell, Jr., 121–146. Thousand Oaks, CA: Sage.

Rayner, C. and L. Keashley. 2005. "Bullying at Work: A Perspective From Britain and North America." In *Counterproductive Work Behavior: Investigations of Actors and Targets*, eds. S. Fox and P.E. Spector, 271–296. Washington DC: American Psychological Association.

Rayner, C., H. Hoel, and C.L. Cooper. 2002. *Workplace Bullying: What We Know, Who Is to Blame, and What Can We Do?* London: Taylor & Francis. https://doi.org/10.1201/b12811.

Reed, K. 2015. "The 5 Dysfunctional Employees Leaders Must Be Aware of at All Times." *Linkedin.* www.linkedin.com/pulse/5-dysfunctional-employees-leaders-must-aware-all-times-kelvin-redd/?trk=articles_directory.

Reich, W., ed. 1990. *Origins of Terrorism: Psychologies, Ideologies, Theologies, States of Mind.* New York, NY: Cambridge University Press.

Renkema, E., M. Broekhuis, M. Tims, and K. Ahaus. 2022. "Working Around: Job Crafting in the Context of Public and Professional Accountability." *Human Relations* 0, no. 0. https://doi.org/10.1177/00187267221104011.

Reynald, D.M. 2016. *Guarding Against Crime.* Ebook. https://doi.org/10.4324/9781315586007.

Rickard, B. n.d. "When Is Bullying Sexual Harassment?" *EduGuide.* www.eduguide.org/article/when-is-bullying-sexual-harassment.

Rinefort, F. and J.A. Petrick. 2004. "Occupational Safety and Health in the United Kingdom, France, Germany and the European Community." *Revista IMES Administracao 21*, no. 60, pp. 23–30.

Rinefort, F. and J.A. Petrick. 2006. "Occupational Safety and Health Trends in the Four East Asian Tigers." *Global Business and Finance Review 11*, no. 1, pp. 79–87.

Rinefort, F., D. Boggs, J. Petrick, and B.M. Farmer. 2014. "The Challenge of Occupational Safety and Health in Greece." *Advances in Management & Applied Economics 4*, no. 3, pp. 89–95.

Rinefort, F.C. and D.D. Van Fleet. 1993. "Safety Issues Beyond the Workplace: Estimate Relationships Between Work Injuries and Available Supervision." *Employee Responsibilities and Rights Journal* 6, no. 1, pp. 1–8. https://doi.org/10.1007/BF01384752.

Rinefort, F.C. and D.D. Van Fleet. June 1998. "Work Injuries and Employee Turnover." *American Business Review*, pp. 9–13.

Rinefort, F.C. and J.A. Petrick. 2015. "India: The Ongoing Challenge of Worker Safety and Health." *The Journal of Global Business Management 11*, no. 2, pp. 114–120.

Rinefort, F.C., D.D. Van Fleet, and E.W. Van Fleet. September 1998. "Downsizing: A Strategy That May Be Hazardous to Your Organization's Health." *International Journal of Management* 15, no. 3, pp. 335–339.

Rinefort, F.C., J.A. Petrick, and V. Schukin. 2001. "Occupational Safety and Health in Russia: Past, Present and Future." *Professional Safety 46*, no. 5, pp. 19–23.

Robert, B. and C. Lajtha. 2002. "A New Approach to Crisis Management." *Journal of Contingency and Crisis Management* 10, pp. 181–191. https://doi.org/10.1111/1468-5973.00195.

Robinson, S.L. and R.J. Bennett. 1995. "A Typology of Deviant Workplace Behaviors: A Multidimensional Scaling Study." *Academy of Management Journal* 38, no. 2, pp. 555–572.

Robotham, D., C.H. Plaza, and S. Windon. 2021. "How to Deal With a Bad Volunteer: Challenges and Solutions." *PennState Extension.* https://extension.psu.edu/how-to-deal-with-a-bad-volunteer-challenges-and-solution.

Rodriguez, J.L. 2020. "Psychosocial Safety Climate, Psychosocial Safety Behavior, and Injury Reporting among Latino and Non-Latino Construction Workers in New York City: A Correlational Study." *ProQuest.* Number 28002199. www.proquest.com/openview/702bae847fab963128dee9e010ee5ed0/1?pq-origsite=gscholar&cbl=18750&diss=y.

Rogers, C.R. 1954. "Toward a Theory of Creativity." *ETC: A Review of General Semantics* 11, pp. 249–260.

Rogers, C.R. 1970. "Towards a Theory of Creativity." In *Creativity: Selected Readings*, ed. P.E. Vernon, 137–152. Harmondsworth, Middlesex, England: Penguin Books. Reprint of Rogers, 1954.

Roloff, J. and R.J. Aßländer. 2010. "Corporate Autonomy and Buyer–Supplier Relationships: The Case of Unsafe Mattel Toys." *Journal of Business Ethics* 97, pp. 517–534. https://doi.org/10.1007/s10551-010-0522-1.

Rosander, M. and M.B. Nielsen. 2023. "Witnessing Bullying at Work: Inactivity and the Risk of Becoming the Next Target." *Psychology of Violence 13*, no. 1, pp. 34–42.

Roscigno, V.J. 2019. "Discrimination, Sexual Harassment, and the Impact of Workplace Power." *Socius: Sociological Research for a Dynamic World* 5, pp. 1–21.

Roscigno, V.J., S.H. Lopez, and R. Hodson. 2009. "Supervisory Bullying, Status Inequalities and Organizational Context." *Social Forces* 87, no. 3, pp. 1561–1589.

Summarized by Sidle, S.D. 2009. "Is Your Organization a Great Place for Bullies to Work?" *Academy of Management Perspectives* 23, no. 4, pp. 89–91.

Rosen, M. 1985. "Breakfast at Spiro's: Drammaturgy and Dominance." *Journal of Management Studies* 11, no. 2, pp. 3184.

Rosenthal, P. and A. Budjanovcanin. 2011. "Sexual Harassment Judgments by British Employment Tribunals 1995-2005: Implications for Claimants and Their Advocates." *British Journal of Industrial Relations* 49, pp. S236–S257. https://doi.org/10.1111/j.1467-8543.2010.00820.x.

Roumeliotis, J.D. 2022. "The Dysfunctional Organization: Weak Company Culture and Negligent Leadership as the Culprits." https://theboldbusinessexpert.com/2022/04/03/the-dysfunctional-organization-weak-company-culture-and-negligent-leadership-as-the-culprits/.

Rozell, E.J. January 23, 2015. "Is Your Workplace Dysfunctional?" *SpringfieldNews-Leader.* www.news-leader.com/story/news/business/2015/01/24/workplace-dysfunctional/22247041/.

Ruby, C.L. 2002. "The Definition of Terrorism." *Asap Analysis of Social Issues and Public Policy* 2, no. 1, pp. 9–14.

Saam, N.J. 2010. "Interventions in Workplace Bullying: A Multilevel Approach." *European Journal of Work and Organizational Psychology* 19, no. 1, pp. 51–75.

Sachs, C., P. Allen, A.R. Terman, J. Hayden, and C. Hatcher. 2014. "Front and Back of the House: SocioSpatial Inequalities in Food Work." *Agriculture and Human Values* 31, no. 1, pp. 3–17.

Saguy, A.C. 2011. "French and U.S. Legal Approaches to Sexual Harassment." *Travail, Genre et Sociétés* 49, pp. 236–257.

Salin, D. 2003. "Ways of Explaining Workplace Bullying: A Review of Enabling, Motivating and Precipitating Structures and Processes in the Work Environment." *Human Relations* 56, no. 10, pp. 1213–1232.

Sanchez, A. 2020. "The High Cost of Toxic Workplace Culture Report Findings." *Linkedin*. www.linkedin.com/pulse/high-cost-toxic-workplace-culture-report-findings-dr-di-ann/.

Sandhu, P. 2023. "9 Signs You're in a Toxic Work Environment—and What to Do About It." *Themuse*. www.themuse.com/advice/toxic-work-environment.

Savas, O. 2019. "Impact of Dysfunctional Leadership on Organizational Performance." *Global Journal of Management and Business Research* 19, no. 1, pp. 37–41.

Schat, A.C.H., M.R. Frone, and E.K. Kelloway. 2006. "Prevalence of Workplace Aggression in the U.S. Workforce: Findings From a National Study." In *Handbook of Workplace Violence*, eds. E.K. Kelloway, J. Barling, and J.J. Hurrell, 47–89. Thousand Oaks: Sage.

Schein, E.H. and W.G. Bennis. 1965. *Personal and Organizational Change Through Group Methods: The Laboratory Approach*. New York, NY: Wiley.

Schmid, A.P. 2011. "The Definition of Terrorism." In *The Routledge Handbook of Terrorism Research*, ed. A.P. Schmid, 39–98. New York, NY: Routledge.

Schmid, A.P. 2012. "The Revised Academic Consensus Definition of Terrorism." *Perspectives on Terrorism* 6, no. 2, pp. 158–159.

Schouten, R., M.V. Callahan, and S. Bryant. 2004. "Community Response to Disaster: The Role of the Workplace." *Harvard Review of Psychiatry* 12, no. 4, pp. 229–237.

Schulte, P.A. 2020. "A Global Perspective on Addressing Occupational Safety and Health Hazards in the Future of Work." *La Medicina del Lavoro* 111, no. 3, pp. 163–165. https://doi.org/10.23749/mdl.v111i3.9735.

Scorza, J. 2018. "Drive Innovation With Psychological Safety." *SHRM Book Blog*. www.linkedin.com/pulse/do-we-need-psychological-safety-psychosocial-whats-elena-lennox/?trk=pulse-article_more-articles_related-content-card.

Scotti, A.J. 1986. *Executive Safety and International Terrorism: A Guide for Travelers*, pp. 43–46. Englewood Cliffs, NJ, NewJersey: Prentice-Hall, Inc.

Sewell, G. and J.R. Barker. 2006. "Coercion Versus Care: Using Irony to Make Sense of Organizational Surveillance." *The Academy of Management Review* 31, no. 4, pp. 934–961. https://doi.org/10.2307/20159259.

Shahidi, F.V., M.A.M.N. Gignac, J. Oudyk, and P.M. Smith. 2021. "Assessing the Psychosocial Work Environment in Relation to Mental Health: A Comprehensive Approach." *Annals of Work Exposures and Health* 65, no. 4, pp. 418–431.

Shapiro, D.L. and M.A. Von Glinow. 2007. "Why Bad Leaders Stay in Good Places." In *Research Companion to the Dysfunctional Workplace*, ed. C.L. Cooper, 90–109. Northampton, MA: Edward Elgar Publishing, Inc.

Shelman, M. and A.J. Connolly. 2012. "The Human Capital Issue: Ensuring the Future of Food and Agribusiness. Editor's Introduction." *International Food and Agribusiness Management Review* 15, no. Special Issue A, pp. 1–2.

Shoben, E.J. 1983. "Applications of Multidimensional Scaling in Cognitive Psychology." *Applied Psychological Measurement* 7, pp. 473–490. https://doi.org/10.1177/014662168300700406.

Shuck, B., K. Rose, and M. Bergman. 2015. "Inside the Spiral of Dysfunction: The Personal Consequences of Working for a Dysfunctional Leader." *New Horizons in Adult Education and Human Resource Development* 27, no. 4, pp. 51–58.

Shullich, R. 2011. "Risk Assessment of Social Media." *International Journal of Electronic Commerce* 2, no. 2, pp. 103–126.

Sims, R.L. and P. Sun. 2012. "Witnessing Workplace Bullying and the Chinese Manufacturing Employee." *Journal of Managerial Psychology* 27, no. 1, pp. 9–26.

Sinclair, J. and M. Cardew-Hall. 2008. "The Folksonomy Tag Cloud: When Is It Useful?" *Journal of Information Science* 34, pp. 15–29. https://doi.org/10.1177/0165551506078083

Sjöblom, K., J.-P. Mäkiniemi, and A. Mäkikangas. 2022. "'I Was Given Three Marks and Told to Buy a Porsche'—Supervisors' Experiences of Leading Psychosocial Safety Climate and Team Psychological Safety in a Remote Academic Setting." *International Journal of Environmental Research and Public Health* 19, no. 19, p. 12016. https://doi.org/10.3390/ijerph191912016.

Slavich, G.M. 2020. "Social Safety Theory: A Biologically Based Evolutionary Perspective on Life Stress, Health, and Behavior." *Annual Review of Clinical Psychology* 16, pp. 265–295. https://doi.org/10.1146/annurev-clinpsy-032816-045159.

Sloan, S. 1986. *Beating International Terrorism; An Action Strategy for Preemption and Punishment*. Maxwell Air Force Base, AL: Air University Press.

Sloan, S. 2000. *Beating International Terrorism; An Action Strategy for Preemption and Punishment*. Revised edition. Maxwell Air Force Base, AL: Air University Press.

Smith, P.K., H. Cowie, R.F. Olafsson, and A.P.D. Liefooghe. 2002. "Definitions of Bullying: A Comparison of Terms Used, and Age and Gender Differences, in a Fourteen-Country International Comparison." *Child Development* 73, pp. 1119–1133.

Smokowski, P.R. and K.H. Kopasz. 2005. "Bullying in School: An Overview of Types, Effects, Family Characteristics, and Intervention Strategies." *Children & Schools* 27, no. 2, pp. 101–110.

Smolinski, J. 2011. "Sexual Harassment Versus Bullying." *AAUW Community*. www.aauw.org/2011/09/29/sexual-harassment-versus-bullying/.

Sorkin, A.R. September 13, 2002. "2 Top Tyco Executives Charged With $600 Million Fraud Scheme." *The New York Times*, Section A, p. 1.

Soule, J.W. 1989. "Problems in Applying Counterterrorism to Prevent Terrorism: Two Decades of Violence in Northern Ireland Reconsidered." *Terrorism* 12, no. 1, pp. 31–46.

Southern Poverty Law Center. 2010. *Injustice on Our Plates: Immigrant Women in the US Food Industry,* Montgomery, Ala.: Southern Poverty Law Center.

Sparks, R.F. 1982. "Paradox of Employee Theft—A Dilemma for Management." *New Jersey Bell Journal* 5, no. 2, pp. 18–27.

Specht, J., A. Kuonath, D. Pachler, S. Weisweiler, and D. Frey. 2018. "How Change Agents' Motivation Facilitates Organizational Change: Pathways Through Meaning and Organizational Identification." *Journal of Change Management* 18, no. 3, pp. 198–217. https://doi.org/10.1080/14697017 .2017.1378696.

Spigener, J., G. Lyon, and T. McSween. 2022. "Behavior-Based Safety 2022: Today's Evidence." *Journal of Organizational Behavior Management* 42, no. 4, pp. 336–359. https://doi.org/10.1080/01608061.2022.2048943.

Spillan, J.E. 2003. "An Explanatory Model for Evaluating Crisis Events & Managers' Concerns in Not-Profit Organisations." *Journal of Contingencies & Crisis Management* 11, pp. 160–169. http://dx.doi.org/10.1111/j.0966-0879.2003.01104002.x.

Staernose, T. 2013. *India Must Have Zero Tolerance for Workplace Sexual Harassment.* www.ilo.org/asia/info/public/WCMS_220527/lang--en/index .htm.

Stanislaw, D. 2022. *5 Symptoms of Organizational Dysfunction.* https:// stanislawconsulting.com/5-symptoms-of-organizational-dysfunction/.

Stein, N. 2003. "Bullying or Sexual Harassment? The Missing Discourse of Rights in an Era of Zero Tolerance." *Arizona Law Review* 45, pp. 783–799.

Stein, N. and K. Mennemeier. 2011. *Addressing the Gendered Dimensions of Harassment and Bullying: What Domestic and Sexual Violence Advocates Need to Know.* [Critical issue brief]. Washington DC: National Resource Center on Domestic Violence and National Sexual Violence Resource Center.

Steinert, C., N. Heim, and F. Leichsenring. 2021. "Procrastination, Perfectionism, and Other Work-Related Mental Problems: Prevalence, Types, Assessment, and Treatment-A Scoping Review." *Frontiers in Psychiatry* 12, p. 736776. https://doi.org/10.3389/fpsyt.2021.736776.

Stieg, C. 2020. "'Psychological Safety' at Work Improves Productivity–Here Are 4 Ways to Get It, According to a Harvard Expert. Make It." www.cnbc.com/2020/10/05/why-psychological-safety-is-important-at-work-and-how-to-create-it.html.

Straus, S. 2012. *Sexual Harassment and Bullying: A Guide to Keeping Kids Safe and Holding Schools Accountable.* Lanham, MD: Rowman & Littlefield Publishers.

Straus, S. 2016. *Is It Bullying or Sexual Harassment?* St. Paul, MN: Minnesota Women's Press. www.womenspress.com/main.asp?SectionID=2&SubSectionID=692&ArticleID=4118.

Straus, S. November 15, 2011. "Bullying vs. Sexual Harassment—Do You Know the Difference?" *Ms. Magazine Blog.* www.msmagazine.com/blog/2011/11/15/bullying-vs-sexual-harassmentdo-you-know-the-difference/.

Strikwerda, L. 2022. "5 Tips for Creating a Safety Committee That Will Make a Difference at Your Company." *WorkforceHub.* www.workforcehub.com/blog/5-tips-for-creating-a-safety-committee-that-will-make-a-difference-at-your-company/.

Stroup, B. (n.d.). "5 Habits of Dysfunctional Leaders." *Velocity Strategy Solutions.* Available at: https://blog.velocitystrategysolutions.com/5-habits-of-dysfunctional-leaders.

Sull, D., C. Sull, and B. Zweig. 2022. "Toxic Culture Is Driving the Great Resignation." *MIT Sloan Management Review.* https://sloanreview.mit.edu/article/toxic-culture-is-driving-the-great-resignation/.

Sutcliffe, K.M., E. Lewton, and M.M. Rosenthal. 2004. "Communication Failures: An Insidious Contributor to Medical Mishaps." *Academy of Medicine* 14, no. 2, pp. 186–194. https://doi.org/10.1097/00001888-200402000-00019.

Sutherland, E.H. 1940. "White-Collar Criminality." *American Sociological Review* 5, pp. 1–12.

Sutton, R. 2010. *The No Asshole Rule.* New York, NY: Business Plus.

Swartz Swidler. 2019. "8 Types of Workplace Harassment (and How to Stop Them)." https://swartz-legal.com/8-types-of-workplace-harassment-and-how-to-stop-them/.

Swendiman, R.A., A.C. Edmondson, and N.N. Mahmoud. 2019. "Burnout in Surgery Viewed Through the Lens of Psychological Safety." *Annals of Surgery* 269, no. 2, pp. 234–235.

Tabak, F. and W. Smith. 2005. "Privacy and Electronic Monitoring in the Workplace: A Model of Managerial Cognition and Relational Trust Development." *Employee Responsibilities and Rights Journal* 17, no. 3, pp. 173–189.

Tams, S., J. Thatcher, V. Grover, and R. Pak. 2015. "Selective Attention as a Protagonist in Contemporary Workplace Stress: Implications for the Interruption Age." *Anxiety, Stress, & Coping* 28, no. 6, pp. 663–686. https://doi.org/10.1080/10615806.2015.1011141.

TandemHR. 2022. "The Importance of Psychological Safety at Work." *TandemHR.* https://tandemhr.com/the-importance-of-psychological-safety-at-work/.

Ten Have, M., S. Van Dorsselaer, and R. de Graaf. 2015. "The Association Between Type and Number of Adverse Working Conditions and Mental Health During a Time of Economic Crisis (2010–2012)." *Social Psychiatry and Psychiatric Epidemiology* 50, pp. 899–907.

Tepper, B.J. 2000. "Consequences of Abusive Supervision." *Academy of Management Journal* 43, no. 2, pp. 178–190.

Tepper, B.J. 2007. "Abusive Supervision in Work Organizations: Review, Synthesis, and Research Agenda." *Journal of Management* 33, no. 3, pp. 261–289.

Tepper, B.J., S.E. Moss, and M.K. Duffy. 2011. "Predictors of Abusive Supervision: Supervisor Perceptions of Deep-Level Dissimilarity, Relationship Conflict, and Subordinate Performance." *Academy of Management Journal* 54, no. 2, pp. 279–294.

Thiede, I. and M. Thiede. 2015. "Quantifying the Costs and Benefits of Occupational Health and Safety Interventions at a Bangladesh Shipbuilding Company." *International Journal of Occupational and Environmental Health* 21, no. 2, pp. 127–136. https://doi.org/10.1179/2049396714Y.0000000100.

Thomas, C. 2018. "Definition of a Dysfunctional Organization: The United Methodist Church." *The Thoughtful Pastor, Patheos.* www.patheos.com/blogs/thoughtfulpastor/2018/11/04/definition-dysfunctional-united-methodist-church/.

Thoring, K. n.d. "The Power of The Workspace to Change Organizational Culture." *Better Innovation Space.* www.betterinnovationspace.com/culture.

Tiwari, B. and U. Lenka. 2016. "Building Psychological Safety for Employee Engagement in Post-Recession." *Development and Learning in Organizations* 30, no. 1, pp. 19–22. https://doi.org/10.1108/DLO-05-2015-0044.

Tomlinson, E.C. and J. Greenberg. 2007. "Understanding and Deterring Employee Theft With Organizational Justice." In *Research Companion to the Dysfunctional Workplace*, ed. C.L. Cooper, 285–301. Northampton, MA: Edward Elgar Publishing, Inc.

Tracy, S.J., P. Lutgen-Sandvik, and J.K. Alberts. 2006. "Nightmares, Demons, and Slaves: Exploring the Painful Metaphors of Workplace Bullying." *Management Communication Quarterly* 20, no. 2, pp. 1–38.

Tsai, Y. 2011. "Relationship Between Organizational Culture, Leadership Behavior and Job Satisfaction." *BMC Health Services Research* 11, p. 98. https://doi.org/10.1186/1472-6963-11-98.

Tucker, S. and N. Turner. 2013. "Waiting for Safety: Responses by Young Canadian Workers to Unsafe Work." *Journal of Safety Research* 45, pp. 103–110. https://doi.org/10.1016/j.jsr.2013.01.006.

Tuckman, B.W. 1965. "Developmental Sequence in Small Groups." *Psychological Bulletin* 63, no. 6, pp. 384–399.

Tuckman, B.W. and M.A.C. Jensen. 1977. "Stages of Small-Group Development Revisited." *Group & Organization Studies* 2, no. 4, pp. 419–427. https://doi.org/10.1177/105960117700200404.

Tulshyan, R. 2021. "Why Is It So Hard to Speak Up at Work?" *The New York Times.* www.nytimes.com/2021/03/15/us/workplace-psychological-safety.html.

Tzeng, J., H.H. Lu, and W.-H. Li. 2008. "Multidimensional Scaling for Large Genomic Sets." *BMC Biometrics* 9, p. 179.

U.S. Department of Agriculture. 2001. *The USDA Handbook on Workplace Violence and Prevention.* Washington DC: Office of Civil Rights. www.dm.usda.gov/workplace.pdf.

U.S. Department of Labor, Bureau of Labor Statistics. 2017. *The Economics Daily: Homicides in Retail Trade, 2003-2008.* U.S. Department of Labor. Available online at https://www.bls.gov/opub/ted/2012/ted_20120104.htm.

Vaez, M., K. Ekberg, and L. Laflamme. 2004. "Abusive Events at Work Among Young Working Adults: Magnitude of the Problem and Its Effect on Self-Rated Health." *Industrial Relations* 59, no. 3, pp. 569–583.

Vaisman-Tzachor, R. 1991. "Stress and Coping Styles in Personnel of a Terrorism Prevention Team." *Journal of Social Behavior and Personality* 6, no. 4, pp. 889–902.

Vaisman-Tzachor, R. 1997. "Positive Impact of Prior Military Combat Exposure on Terrorism Prevention Work: Inoculation to Stress." *International Journal of Stress Management* 4, pp. 29–45. https://doi.org/10.1007/BF02766071.

Van Fleet, D.D., and E.W. Van Fleet. 2006. "Internal Terrorists: The Terrorists Inside Organizations." *Journal of Managerial Psychology* 21, no. 8, pp. 763774.

Van Fleet, D.D. and E.W. Van Fleet. 1996. *Workplace Violence: Moving toward Minimizing Risks (Curriculum Module 96-002).* Cincinnati, OH: Minerva Education Institute.

Van Fleet, D.D. and E.W. Van Fleet. 2007. "Preventing Workplace Violence: The Violence Volcano Metaphor." *Journal of Applied Management and Entrepreneurship* 12, no. 3, pp. 17–36.

Van Fleet, D.D. and E.W. Van Fleet. 2010. *The Violence Volcano: Reducing the Threat of Workplace Violence.* Charlotte, NC: Information Age Publishing.

Van Fleet, D.D. and E.W. Van Fleet. 2012. "Towards a Behavioral Description of Managerial Bullying." *Employee Responsibilities and Rights Journal* 24, no. 3, pp. 197–215.

Van Fleet, D.D. and E.W. Van Fleet. 2014. "Future Challenges and Issues of Bullying in the Workplace." In *Bullying in the Workplace: Causes, Symptoms, and Remedies,* eds. L.M. Crothers and J Lipinski, 550–577. New York, NY: Routledge/Taylor and Francis.

Van Fleet, D.D. and E.W. Van Fleet. 2022. *Bullying and Harassment at Work: An Innovative Approach to Understanding and Prevention.* Northampton, MA: Edward Elgar Publishing Inc.

Van Fleet, D.D. and R.W. Griffin. 2006. "Dysfunctional Organization Culture: The Role of Leadership in Motivating Dysfunctional Work Behaviors." *Journal of Managerial Psychology* 21, no. 8, pp. 698–708.

Van Fleet, D.D., E.W. Van Fleet, and G.J. Seperich. 2014. *Agribusiness: Principles of Management.* Clifton Park, NY: Delmar/Cengage Learning.

Van Fleet, D.D., L. White, and E.W. Van Fleet. 2018. "Baseballs or Cricket Balls: On the Meanings of Bullying and Harassment." *Journal of Human Resource and Sustainability Studies* 6, no. 1, pp. 131–148.

Van Fleet, E.W. and D.D. Van Fleet. 1998. "Terrorism and the Workplace: Concepts and Recommendations." In *Dysfunctional Behavior in Organizations: Violent and Deviant Behavior*, eds. R.W. Griffin, A. O'Leary-Kelly, and J. Collins, 165–201. Vol. 23, Part A. Greenwich, CT, Connecticut: JAI Press.

Van Fleet, E.W. and D.D. Van Fleet. 2007. *Workplace Survival: Dealing With Bad Bosses, Bad Workers, Bad Jobs.* Frederick, MD: PublishAmerica.

Van Fleet, E.W. and D.D. Van Fleet. 2010. *The Violence Volcano: Reducing the Threat of Workplace Violence.* Charlotte, NC: Information Age Publishing.

Van Fleet, E.W. and D.D. Van Fleet. 2014. *Violence at Work: What Everyone Should Know.* Charlotte, NC: Information Age Publishing.

Van Jaarsveld, D.D., D.D. Walker, and D.P. Skarlicki. 2010. "The Role of Job Demands and Emotional Exhaustion in the Relationship Between Customer and Employee Incivility." *Journal of Management* 36, no. 6, pp. 1486–1504. https://doi.org/10.1177/0149206310368998.

Vardi, Y and E. Weitz. 2016. *Misbehavior in Organizations.* New York, NY: Routledge.

Vardi, Y. and Y. Wiener. 1996. "Misbehavior in Organizations: A Motivational Framework." *Organizational Science* 7, no. 2, pp. 151–165.

Vartia M.A. 2001. "Consequences of Workplace Bullying With Respect to the Well-Being of Its Targets and the Observers of Bullying." *Scandinavian Journal of Work, Environment & Health* 27, no. 1, pp. 63–69.

Veiga, J.F., T.D. Golden, and K. Dechant. 2004. "Why Managers Bend Company Rules." *Academy of Management Perspectives 18*, pp. 84–90.

Ventiv Technology. 2023. "How Stress Impacts Workplace Safety." www.ventivtech.com/blog/how-stress-impacts-workplace-safety.

Viegas, F.B. and M. Wattenberg. 2008. "Tag Clouds and the Case for Vernacular Visualization." *Interactions* 15, pp. 49–52. https://doi.org/10.1145/1374489.1374501.

Villena, V.H., T.Y. Choi, and E. Revilla. November–December 2016. "Managing the Dark Side of Collaborative Buyer-Supplier Relationships." *Supply Chain Management Review*, pp. 50–55. https://ssrn.com/abstract=2773637.

Vinney, C. 2021. "What Are the Different Types of Bullying?" www.verywellmind. com/what-are-the-different-types-of-bullying-5207717.

Walek, T. 2018. "Concept, Origin and Classification of Terrorist Phenomena." *Securitologia* 2, pp. 107–119.

Wallace, J. and K.P. Gaylor. 2012. "Study of the Dysfunctional and Functional Aspects of Voluntary Employee Turnover." *S.A.M. Advanced Management Journal* 77, no. 3, pp. 27–36.

Wegner, A. n.d. "How to Create Psychological Safety at Work: 5 Steps." www .babbelforbusiness.com/blog/how-to-create-psychological-safety-at-work/.

Weinberg, L., A. Pedahzur, and S. Hirsch-Hoefler. 2004. "The Challenges of Conceptualizing Terrorism." *Terrorism and Political Violence* 16, no. 4, pp. 777–794. https://doi.org/10.1080/095465590899768.

White, P. 2017. "Can a Christian-Led Business Be a Toxic Workplace?" *Convene.* www.convenenow.com/blog/2017/01/23/can-a-christian-toxic-workplace.

Widerszal-Bazyl, M. and M. Cieślak. 2000. "Monitoring Psychosocial Stress at Work: Development of the Psychosocial Working Conditions Questionnaire." *International Journal of Occupational Safety and Ergonomics* 6, no. sup1, pp. 59–70. https://doi.org/10.1080/10803548.2000.11105108.

Wiefling, K. 2019. "The Global Epidemic of Disengaged Employees & Dysfunctional Organizations." *Global Company Culture Association.* https:// globalcompanycultureassociation.com/resource/gcca-articles/the-global-epidemic-of-disengaged-employees-dysfunctional-organizations/.

Wilkie, D. 2019. "Why Is Workplace Theft on the Rise?" *SHRM.* www.shrm. org/resourcesandtools/hr-topics/employee-relations/pages/workplace-theft-on-the-rise-.aspx.

Wilkinson, C.W. 2001. "Violence Prevention at Work. A Business Perspective." *American Journal of Preventative Medicine* 20, no. 2, pp. 155–160. https:// doi.org/10.1016/s0749-3797(00)00292-0.

Williams, K.D. 2007. "Ostracism." *Annual Review of Psychology* 58, pp. 425–452.

Wilson, C.R. 2021. "Workplace Bullying: 24 Examples & Ideas to Support Adults." https://positivepsychology.com/workplace-bullying/.

Wolf, W. 2016. "Nine Signs of a Dysfunctional Organization." *Linkedin.* www .linkedin.com/pulse/nine-signs-dysfunctional-organization-willie-wolf-m-p-a/.

Wollan, M.L., F.C. Rinefort, and J.A. Petrick. 2013. "The Challenge of Workplace Health and Safety in Croatia." *The Journal of International Management Studies* 8, no. 1, pp. 77–83.

Woolf, M. 2021. "Workplace Bullying Is on the Rise [2021 Study]." *Myperfectresume.* www.myperfectresume.com/career-center/careers/basics/workplace-bullying-in-2021.

Workhuman Editorial Team. 2022. "What Are the Most Important Elements of Organizational Culture?" *Workhuman*. www.workhuman.com/blog/key-elements-of-organizational-culture/.

Wrzesniewski, A. and J.E. Dutton. 2001. "Crafting a Job: Revisioning Employees as Active Crafters of Their Work." *Academy of Management Review* 26, no. 2, pp. 179–201.

Wu, J., Z. Zheng, and J.L. Zhao. 2021. "FairPlay: Detecting and Deterring Online Customer Misbehavior." *Information Systems Research* 32, no. 4, pp. 1323–1346.

Xiao, B., C. Liang, Y. Liu, and X. Zheng. 2022. "Service Staff Encounters With Dysfunctional Customer Behavior: Does Supervisor Support Mitigate Negative Emotions?" *Frontiers in Psychology* 13, p. 987428. https://doi.org/10.3389/fpsyg.2022.987428.

Xu, G. and L. Li. 2013. *Social Media Mining and Social Network Analysis: Emerging Research*. Hershey, PA: Information Science Reference. https://doi.org/10.4018/978-1-4666-2806-9.

Yamada, D.C. 2004. "Crafting a Legislative Response to Workplace Bullying." *Employee Rights and Responsibilities Journal* 8, pp. 475–521.

Yazbak, K. 2017. "New CEO. Dysfunctional Organization. Now What?" *Viewcrest Advisors*. https://viewcrestadvisors.com/new-ceo-dysfunctional-organization-now-what.

Yip, J.A., E.E. Levine, A.W. Brooks, and M.E. Schweitzer. 2021. "Worry at Work: How Organizational Culture Promotes Anxiety." *Research in Organizational Behavior* 40, pp. 100–124.

Yones, M.n.d. "Dysfunctional Leadership & Dysfunctional Organizations." *International Institute of Management (https://www.iim-edu.org/), Executive Journal.* www.lesaffaires.com/uploads/references/1281_Dysfunctional LeadershipDysfunctionalOrganizations.pdf.

Yunos, Z. and S. Sulaman. 2017. "Understanding Cyber Terrorism From Motivational Perspectives." *Journal of Information Warfare* 16, no. 4, pp. 1–13.

Zaleski, O. 2017. "Inside Hampton Creek's Empty Boardroom." *Bloomberg*. www.bloomberg.com/news/articles/2017-07-25/inside-hampton-creek-s-empty-boardroom#xj4y7vzkg.

Glossary

Everyone, Especially Managers, Should Be Familiar With These Terms

It Might Be Useful to Copy These for Reference, Especially in Meetings or Group Discussions

360 Degree Feedback: Feedback is obtained from an employee's subordinates, peers, colleagues, and supervisor, as well as a self-evaluation by the employee themselves is gathered.

Abjection: The separating of an individual from the group through statements of disgust.

Absenteeism: Intentional or habitual absence from work.

Abuse: Any action that intentionally harms or injures another person.

Accommodation: Making special circumstances for someone.

Accountability: Answerability for actions, decisions, and performance.

Activate: To make active; cause to function or act.

Active Shooter/Hostile Intruder Threat: A person or persons with a homicidal intent who enter the workplace in retaliation for the specific objective of killing those he/she has targeted. The hostile intruder could be armed with a handgun, shotgun, machine gun, knife, or machete. This person typically has no intention of getting apprehended and will continue until he/she stops or is stopped by police.

Affect: An emotion that changes or influences what you do or think.

Affected Area: This is the general space or area where the unrestrained hostile intruder is roaming until contained.

Affirmative Action: Plans of action undertaken by organizations to comply with human rights legislation by actively striving to recruit, hire, train, develop, and promote women and members of minority groups.

Age Discrimination: Discrimination based on age; see also, discrimination.

Agent: A person who acts for or in the place of another person.

Aggravation: A source or cause of annoyance or exasperation.

Aggressive: Pursuing one's aims and interests forcefully, sometimes unduly so.

Aggressor: A person who says or does hurtful things.

Aggrieved Person: Someone who has been discriminated against in some way.

Agreeableness: The tendency to get along with other people.

Ambiguous Information: Information that can be interpreted in multiple and often conflicting ways.

Anger-Related Incidents: Sudden display of aggression, impulsivity, or disruptive behavior.

Antibias: A commitment to avoid prejudice, stereotyping, and all forms of discrimination.

Antisocial: Not sociable; not wanting the company of others.

Anxiety: A feeling of worry, nervousness, or unease, typically about an imminent event or something with an uncertain outcome.

Assault: Intentionally putting someone in reasonable apprehension of an imminent harmful or offensive contact; physical injury is not required.

Backbiting: Malicious talk about someone who is not present.

Backstabbing: Verbal attack against someone who is not present, especially by a so-called friend.

Battery: The actual act that causes physical harm.

Bias: A tendency to believe that some people, ideas, and so on are better than others that usually results in treating some people unfairly.

Bigotry: Obstinate or intolerant devotion to one's own opinions and prejudices.

Bothering: Annoying or pestering someone.

Burnout: A state of emotional, physical, and mental exhaustion caused by excessive and prolonged stress.

Bystander: A person who witnesses bias or an incident.

Capital: Anything that confers value or benefit to its owners, such as its equipment or machinery, intellectual property like patents, financial assets, or its employees.

Civil Lawsuit: A court-based process through which Person A can seek to hold Person B liable for some type of harm or wrongful act.

Climate: The social environment of the organization.

Codes of Conduct: Meaningful symbolic statements about the importance of adhering to high ethical standards in an organization.

Coercion: Using power or force to impose an unwanted behavior.

Cohesiveness: The extent to which members of the group are motivated to remain together.

Compensation: Wages and salaries paid to employees for their services.

Competitive Advantage: The ability of one organization to outperform other organizations because it produces desired goods or services more efficiently and effectively than they do. The component of strategy specifies the advantages that the organization holds relative to its competitors.

Complainant: A person, group, or company that makes a complaint, as in a legal action (see also plaintiff).

Complaint: A complaint is an allegation of illegal discrimination.

Compliance: Going along with the boss's request but without any stake in the result.

Compromise: An agreement or a settlement of a dispute that is reached by each side making concessions.

Conflict of Interest: A situation where the employee's decision may be compromised because of competing loyalties.

Conflict: Active disagreement between people with opposing opinions or principles.

Consultants: Consultants are all consultants, vendors, or contractors engaged with over a predetermined period of time and their safety and security might be in jeopardy.

Cyberbullying: Willful and repeated harm inflicted through the use of computers, cell phones, or other electronic devices.

Damages: A remedy in the form of a monetary award to be paid to a claimant as compensation for loss or injury.

Defaming: Making a false statement that injures someone's reputation or standing within a group.

Defendant: A person, company, and so on against whom a claim or charge is brought in a court; person, or entity being sued (see plaintiff).

Denigration: Sending or posting gossip or rumors about a person that damages that person's reputation or friendships.

Discipline: Punishment inflicted by way of correction and training.

Discrimination: Unfair treatment of one person or group of people because of the person or group's identity (e.g., race, gender, ability, religion, culture, etc.).

Disparate Impact: One group receives less favorable results than another.

Disparate Treatment: One group is subjected to inconsistent application of rules and policies relative to others.

Disruptive: Behavior that causes difficulties that interrupt performance or prevent it from continuing.

Diversity: Differences among people in age, gender, race, ethnicity, religion, sexual orientation, socioeconomic background, and capabilities/disabilities.

Due Diligence: Reasonable steps taken by a person in order to satisfy parties and to avoid harm to those involved.

Duress: Threats, violence, constraints, or other action brought to bear on an individual to do something against their will or better judgment.

Dysfunctional Organization: An organization that undermines the purpose, health, wholeness, safety, solidarity, and worth of an organization or its stakeholders.

EAP: Emergency Action Plan; also known as an Emergency Preparedness Plan.

EEOC: The U.S. Equal Employment Opportunity Commission is responsible for enforcing federal laws that make it illegal to discriminate.

Effectiveness: Doing the right things in the right way at the right times. A measure of the appropriateness of the goals an organization is pursuing and of the degree to which the organization achieves those goals.

Empathy: The ability to identify and share feelings with someone.

Empire-Building: Attempting to enlarge the size, scope, and influence of an individual or organization's power.

Enabling Factors: Those things that improve your ability to manage unacceptable behavior that could lead to violence.

Equal Employment Opportunity Commission (EEOC): Agency responsible for enforcing federal laws regarding discrimination or harassment against job applicants or employees in the United States.

Equality: Having the same or similar rights and opportunities as others.

Equity: The quality of being fair or just.

Eroding Factors: Those things that impede your ability to reduce unacceptable behavior that could lead to violence.

Ethics: A moral philosophy or code of morals practiced by a person or group of people.

Ethnic Group: People who share a common religion, color, or national origin.

Evidence: The means by which any alleged matter is established or disproved.

Exclusion: Intentionally excluding someone from a group or its activities.

Fair Labor Practices: Equitable practices concerning hiring, wages, union relations, etc.

Feedback: Response from the receiver of a message to the sender of that message; for instance, telling the employee the results of his or her performance appraisal.

Gossiping: Spreading information usually incorrect about a person.

Grievance: A written statement or complaint filed by an employee with the union concerning the employee's alleged mistreatment by the company.

Group Cohesiveness: The degree to which members are attracted or loyal to a group.

Group Decision Making: Choosing among alternatives by teams, committees, or other types of groups rather than by one individual.

Group Norms: Shared guidelines or rules for behavior that most group members follow.

Group: Two or more people who interact regularly to accomplish a common goal.

Groupthink: Phenomenon that happens when the maintenance of cohesion and good feelings overwhelms the purpose of the group. A pattern of faulty and biased decision making that occurs in groups whose members strive for agreement among themselves at the expense of accurately assessing information relevant to a decision.

Grudge: A feeling of ill will or resentment.

Harassment: Making any profane or antagonizing remarks to attempt to annoy, anger, harass, and impede movement or any act involving nuisance phone calls, or annoying pranks.

Harm: physical or psychological damage or injury.

Hostile Intruder (Active Shooter): An unrestrained individual within a contained area exercising the use of lethal force and posing immediate risk of death or serious injury to area occupants, regardless of the type of lethal weapon involved.

Hostile Work Environment: The workplace creates an environment that is difficult or uncomfortable for another person to work in, due to discrimination.

Hubris: *An extreme and unreasonable feeling of pride and confidence in yourself.*

Human Resource Management (HRM): Activities that managers engage in to attract and retain employees and to ensure that they perform at a high level and contribute to the accomplishment of organizational goals.

Ignore: Refuse to take notice of or acknowledge; disregard intentionally.

Inconsistency: A communication problem that exists when a person sends conflicting messages.

Inequality: An unfair situation when some individuals have more rights or better opportunities than others.

Inequity: Lack of fairness.

Informal Organization: The overall pattern of influence and interaction defined by all the informal groups within an organization. The system of behavioral rules and norms that emerge in a group.

Initiative: The ability to act on one's own, without direction from a superior.

Injustice: A situation in which the rights of a person or a group of people are ignored, disrespected, or discriminated against.

Intention: Something that you want and plan to do.

Internal Terrorism: Behavior that involves the intent to evoke fear or extreme stress for the purpose of bringing about a change that benefits the perpetrator.

Interpersonal Communication: Communication between people, especially small numbers of people, either orally, in writing, or nonverbally.

Intimidation: Making others afraid or fearful through threatening behavior.

Jealousy: Feeling or showing envy of someone or their achievements and advantages.

LGBTQ: An acronym that collectively refers to individuals who are lesbian, gay, bisexual, transgender, or queer. It is sometimes stated as LGBT (lesbian, gay, bisexual, and transgender), GLBT (gay, lesbian, bi, and transgender).

Life Stress: Events or experiences that produce severe strain, for example, bullying or harassment on the job.

Litigation: The process of resolving disputes by filing or answering a complaint through the court system.

Lockout: Exclusion of a person from a group.

Mediation: A process wherein the parties meet with a mutually selected impartial and neutral person who assists them in the negotiation of their differences.

Menace: A person whose actions, attitudes, or ideas are considered dangerous or harmful.

Mentor: An experienced and trusted adviser.

Mindset: An established set of attitudes held by someone.

Minority: A smaller group within a state, region, or country differs in race, religion, or national origin from the dominant group.

Molestation: Sexual assault or abuse of a person, especially a woman or child.

Molesting: Assault or abuse (a person, especially a woman) sexually.

Murder: The premeditated killing of a person by another person.

Name-Calling: The use of words to hurt, belittle, or be mean to someone or a group.

Narcissism: Self-centeredness; *an extreme and unreasonable feeling of pride and confidence in yourself.*

Negotiation: A method of conflict resolution in which the parties in conflict consider various alternative ways to allocate resources to each other in order to come up with a solution acceptable to them all.

Negotiator: The role that a manager plays when attempting to work out agreements and contracts that operate in the best interests of the organization.

Networking: The exchange of information through a group or network of interlinked computers.

NIOSH: The National Institute for Occupational Safety and Health is part of the CDC charged with developing new knowledge in the field of occupational safety and health and transferring that knowledge into practice.

NLRB: National Labor Relations Board.

Nonverbal Communication: Gestures and facial expressions that do not involve speaking but can also include nonverbal aspects of speech (tone and volume of voice, etc.).

Norm: A standard of behavior that the group develops for its members.

Normality: The condition or state of being usual, typical, or expected (normal).

Occupational Deviant Behavior: Self-serving deviant acts that occur at the workplace.

Offense: A perceived insult to or disregard for an individual.

Organizational Culture: Values and behaviors that contribute to the unique social and psychological environment of a business.

Organizational Environment: The set of forces and conditions that operate beyond an organization's boundaries but affect a manager's ability to acquire and utilize resources.

Organizational Politics: Activities that individuals engage in to increase their power and to use power effectively to achieve their goals and overcome resistance or opposition.

OSHA: Occupational Safety and Health Administration charged with ensuring safe and healthful working conditions for workers by setting and enforcing standards and by providing training, outreach, education, and assistance.

Ostracism: Being excluded from a group.

Overt Discrimination: Knowingly and willingly denying diverse individuals access to opportunities and outcomes in an organization.

Pain and Suffering: The physical or emotional distress resulting from an injury.

Paranoia: Unjustified suspicion or distrust.

Participative Management: Giving employees a voice in how things are done in organizations.

Perception: The recognition and interpretation of sensory information.

Perpetrator: A person who engages in unacceptable behavior or who carries out a harmful, illegal, or immoral act.

Persecution: Persistent annoyance, hostility, or ill-treatment, especially because of race or political or religious beliefs.

Personal Injury: Physical injury inflicted to a person, as opposed to damage to property or reputation.

Pestering: Troubling or annoying an individual with frequent or persistent requests or interruptions.

Physical Assault(s): Actually, hurting someone; also, legally—intention, coupled with a present ability, of actual *violence* against a person, as by pointing a weapon at him when he is within reach of it (legal-dictionary. thefreedictionary.com). Shoving, pushing, hitting, kicking, fighting, and armed robbery.

Plaintiff: A person or entity filing a lawsuit (see defendant).

Power Imbalance: A situation where one person or group has an advantage over others.

Power: An individual's ability to control or direct others.

Prank(s): Mischievous act(s) intended to harm or embarrass someone.

Prejudice: Judging or having an idea about someone or a group of people before you actually know them.

Prima Facie: This Latin for *on first view* or *at first appearance*. In EEO cases, complainants present evidence and arguments to support a claim of discrimination.

Professional Ethics: Standards that govern how members of a profession are to make decisions when the way they should behave is not clear-cut.

Property Damage: Injury to real or personal property through another's negligence, willful destruction, or by some act of nature. In lawsuits for damages caused by negligence or a willful act, property damage is distinguished from personal injury (dictionary.law.com).

Protected Class: Groups protected from employment discrimination by law.

Psychological Trauma: An emotional response to a terrible event like an accident, rape, or natural disaster. Immediately after the event, shock and denial are typical (www.apa.com).

Public Apology: Apologizing in the presence of others.

Punishment: Administering an undesired or negative consequence when dysfunctional behavior occurs; reprimands, discipline, fines, and so on, which are used to shape behavior by causing a reduction in unwanted behaviors.

Punitive Damages: Damages assessed in the legal process to punish a defendant and to prevent him or her from hurting others by the same or similar actions.

Pushing: Shoving someone usually with a hand.

Quid Pro Quo: A manager or other authority figure offers or merely hints that he or she will give the employee something (a raise or a promotion) in return for that employee's satisfaction of a sexual demand.

Racism: Prejudice and/or discrimination against people because of their racial group; see also, discrimination.

Rareness: The capability of managing the contributing factors to unacceptable behavior that might lead to violence within the organization.

Reasonable Person Standard: A test in personal injury cases that jurors use to determine if a defendant acted as other people would have in the same situation.

Recruiting: The process of attracting a pool of qualified applicants who are interested in working for the company.

Resistance: The negative, uncooperative response of people when their boss attempts to influence them.

Retaliation: An employer punishes an employee for engaging in legally protected activity; an employee or former employee engages in acts to damage an employer.

Rumor(s): Unofficial pieces of information of interest to organizational members but with no identifiable source; a story or report of uncertain or doubtful truth.

Sabotage: Acting to deliberately destroy, damage, or obstruct (something), especially in retaliation.

Safe Harbor Rooms (Safe Rooms): A predetermined interior, windowless area/ room, or any room of the office/facility that can provide a temporary barrier in protecting occupants from external dangers posed by a hostile intruder(s).

Sexual Harassment: Unwelcome sexual advances, requests for sexual favors, or other verbal or physical conduct of a sexual nature.

Shelter-in-Place (Immediate Protective Measures): A defensive action employees and others can take to protect themselves against a hazard such as a hostile intruder armed and in circumstances in which there has been an insufficient warning to escape and evacuate the offices, facilities, buildings, work areas or safely enter the safe harbor room.

Shunning: An act of social rejection or emotional distancing.

Stalking: Following someone stealthily to cause them fear.

Stereotype: False idea that all group members are the same and/or think and behave in the same way.

Stress: A feeling of emotional strain and pressure.

Swearing: Using offensive language.

Tagout: Disabling machinery so it cannot be used.

Target: Someone who is subject to unacceptable behavior or treated in hurtful ways by a person or a group on purpose and over and over.

Team Building: A series of activities and exercises designed to enhance the motivation and satisfaction of people in groups by fostering mutual understanding, acceptance, and group cohesion.

Team: A group whose members work intensely with each other to achieve a specific, common goal or objective.

Teasing: Persistently annoying someone, especially with jokes that may even be about them.

Terror: Violence or threats of violence used for intimidation or coercion.

Terrorism: Intimidation or coercion by instilling fear.

Theft: Stealing; robbing.

Threat: The implication or expression of intent to inflict physical harm or actions that a reasonable person would interpret as a threat to physical safety or property.

Tolerance: The willingness to accept opinions, behaviors, and characteristics different from one's own.

Turnover: The number or percentage of workers who leave an organization and are replaced by new employees.

Value: The organization's productivity and its value to customers, clients, and employees.

Vandalism: Deliberate destruction of or damage to property.

Vengeance: Infliction of injury, harm, humiliation, or the like, on a person by another who has been harmed by that person.

Verbal Abuse: Making profane or antagonizing remarks in an attempt to annoy anger or harass.

V-REEL: Framework, originally developed for strategic analysis in organizations (Flint 2018), provides a unique way of thinking about the causes of unacceptable behavior that might lead to violence and how to eradicate it. It consists of five components—value, rareness, eroding factors, enabling factors, and longevity.

Vulnerable Individuals: Those who are or may be for any reason unable to take care of themselves, or unable to protect themselves against significant harm or exploitation.

Whistleblower: A person who reports illegal or unethical behavior.

Withdrawal: Avoiding people and activities you would usually enjoy; social isolation.

Workplace Violence: Behavior in which an employee, former employee, visitor, or service provider to a workplace inflicts or threatens serious harm, injury, or death to others at the workplace or inflicts damage to property. This behavior is pertinent in workplaces as defined as an official workplace or company-sponsored event.

Zero Tolerance: A standard that establishes that any behavior, implied or actual, that violates the policy will not be tolerated.

About the Author

David D. Van Fleet is a Professor Emeritus at Arizona State University. He has over 50 years of experience in the practice, teaching, and research of management and organizations. He taught at the University of Tennessee, the University of Akron, Texas A&M University, and Arizona State University. He taught human relations management, organizational behavior, management, and leadership. He draws upon this impressive career to provide examples, analyses, and recommendations for dealing with dysfunctional organizations. He has been listed in *Who's Who in the World* (2004), *Who's Who in America* (2003), *Who's Who Among America's Teachers* (2002), and *Who's Who in the Management Sciences* (2000).

He has published over 100 journal articles or book chapters, including *What Members Need in Work Situations: Two Samples of Essential Managerial Leadership Behaviors* (Journal of Managerial Issues, 2022); *Baseballs or Cricket Balls: On the Meanings of Bullying and Harassment* (Journal of Human Resource and Sustainability Studies, 2018); *Future Challenges and Issues of Bullying in the Workplace*, in Laura M. Crothers and John Lipinski (eds.), *Bullying in the Workplace: Causes, Symptoms, and Remedies.* 2014, Taylor & Francis; *Towards a Behavioral Description of Managerial Bullying* (Employee Responsibilities and Rights Journal, 2012); *Preventing Workplace Violence: The Violence Volcano Metaphor* (Journal of Applied Management and Entrepreneurship, 2007); *Internal Terrorists: The Terrorists Inside Organizations* (Journal of Managerial Psychology, 2006); *Terrorism and the Workplace: Concepts and Recommendations* (in Dysfunctional Behavior in Organizations, JAI Press, 1998); *Terrorism and the Workplace: Concepts and Recommendations*, in R. W. Griffin, A. O'Leary-Kelly, and J. Collins (eds.), *Dysfunctional Behavior in Organizations: Violent and Deviant Behavior.* 1998, 23, Part a. JAI Press; and *Workplace Violence: Moving Toward Minimizing Risks* (Project Minerva publication, funded by OSHA,1996).

His books are:

Albanese, R. and D.D. Van Fleet. 1983. *Organizational Behavior: A Managerial Viewpoint*. Hinsdale, Illinois: Dryden.

Griffin, R.W. and D.D. Van Fleet. 2013. *Management Skills: Assessment and Development*. Mason, OH: South-Western/Cengage Learning.

Nater, F., D.D. Van Fleet, and E.W. Van Fleet. 2023. *Combating Workplace Violence: Creating and Maintaining Safe Work Environments*. Charlotte, NC, North Carolina: Information Age Publishing.

Van Fleet, D. D. 1988. *Contemporary Management*. 1st edition; Boston: Houghton Mifflin.

Van Fleet, D.D. 1991. *Behavior in Organizations*. Boston: Houghton Mifflin, in collaboration with G. Moorhead and R.W. Griffin.

Van Fleet, D.D. 1991. *Contemporary Management*. 2nd edition; Boston: Houghton Mifflin, in collaboration with R.W. Griffin.

Van Fleet, D.D. 2020. *Quality Time: Productivity Through Time Management*. Charlotte, NC, North Carolina: Information Age Publishing.

Van Fleet, D.D. and E.W. Van Fleet. 2010. *The Violence Volcano: Reducing the Threat of Workplace Violence*. Charlotte, NC, North Carolina: Information Age Publishing.

Van Fleet, D.D. and E.W. Van Fleet. 2022. *Bullying and Harassment at Work: An Innovative Approach to Understanding and Prevention*. Northampton, MA, Massachusetts: Edward Elgar Publishing.

Van Fleet, D. D. and T.O. Peterson. 1994. *Contemporary Management*. 3rd edition ed. Boston: Houghton Mifflin, in collaboration with R.W. Griffin.

Van Fleet, D.D., E.W. Van Fleet, and G.J. Seperich. 2014. *Agribusiness: Principles of Management*. Clifton Park, NY, New York: Delmar/Cengage Learning.

Van Fleet, D.D. and G.A Yukl. 1986. *Military Leadership: An Organizational Behavior Perspective*. Greenwich, Connecticut: JAI Press, Inc.

Van Fleet, E.W. and D.D. Van Fleet. 2007. *Workplace Survival: Dealing with Bad Bosses, Bad Workers, Bad Jobs*. Frederick, MD, Maryland: PublishAmerica.

Van Fleet, E.W. and D.D. Van Fleet. 2014. *Violence at Work: What Everyone Should Know*. Charlotte, NC, North Carolina: Information Age Publishing.

Index

Note: Page numbers followed by "f" refer to figures and "t" refer to tables.

www.ingramcontent.com/pod-product-compliance
Lightning Source LLC
Chambersburg PA
CBHW061152220326
41599CB00025B/4454